VARIETIES OF
CHRISTIAN APOLOGETICS

VARIETIES OF
CHRISTIAN APOLOGETICS

Bernard Ramm

BAKER BOOK HOUSE
Grand Rapids, Michigan

ISBN: 0-8010-7610-2

First Printing, January 1962
Second Printing, August 1965
Third Printing, September 1968
Fourth Printing, February 1973
Fifth Printing, December 1974

PHOTOLITHOPRINTED BY CUSHING - MALLOY, INC.
ANN ARBOR, MICHIGAN, UNITED STATES OF AMERICA
1974

DEDICATION

It is with sincere Christian affection that we dedicate this volume to our dear friend in Christ,

Rev. Eric N. Lindholm

pastor of the Lakeside Baptist Church of Oakland, California. A wise counselor, beloved pastor, and student of apologetics.

PREFACE
TO THE REVISED EDITION

This volume intends to be a textbook for the study of Christian apologetics, or more broadly, for a study of the philosophy of religion. The first edition met such a need and when it was exhausted it was decided to rewrite the book to make it serve much better as a text. We have done certain things to achieve this. We have eliminated critical footnotes in order that the student might keep his attention directly upon the body of the text. Matters of critical comparison are of value only after basic mastery of a subject matter has been achieved. Some of the passages of the first edition which we judged as obscure or overly philosophical we have rewritten for the sake of simplicity and clarity.

In the first edition the last two men discussed were C. Van Til and E. J. Carnell. Many reviewers and friendly critics suggested that I stay more in the classic examples of apologists, so accordingly I have substituted chapters on Calvin and Kuyper. The first chapter has been extensively reworked to make it a digest of apologetics.

I profited from the work of other scholars in writing the first edition and what I have learned from them has (I trust) carried over into the second. Dr. Emille Cailliet of Princeton read the chapter on Pascal; Dr. Paul Holmer on Kierkegaard; Dr. Paul Jewett on Brunner; Francis J. Marien, S. J., on Aquinas and Augustine; Dr. Van Til on Butler; Dr. Buswell on Tennant. Dr. Carnell read the first edition in typescript form and offered extensive criticisms. Dr. Robert Otto, then of Bethel College, read the typescript in part. Special thanks should also be extended to Eric Lindholm who read the entire manuscript in the first edition. Of course errors of substance and interpretation belong to me and not to my kind critics.

The chapters are not meant to be authoritative interpretations but it is trusted that they are accurate summaries of the men's thought. Consequently we engaged in the absolute minimum of critical remarks and where two or more interpretations of some point were possible we attempted to stay with the more generally accepted one.

Bernard Ramm

Covina, California
June, 1961

SUGGESTIONS TO TEACHERS

Besides the traditional methods of using a text the following alternatives are suggested:

1. Students may be requested to write papers on various topics such as faith or revelation or natural theology by comparing what the different apologists have said on these subjects.

2. The book may be read in historical order and thus be a kind of history of apologetics. Augustine represents the patristic period; Thomas, the scholastic period; Calvin, the Reformation; Pascal and Butler, the post-Reformation period; and then Kierkegaard, Kuyper, Tennant, and Brunner for the modern period. The teacher should also note the different church communions these apologists represent, and their theological alinements.

3. The class may be divided so that two or three members each specialize in one of the nine apologists of the book. Then debates may be held in which the debaters defend the position of the man they have chosen. Thus the followers of Kierkegaard would challenge the followers of Tennant on Tennant's notion that there can only be one kind of faith for both science and religion; or the followers of Calvin would attack the followers of Thomas at the point of Thomas' natural theology.

4. Each member of the class volunteers to master one apologist of his choosing. The final exam (or one of the exams) would then be intensive questions about this one man, especially correlating his opinions with modern problems. For example, "how would Augustine criticize modern positivism?"; "How do you think Thomas would react to contemporary science?"

PERMISSION TO QUOTE

We extend our thanks to the following firms for permission to quote from their copyrighted books.

The Westminster Press: E. Cailliet and J. Blankennagel, *Great Shorter Works of Pascal* (1948). Emil Brunner, translated by Olive Wyon, *Revelation and Reason* (1946).

Cambridge University Press. F. R. Tennant, *Philosophical Theology* (1928 and 1937). F. R. Tennant, *Philosophy of the Sciences*.

CONTENTS

Part I

Systems Stressing Subjective Immediacy

Part II

Systems Stressing Natural Theology

Part III

Systems Stressing Revelation

Chapter I
BRIEF INTRODUCTION
TO CHRISTIAN APOLOGETICS

I. THE CONCEPT OF SYSTEM IN APOLOGETICS

The historical origin of apologetics is to be found in the legal procedures in ancient Athens. The plaintiff brought his accusation (*katēgoria*) before the court. The accused had thè right of making a reply (*apologia*) to the accusation. The reply was an effort to show the falsity of the accusation; hence the accused attempted to "speak off" the charge. Hence we have the verb *apologesthai*, "to make reply, to give an answer, to legally defend one's self"; and the noun *apologia*, "the answer given, the defense made"; and *apologētikos* which refers to the art or skill of making one's reply or answer.

The classical example of the apology is of course the famous *Apology* of Socrates before the Athenian court of law preserved for us in the *Dialogues* of Plato. The social use of the word in the sense of excusing one's self for some miscue or blunder is secondary in classical Greek, although it is the popular meaning in contemporary language.

Both the verb (*apologesthai*) and the noun (*apologia*) occur in the New Testament but they are never translated either by "to make apologetical defense" or to make an "apology." Such expressions as "to make reply," or "to give answer," or "to make one's defense" are used.

Besides noting that the vocabulary of apologetics is to be found in the New Testament we also note considerable apologetical activity. For example on numerous occasions Jesus was *accused* of some fault by the Jews, and to this *accusation* our Lord made his defense (*apologia*) even though it was not named as such. A beautiful example of the apologetical activity of Christ may be seen in Matthew 22 where three leading questions were asked of him by the three leading Jewish sects of the day. In each instance our Lord made reply (*apologia*) and gave a most judicious answer.

The apologetic activity of Paul may be observed in the closing chapter of the book of Acts. He defended himself before the mob in Jerusalem (Acts 22:1 ff.), before the Jewish council (Acts 23:1 ff.), before Felix (Acts 24:1 ff.), and before Festus and Agrippa (Acts 26:1 ff.). The apologetic activity carries over into

his epistles too. Paul defends his gospel and apostleship in Galatians 1 and 2, and in I Corinthians 9 he answers the accusation
(*kategōria*) that he is not an apostle with a defense (*apologia*)
that he is. Returning to this theme in II Corinthians 13 he makes
another defense (*apologia*) of his apostleship.

Peter wrote: "But in your hearts reverence Christ as Lord. Always be prepared to make a defense to any one who calls you to
account for the hope that is in you" (I Peter. 3:15). The word
"defense" is the Greek word, *apologia*. Here is a direct exhortation
by an apostle for Christians to engage in apologetics. An *apologia*
may be a formal court defense as it was in Paul's case (this is
certainly the meaning in II Timothy 4:16 where Paul speaks of
his "first defense"); or it may mean an informal defense of one's
faith, which is perhaps the meaning of Peter.

The apologetic activity of Christ and his apostles was continued
in the early church. It too was subjected to a variety of accusations—Christians were cannibals, or immoral, or they were under-
mining the Roman empire, or they were gullible—and to these
accusations its great leaders gave their defense (*apologia*). In fact
the earliest theologians of the church were called *apologists* and
the greatest treatise of the pre-Augustinian era was Origen's
famous work, *Against Celsus*.

However, it gradually became evident that any defense of the
faith must be built upon the positive affirmations of the faith.
They came to see that any particular *apologia* had to be made
from a definite position. They saw that it was necessary to find
that place from which *any* and *all* attacks were to be answered.
The problem of the *apologia* was at its deepest the problem of
the truthfulness of the Christian faith, the problem of the objectivity of the Christian claims, and the problem of the knowledge of God.

In the apologists of the first two centuries we can observe apologetics on the way to self-consciousness. The great Christian writers
saw certain elements within the Christian faith which seemed to
them to have verification-bearing force. For example, the antiquity
of the Hebrew religion in contrast to the proposed recency of
Greek and Roman religion seemed to them to express its divine
origin. Furthermore they saw many parallels in the writings of
Plato to the thought of Moses. They therefore concluded that
Plato copied from Moses, and thus the virtue of the great Greek
philosopher transfers to the Christian Scriptures. However, that
which impressed them the most was the fulfilment of Old Testament prophecies in the person of Jesus Christ, in the salvation he
obtained, and in the Christian Church.

Apologetics comes of age with Augustine. He saw to the bottom of the issue, namely, that the fundamental issues in Christian apologetics were the truthfulness of the claims made, and the reality of the possession of a knowledge of God. Here the *apologia* gives way to apologetics. There are apologetical elements in most of Augustine's writings but his masterpieces are *The City of God*, and, *The Confessions*. In wrestling with the twin problems of the truth of Christianity and the problem of knowledge in Christian faith Augustine laid the foundations of Christian apologetics. This is not meant to detract, however, from the great *apologia* of Origen (*Contra Celsus*) which was the greatest work of the early Church of a more defensive nature.

Christian apologetics is the strategy of setting forth the truthfulness of the Christian faith and its right to the claim of the knowledge of God. Some apologists emphasize the principle of verification in apologetics (e.g., Butler who argued that we are given reason to test a revelation), and others the principle of the knowledge of God (e.g., Calvin, Warfield).

However, not all Christian apologetics comes with a clear label. It must be said *first* of all that every *apologia* implies an *apologetics*; or, every attempt to defend the faith is based upon certain tacit assumptions about the truth of the faith. *Secondly*, a broad philosophical treatise may virtually be an apologetics. Kant's three great *Critiques* represent a defense of Christianity morally interpreted. Or we may mention Bishop Berkeley who saw in his spirited defense of a spiritual universe and the destruction of materialism a vindication of Christian belief. *Thirdly*, apologetics may be written under the rubric of the philosophy of religion (or some other similar title). Thus Brightman's apologetics is in his work, *A Philosophy of Religion*. B. P. Bowne preferred the older caption of *Theism*. E. R. Tennant employed the more ambitious title of *Philosophical Theology*. Mullins chose the more earthly title, *Why is Christianity True?* Barth's system must be unearthed from his massive *Church Dogmatics*. However, whatever deals with *truth* or with *knowledge* with respect to the Christian faith is apologetical in scope and content. We must not permit titles of books to hide the subject matter.

The serious question in apologetics is the question of strategy. How is truth applied to Christianity? What constitutes a demonstration that a Christian does possess knowledge? Is geometry our model? Or are theological truths more like poems which must be felt equally as much as understood? Or are theological claims much like the probability statements of science? This question of strategy is basic bedrock in Christian apologetics. Unless an apologist is clear at this point he jeopardizes his entire system. Unless he is clear here he will find it difficult to be clear elsewhere.

The purpose of this book is to set forth a number of fundamental positions in Christian apologetics as a means of clarifying the fundamental problem of apologetics. In doing this we follow the pattern of such works as Burtt's *Types of Religious Philosophy*, Hocking's, *Types of Philosophy*, and Mackintosh's *Types of Modern Philosophy*. Such a comparative study not only elucidates the fundamental problems of apologetics, but shows the varieties of the forms of argumentation which have been employed in apologetics, and also illustrates the consequences of one's assumptions. Our approach is then comparative, namely, *an investigation of types of apologetic systems*.

A system can be of two different kinds: (i) a system may be a very tightly organized set of propositions which are carefully interrelated. In philosophy Hegel is the prime example of this kind of system. (ii) A system may mean an interpretation of some subject matter which is guided by certain fundamental assumptions with no attempt made rigorously to coordinate everything that is said. Rather it means a cluster of axioms and assumptions which function as guides and directives for the discussions and thus serve to unify and integrate the discussions. We are using the word system in this second sense.

Upon an examination of a treatise on apologetics it is soon apparent that the author is working with a group of closely related assumptions. The apologist finds one theory of truth more suitable to his purposes than another, and with this theory of truth he finds some metaphysical system which is congenial to it. He then proceeds to interpret the Christian faith from a perspective which is cordial to his theory of knowledge and doctrine of metaphysics. And so we can see his system taking shape. We also note systematic correlations when we study his assertions about man, sin, human reason, and miracles.

However, as we move from treatise to treatise examining the fundamental core of assumptions we find that they tend to group themselves into families, i.e., into types. Sometimes this relationship is rather close. For example, the same fundamental insights of Augustine are repeated in Anselm. Other times the relationship is there but more distant. There is a strong empirical strain in Aquinas and Butler, but Aquinas builds on the philosophy of Aristotle whereas Butler builds on Locke. But Butler is far closer to Aquinas than he is to Anselm.

We have found at least three major families among the various apologists. Although a classification which would subsume all apologists under some group or other would run up to ten or twelve distinct types we can at least subsume some of the greater apologists under a three-fold classification. And if a student can master these three types he is in a position to understand with some degree of comprehension any other type. For example, we do not treat the *evidential school*. The *evidential school* would say that the Christian faith is verified apart from sophisticated philosophical considerations, but rests solidly on fulfilled prophecies, miracles, and the resurrection of Christ. But many apologists absorb evidences into their apologetic system at some point, and if we understand how and why they do this we can readily understand the structure of the argument in the *evidential school*.

These three types of apologetic systems are as follows.

(i) *Some systems stress the uniqueness of the Christian experience of grace.* If a learned philosopher were to have a debate with a pious peasant the peasant would consider his most trenchant proof for the truthfulness of Christianity to be his own personal experience. Christianity is in his heart! He was *there* when it happened. It is the apologetic of one's personal testimony. It is the kind of apologetic argued from the conversions of famous people or wicked sinners. However, it is usually theologically and philosophically very naive.

However, men of considerable genius and acumen have taken this type of argument and have given it a profound apologetical and theological grounding. These men reason that the experience of religion is so profound or so unique or self-validating that the experience itself is its own proof. For example, what is the proof that one is in love? Is it rational analysis? As Pascal asked, Can a man really *argue* that he should be loved? Certainly the intellectual perception of the structure of love is not love itself. The inward experience of being in love is its own proof. Of course the validation of Christianity is more complex than the structure of "being in love" but the experience of being in love illustrates that kind of entity which can only be known by the experience itself. To exemplify this kind of apologetics we have chosen Pascal who develops a very remarkable and subtle doctrine of the *heart*, Kierkegaard who breaks new ground in apologetics with a doctrine of *existential faith*, and Brunner who unites Kierkegaard's *existential faith* with the theological concept of *encounter* characteristic of the crisis theology.

The family-characteristics of this type are briefly as follows: (a) A great stress is laid upon the inward and subjective experience of the gospel; (b) there is frequently a marked hostility towards traditional philosophy and a sympathy for an existential philosophy; (c) much emphasis is placed upon the supra-rational or paradoxical character of Christian teaching; (d) there is a rejection of natural theology and theistic proofs; (e) there is an emphasis on the transcendence of God and the hiddenness of God; and (f) there is a strong doctrine of blinding effects of sin.

(ii) *Some systems stress natural theology as the point at which apologetics begins.* At root this school has deep trust in the powers of human reason in the area of religious knowledge. It does not seek a sharp differentiation among ways of knowing or kinds of truth. It more or less puts religion and science on the same continuum. Science and theology interpret the *same* data only using different categories. Therefore apologetic statements have the same sort of generality and the same sort of status of verification as do scientific laws. As representatives of this school we have chosen Aquinas who builds from the empirical philosophy of Aristotle, Butler who works narrowly with the theory of probability and Locke's empiricism, and Tennant who makes a tremendous attempt to put religious statements upon the same sort of empirical foundation as scientific ones.

The characteristics of this family are: (a) a robust faith in the rational powers of the mind to find the truth about religion; (b) an effort to ground faith in empirical foundations; (c) a belief that the *imago Dei* (image of God in man) was weakened but not seriously damaged by the Fall and sin; and that (d) religious propositions enjoy the same kind of verification that scientific assertions do. Therefore faith in God is just as rational and credible as faith in confirmed scientific law.

(iii) *Other systems stress revelation as the foundation upon which apologetics must be built.* It should be apparent by now that these systems share certain assumptions. We have been stressing what these systems do not have in common. In attempting to be *Christian* apologetics they naturally share many common postulates. For example, all three types accept revelation. But the revelational school believes that the first school is too subjectivistic. Apologetics must have its principle anchorage in God's truth and not man's experience. It criticizes the second school for not seriously evaluating man's depravity. If sin prevents general revelation from speaking the truth of God then no natural theology is possible. Apologetics must commence with God's redemption and God's word of special revelation. For spokesmen of this type of apologetic system we have chosen Augustine with his elaborate doctrine of illumination; Calvin with his great doctrine of the witness of the Spirit; and Kuyper who attempted a fresh statement of the Augustinian-Calvinistic tradition in the light of more recent knowledge.

Common theses in this family are: (a) The conviction that faith precedes understanding; (b) that once we do believe we are to seek understanding as comprehensively as we can; (c) that the personal experience of the gospel is anchored in the objective work of Christ, the objective justification of God, and the objective word of God; (d) that a special act of the Spirit is indispensable for Christian faith and enlightenment; (e) that human depravity has made human reason as it functions within a depraved soul untrustworthy; and that (f) the issue of truth in religion must suffer no dilution.

II. THE MAJOR PROBLEMS OF CHRISTIAN APOLOGETICS

In that the major portion of this book is a review of apologetic systems it is advisable to supplement this material with a brief survey of the typical problems of Christian apologetics. There are certain issues to which every apologist must speak—or at least to which many apologists have spoken. Unless one is somewhat familiar with these topics he will find interaction with Christian apologetics somewhat difficult. Some of these typical problems are as follows:

1. *What is the relationship between philosophy and Christianity?* The early theologians of the Christian Church were directly confronted with this problem and gave differing answers. The most negative form of this relationship was expressed by those Church Fathers who believed that philosophy was inspired by demons. Tertullian is taken in the history of Christian thought as the most consistent representative of those who would have nothing to do with philosophy. Jerusalem and Athens! What have they to do with each other? Nothing!

Just the opposite in the early Church were the opinions of the Alexandrians (Origen, Clement) who felt that the best of Greek philosophy was inspired by the Logos. Just as the Old Testament was the introduction to Christ the Word for the Jews, so the Logos in Greek philosophy was the introduction to Christ for the Greeks. These men had no hesitation in affirming that the noble Greek philosophers were Christians.

A more positive attempt to rethink the issue occurs in Augustine. Augustine saw a role in philosophy of servant or help to theology. One could use philosophy without bestowing upon it a divine status. The opinion of Thomas offers a criticism to that of Augustine's position. The view that Augustine takes does not really give philosophy a status of integrity of its own. Thomas seeks to remedy this by giving philosophy an independent status. However he said more than this. He gave a special place to the philosophy of Aristotle and saw in the latter's philosophy the unique tool for the writing of Christian apologetics and theology.

Thomas' thesis that there is a philosophy congenial for the defense of Christianity and the exposition of Christian theology has occured many times in different versions in the history of Christian theology. Kierkegaard found a real congeniality between his existentialism (of the *Philosophical Fragments*) and Christian faith. Albert Ritschl found the Kantian philosophy remarkably suited for his theology, as did Biedermann the Hegelian philosophy. Bowne and Brightman both found the philosophy of personalism the natural cohort and ally of Christian faith.

Pascal, however, suggests another alternative, namely that philosophy has a right of its own but outside of the Christian faith. It can be pursued like physics or geography and so exist in its own right and integrity. But any attempt to make it the cohort of the Christian gospel is fateful.

Barth offers yet another variation. In that all thinking (in science or theology) is governed by principles, and helped by them the Christian theologian cannot help but also use principles. Accordingly the theologian cannot escape the use of philosophical methods or principles or categories. But no philosophy corresponds exactly with the divine revelation. So to use one philosophy exclusively as Thomas did was very wrong. Even though we may use philosophical methods we must always be prepared to alter them or correct them as light is thrown upon them from our study of Sacred Scripture. Furthermore, God in his sovereignty may use any philosophy to correct a false opinion. Thus even materialism may bring us to our senses that "The Word became flesh" when we might be charmed by a highly spiritualized philosophy which would think it abhorrent that the Word could be made flesh. Accordingly Barth demands that we be ready to reckon with *any* philosophy, but the autonomy of the Christian revelation means that we can form no permanent alliance with any particular philosophy.

2. *What is the value of theistic proofs?* A theistic proof is a proof for the existence of God, e.g., God as the First Cause. The position of Thomas is that the theistic proofs are valid. They do *demonstrate* that God is. Since then it has become official Roman Catholic dogma that the natural reason without the help of the Holy Spirit can demonstrate the existence of God.

A second position is that the proofs are not absolutely compelling. They are reasonable and worthy surmises. What they lack in complete formal validity they make up for when supplemented by moral conviction or religious insight. This was the attitude towards the theistic proofs of the great Princeton theologian, Charles Hodge, and the Southern Baptist apologist, E. Y. Mullins.

A third position is that the proofs are logically invalid and no amount of moral insight or religious conviction can rescue them. Somewhere in the argument there is a violation of a principle of logic, or the ambiguous use of some term. Thus "fire causes heat" is not the same order of meaning as "God causes the universe." If we believe in God then it must be on some other grounds than the theistic proofs.

A fourth position affirms that the mere proof of the existence of God is inconsequential. The real issue is whether we possess a knowledge of God or not which leads us to the love, worship, and service of God. A proof just does not say enough! This was essentially Calvin's view.

The fifth position is that of men like Kierkegaard, Pascal, Brunner and Barth. To them the theistic proofs are *irreligion*. They represent man's method of opposing the truth of God. It is a kind of fighting fire with fire. We make a religion of our own to keep God's truth at a distance. Theistic proofs are at best mental exercises. They treat solely with a philosophical abstraction, but never with the Living God of biblical revelation or the gospel of Jesus Christ.

3. *Must the apologist work with some theory of truth?* A theory of truth is some principle which a philosopher adopts which, when applied to claims to knowledge or truth, will separate the true from the false. One such theory is the correspondence theory of truth. A proposition is true, it claims, if the fact or facts it asserts are found to be so; or, to put it otherwise, a proposition is true if the fact or facts it asserts correspond to reality. In that the apologist is dealing with facts, truth, and knowledge, it would appear mandatory that he have a certain theory of truth.

It may be laid down as an axiom that when an apologist accepts a certain philosophy as basic to Christian apologetics he thereby adopts the theory of truth within that philosophy. The classical example is Thomas who adopts Aristotle and works within his system at all cardinal points save those that touch vitally on special revelation.

It would represent years of work to investigate every apologist of worth and decipher from his writings that theory of truth which he used as his guiding instrument. We must limit ourselves to obvious examples.

One class of apologists employs some principle of truth already existing among philosophers. Bishop Butler employed the theory of probability as his theory of truth. Brightman employed a two-pronged theory of truth (and Carnell similarly on independent grounds) : namely, a logical test of consistency, and a material test of conformity to fact. Gordon Clark, however, restricts himself solely to consistency, i.e., the priority of the law of non-contradiction. Tennant generally follows Butler but adds to Butler the precision in logical theory which has come with the development of science. Thus to Tennant the general canons of truthfulness in science are the general canons for truthfulness in theology.

A second class of apologists does not think it is possible to apply a general theory of truth to the specific character of Christian revelation. They feel that a special canon of truthfulness applies to Christian faith. Thus Kierkegaard emphasized that the paradox was the sign of truth in theology. He was followed closely by the neo-orthodox theologians in their earlier days especially when they emphasized the *dialectical* character of Christian theology. For every "yes" there must be a "no." For example in contemporary physics we have the wave-theory and the particle-theory of matter. In some experiments matter acts like a wave, and in others, like a particle. Yet we cannot bring the two together. So, theological statements have this sort of structure, i.e., they talk of both sides of the truth but not of the center. Those who follow Martin Buber affirm that in that there are two ways of knowing there are two criteria of truthfulness. Buber said persons know each other in the relation of I-Thou (this is one word to Buber), and that persons know objects in the relation of I-it (this too is one word) . Hence the world of personal relationships operates differently from the world of person-object relationships, and to confuse these two ways of knowing is to create theological confusion.

One may become intensely and radically theological at this point and assert that God makes himself known to us in such a way that we cannot doubt it, even though we cannot spell out the theory of knowledge or the theory of truth which must accompany such conviction. I presume that this is the position of Calvin, Luther, and in a very radical form, Karl Barth. Brunner, to the contrary, finds support for his views in Kierkegaard and Buber. His work *Warheit als Begegnung* (truth as encounter or meeting) is held as a rather faithful theological counterpart to Buber's work, *I and*

Thou. There is some justification, on the other hand, of calling Calvin and Luther's view, "The Epistemology of the Holy Spirit."

4. *What is the importance of the doctrine of sin for apologetics?* Man wishes to know God. What happens to the possibility of knowing God if the knower (man) is sinful and corrupt? Does the human reason function as reliably in the shadow of human depravity as it would apart from depravity?

At one extreme we find the monk Pelagius. In his view there is really no depravity in man, so theorectically the human mind is as intact after sinning as it was before. There are few who would defend this position today.

In the center we find Roman Catholic theology. According to this position human nature was complete before God graced it with original righteousness. Therefore after the entry of sin and the fall of man human nature is still complete even though deprived of original righteousness. Certainly shadows have fallen over it. Man is depraved to the extent that he needs God's revelation to learn the way of salvation, and God's grace to trust the Savior. But this yet leaves a large territory in which the human mind is competent. It may create a true philosophy (Aristotle) ; it may prove the existence of God; it may demonstrate the immortality of the soul; it may create a system of ethics based upon natural law; and it may prove the divine origin of the Roman Catholic Church.

The Reformers looked at the matter much differently. Roger Mehl says in his great work, *La Condition du Philosphe Chrétien*, that the Reformers refused to think of human reason apart from the doctrine of human depravity. Man does not think abstractly. The total man thinks, and if the total man suffers depravity, his reason is buried within this depravity as is any other human faculty. Therefore, the Reformers could not accept the position of the Roman Catholic Church because her theologians failed to see the proper implications of human sinfulness for the status of the human rational power. Therefore we find in the Reformers a much stronger doctrine of grace and revelation necessary to counterbalance this depravity.

However, other sons of Calvin have felt that if human depravity were unrelieved in the sinner then the sinner was in no sense guilty. Or if the sinner was so blind that he could see nothing, why preach? They felt that human depravity was modulated by *common grace*. Fallen man can follow the basic arguments of Christian evidences and of the theistic proofs, for God has restrained sin so that humanity can in its sinfulness yet perceive some rays of light.

5. *What is the character of revelation?* The nineteenth Psalm speaks of the glory of God in the heavens and the judgments of God in the law. This is taken to mean that there is a general revelation for all men seen in the radiance of the sun by day and the beauty of the stars by night; and that there is a special revelation in Sacred Scripture. What, then, is the relationship of these two revelations?

The Roman Catholic position is that the general revelation of nature may be so read by man apart from Christ and apart from grace that he can prove that God is, and know some of his attributes. Then with the grace of Christ and the Spirit he believes in the Christian truth and so receives special revelation. Hence grace fulfills and completes nature. Furthermore, the emphasis upon special revelation is that it yields itself readily to dogmatic formulations. These dogmatic formulations defined by the Church as necessary for salvation (*de Fide*) must be believed by all Catholics. Faith in revelation is thereby essentially assent to these *de Fide* dogmas. Faith to the Roman Catholic theologians is *theological* in that it means accepting dogmas of the Church as true.

Luther and Calvin readily agreed that God is the Creator of heaven and earth. There was no doubt in their minds that nature was a general revelation of God. But a knowledge of God is a product of a datum and a knower. Only as there is a reliable datum and a reliable knower does knowledge emerge. However, this is not the case with reference to general revelation. The datum is there (creation) but the knower is a sinner! Therefore the true knowledge of God does not exist. Only in special revelation is the sinner purified so that he can recover the truth of God in general revelation.

However, Kierkegaard and the neo-orthodox theologians have added another facet to the discussion of revelation. According to them revelation is an *event* which involves God and man. Without *both* partners revelation does not really occur. In traditional Roman Catholic and Protestant doctrines revelation was the truth of God recorded in Scripture which became real or personal through faith and the Holy Spirit. Hence, revelation is what God says; illumination is our proper reception of revelation. But according to recent thought revelation must include illumination or else it is not even revelation. Thus the Bible is not revelation in itself. It is a "potential" of revelation. Its doctrines are not theologically truths but "behests" or "invitations" or "prescripts." When we believe them with the help of the Spirit *then* revelation occurs. Accordingly that which theologians traditionally called revelation, these writers rename as *signs* or *witnesses* of revelation.

6. *What kind of certainty does Christianity offer?* How sure are we that we are sure? All are familiar with the Roman Catholic claims to infallibility. The faithful Catholic believer himself is fallible enough but in virtue of the infallibility of the mother Church he enjoys "passive infallibility." What assurance does the Protestant believer have?

Men like Butler and Tennant argue that the Christian faith has the same kind of certainty as we have for any judgment of life. Life is not made up of absolutes and none of our lives is guided by absolutes. Our lives are guided by principles graced with a high degree of probability. Even if Christianity were absolute in its truth-status we as imperfect creatures would only *probably* know this. Why attempt to settle for more than that which the rest of life demands?

On the other hand some apologists think that it is slightly blasphemous to say, "I believe in God—probably." So Frank argues in his *System of the Christian Certainty* that along with the sense of surety of our salvation, God gives the Christian an additional gift of the certainty of the Christian faith as true. Van Til reasons that it is the very nature of the Christian faith to impart a sense of real certainty, and not merely probability. Of course the Roman Catholic apologists believe that the claims of Christianity are *demonstrable* and therefore yield maximum certainty.

Most apologists settle for some sort of distinction between certainty and certitude. By certainty they mean the amount of evidence of all kinds *for Christianity*. This can never be absolutely conclusive but it can be very convincing. With reference to certainty then the Christian faith possesses a high degree of probability. Certitude is our inward attitude. Here the Christian has complete assurance that Christianity is true. The witness of the Holy Spirit confirms him in the reality of his faith. It is very prudent to say in a lecture on Christian evidences that Christianity is true—probably. But in one's prayers one would not say, "The Lord is my shepherd—probably."

However, Kierkegaard would maintain that Christian faith is held with a profound degree of certainty as the truth as the believer looks within his own heart, but that the so-called external evidence is yet very ambiguous! Barth's opinions are somewhat difficult to classify for at times he stresses the objectivity and historical credibility of the great saving actions of God as sturdily as any orthodox theologian, yet at other times he emphasizes the complete ambiguity of the biblical history as far as historical research is concerned. Only in hearing the magisterial Word of God in Scripture is the ambiguity of the Scriptures resolved. There is still a Kierkegaardian overtone to Barth's thought at this point.

7. *Is there a common ground between believer and unbelievers which forms a point of contact for conversation and argumentation?* If a Christian draws a circle before the non-Christian and says, "the matters in this circle are common to both of us, so let us debate them to a conclusion," then it could be said to him, "You have conceded that there is some territory—namely that circle which you just drew—about which God has spoken no word, and therefore the argument may go one way or the other; but in that God is sovereign Creator no such circle exists and the argument can go only one way, namely, God's way."

Then the Christian who drew the circle replies: "If no such common ground exists, then no matter what I say to the non-Christian, it will sound like meaningless chatter. God does not expect a man to believe meaningless chatter; so some circle must exist for Christian communication."

There is the paradox: grant the circle and deny God's sovereignty; deny the circle and eliminate any communication of the gospel.

In modern times Van Til has been an unusually sturdy defender of the thesis that God's will pertains to the *entire* universe so that no such circle of common ground may be drawn. Barth comes to a similar position but for a different reason. If such a neutral or common ground exists the sinner will use it as a fulcrum against revelation. He will not properly use it but will abuse it. It will be his stance for uttering criticisms of God's truth. Revelation builds its own beachhead within the sinner.

However, other theologians do not take such a radical stance. They believe that *general revelation*, especially in its form of moral consciousness in man, yet remains in force and forms the point of contact between man and grace. Others would say that common grace overcomes our depravity so that we may see the truth of general revelation which in turn leads us to special revelation.

Carnell's resolution of the problem is that in areas of common knowledge and research, believer and unbeliever can communicate, for there is nothing Christian or non-Christian about the laws of logic and rules of procedure in science. But as soon as the discussion presses into areas which deal with men's basic presuppositions the common ground ends. Sinner and saint do not stand on common ground in the discussion of Jesus Christ.

Recently Bultmann has urged a new kind of common ground, namely that of existential philosophy. It is the function of existential philosophy to discuss *how* man exists. Every subject matter is grasped by some sort of *how*, and this *how* Bultmann calls "pre-understanding" or "fore-understanding" (*Vorverständnis*). This "pre-understanding" of the problems and factors of human existence is the common ground between the evangelist and the sinner.

8. *What is the character of faith?* Where is the supreme locus of faith? If it be granted that the entire man believes, it might be asked which part of man believes the most. Is faith basically located in the mind? This has been argued for certain. Faith, we are told, is a response to credible evidence. If I am asked what is the color of the shirt I am wearing, I can answer from knowledge. This is not faith. But if Sam tells me Jim is wearing a blue shirt, I believe this because Sam is a veracious person. Thus Augustine treated faith as response to assertions to which we ourselves cannot bear direct witness but which we receive on credible authority. Such a definition can be given an even more intellectual turn. It can be argued that faith is the belief in *anything* which has sufficient evidence. Thus asserting that I am wearing a white shirt is also a matter of faith. In fact it is a stronger faith, because for this I have the validation of my own senses whereas I know that Jim has a blue shirt only through the word of Sam.

Thomas Aquinas made a sharper distinction between faith and knowledge than did Augustine. According to Thomas we cannot *know* and *believe* the same proposition at the same time. We *know* all those things which come into the orbit of our knowing faculties; we *believe* all those things that come into our orbit in virtue of divine revelation.

To others faith is fundamentally an act of the will under moral guidance. If faith were in truths clearly proved it would be without merit. Only when there is venture is faith spiritual. Thus the case for Christianity is never closed or finished. There is an open end to it and this open end the man of faith fills up with his will to believe. Thus faith is essentially an act of the will.

To others faith is located in the emotions. This at least was Kierkegaard's existentially motivated definition of faith. The chief chore of faith to Kierkegaard is to transform the self. Only a profound inward movement could work this change. Therefore he located it among the emotions for from the supreme excitation of the emotions comes the necessary Christian transformation of the self.

Some men inspired by Kierkegaard have nonetheless gone beyond Kierkegaard (perhaps more influenced here by Buber). God comes to man with the *address* of his word. An address calls for a *reply*.

If the address is the magisterial Word of God, faith is the reply. Thus faith is the correlate of revelation. In that faith is here *decision* it is partially located in the will, and in that faith is here somewhat *existential* it is partially located in the emotions.

9. *What is the status of Christian evidences?* By Christian evidences is meant all of those reasons from the nature of Scripture, from the person of Christ, and from the history of the Church which seem to argue for the divine origin of the Christian faith. The basic elements are the fulfilment of prophecy, miracles, and the resurrection of Christ.

First we may note the "evidentialists." The evidentialist accepts Christian evidences as the God-given means of certifying the Christian faith to ordinary people and apart from sophisticated arguments. Any person graced with common sense and free from prejudice can ascertain that Jesus rose from the dead and can perceive in this the divinity of the Christian religion.

Calvin saw it differently. The very point is that man cannot be free from prejudice for sin is a deep, permanent prejudice against the truth of God. Only the Holy Spirit can prevail in the heart and *then* we may appeal to Christian evidences. Other Calvinists (e.g., Warfield) maintain that the unbeliever must be given something when he asks *why* he must believe. Although Christian evidences do not replace the Holy Spirit, neither does the Holy Spirit replace Christian evidences.

Those who approach apologetics with a strong philosophical bent make short work of apologetics. They maintain that Christian evidences are accepted or rejected in terms of one's philosophical position. The real issue then is arguing philosophical position, and not Christian evidences. In the final analysis evidences are immaterial to Christian apologetics.

10. *What is the relationship between faith and reason?* This is one of the most customary formulations of the problem of Christian apologetics. Yet it is a most ambiguous formulation. The question really contains a cluster of questions. First of all we note that *faith* is a manner in which we accept something or receive something; so the real issue is not between faith and reason but between reason and *that which faith accepts*. Complicating the question is the further fact that *reason* is not some common concept about which there is universal agreement. One must specify which theory of reason he is talking about!

What the question really asks is, What is the relationship between that which we know by revelation and that which we know by other ways of knowing? Thus it is the question of the relationship of revelation and philosophy, revelation and scientific knowledge, revelation and historical knowledge, revelation and biblical criticism. To what extent is revelation under the canons of logic, evidence, fact, and to what extent is logic, evidence, fact under revelation?

We have a variety of opinions at this point. Some theologians argue that reason leads up to revelation but must stop there. Reason and revelation do not conflict, but revelation advances into an area where reason can no longer serve as arbiter. Others would say that reason and revelation inevitably conflict. In that reason is the work of sinful man and revelation the gift of a righteous God their encounter can only be one of believing submission or violent opposition.

Again it is argued that in all matters of fact (history, criticism, logic) revelation must yield to the corrective voice of reason; but in all matters of revelation (as salvation, the person of Christ) reason must yield to revelation.

BIBLIOGRAPHY

Brunner, E., *Revelation and Reason*
Carnell, E. J., *An Introduction to Christian Apologetics*
Casserly, J. V. L., *Graceful Reason*
Clark, G., *A Christian View of Men and Things*
Hick, J., *Faith and Knowledge*
Mullins, E. Y., *Why is Christianity True?*
Myers, E. D., editor, *Christianity and Reason*
Richardson, A., *Christian Apologetics*
Smith, W. M., *Therefore Stand*
Sweet, L., *The Verification of Christianity*
Van Til, C., *The Defense of the Faith*
Warfield, B. B., "Apologetics," *The New Schaff-Herzog Encyclopedia of Religious Knowledge*

Part I

Systems Stressing Subjective Immediacy

I. PASCAL AND THE HEART

II. KIERKEGAARD AND INWARDNESS

III. BRUNNER AND REVELATION

Chapter II

BLAISE PASCAL (1623-1662)

The world is full of lovers of Pascal. Who Loves Descartes?
Who loves Kant?—Morris Bishop in *Pascal, The Life of Genius*

Pascal ranks as one of the greatest geniuses France has ever produced. He was a man of superlative mental powers, but also a great Christian saint. He was truly a splash of genius—mathematician, scientist, man of letters, linguist, exegete, saint, mystic, controversialist and apologist. His great powers of abstract thought manifested themselves in his work as a theoretical mathematician. Vexed with the problem of moving around Paris he invented public transportation showing that the theoretical was not divorced from the practical. He also was a deeply mystical person. His paragraph on "Fire" is one of the classics in the history of mysticism. In science he distinguished himself by demonstrating with repeated experiments that nature does not abhor a vacuum but air exerts pressure. He had sufficient linguistic gifts to engage in serious biblical exegesis.

Pascal wrote no system of apologetics. However as David collected materials for the temple so Pascal collected materials for an apology. His inspirations were written down on whatever was handy—sometimes in legible hand and other times in an illegible scrawl. Sometimes he scribbled in haste and at other times he deliberately composed his lines. These scraps, edited and bound together, are called Pascal's *Pensées* (French, "thoughts"). They present no connected system and therefore constructing a unified view of Pascal is a task of literary palaeontology, and entire treatises of intensive scholarly research have been devoted to this task. What the *Pensées* lack in organizational form they certainly atone for in their genius. Pascal's name ranks with the greatest in the history of Christian apologetics.

I. INTRODUCTION

1. *His problem.* Pascal lived in the seventeenth century when the French nation was increasingly drifting into deism, indifferentism, and eventually materialism and revolution. On the one hand were sophisticated people who would have nothing to do with Christianity but spent their time gambling or going to the drama or play-

ing billiards—to reconstruct the picture from Pascal's barbed remarks. Their attitude towards Christianity was one of placid indifference and deliberate ignoration. Others were drunk with the Cartesian wine hoping that the application of the geometrical method to the problems of philosophy would readily solve them.

Pascal's problem was to evangelize men of these different dispositions—atheists, deists, skeptics, and Epicureans. The indifferent and the atheistic had to be shocked into spiritual sensibility: the libertines must be awakened to spiritual responsibility; and the Cartesians must be routed from the field.

2. *His diagnosis.* Why was it that such secular and anti-Christian diseases plagued France? Why was it not one Christian nation rejoicing in the one true faith? Part of Pascal's greatness was his analysis of the causes of unbelief in his own generation and in his own country.

(1) Turning to his Bible Pascal found reference to God as *Deus absconditus* (the Hidden God, Isaiah 45:15). God was not like gold to be found by diligent and systematic research. He was the Hidden God. He was hidden because man is a sinner and has forfeited his right to divine fellowship. A cannonade is here leveled at the deists. The deists thought that all of Nature was a book of God to be easily read on every page. Not so to Pascal! Sin had clouded the mind of man, had broken the divine-human fellowship, *and God had gone into hiding!* Therefore, the way back to God was no simple matter. The corruption of man through sin coupled with the moral nature of God meant that recovery and redemption were no easy matter. Let no man think that God is near us and available to us like the air we breath. God is the Hidden God!

(2) Casting a shrewd glance over current philosophic thought Pascal discovered men uncritically accepting the complete ability of reason to solve their religious problems. Thus men were not becoming Christians because they thought that Christianity was irrational. Men were refusing *revelation* because they believed that they had a more reliable resource in *reason*.

However, *reason* meant something very specific to Pascal. He means reason as exemplified in the philosophy of Descartes. It was the reason of mathematical induction, the reason of logical inference, the reason of the metaphysical methodology of Descartes. Fundamental axioms, rules, definitions and symbols are postulated, and from these theorems are deduced. By an imitation of this geometric-like procedure Descartes hoped to reconstruct philosophy. It was one of Pascal's most fundamental convictions that men were abusing a method which was designed for geometry and science but which was totally inapplicable to Christian faith. Therefore reason (in this Cartesian sense) must also be put in its place.

(3) Furthermore, the Frenchman of his times was failing to understand himself and in failing to understand himself he was exasperatingly indifferent to Christian faith. Pascal felt that man had become numb to the issues of life, existence, immortality and God. Man smug in himself fails to understand himself. The self-satisfied man looks at the Christian faith as the troubler in Israel and not the redeemer in Israel. It was part of Pascal's strategy to blast Frenchmen out of this smugness and show the vanity (i.e., emptiness) of men.

II. THE CURE

Having made the proper diagnosis how did Pascal set himself to his task of bringing men around to the serious consideration of the Christian faith? Although there were traditional apologetic materials to draw from Pascal salvaged little from them. Part of Pascal's novelty and part of his contribution to Christian apologetics is the manner in which he attempted to reënlist the French people in the cause of Christian faith. He employed the following methods:

1. *Existential shock and appeal.* Pascal's existentialism before existentialism is well known. Pascal's use of existential shock was perhaps the biggest weapon in his arsenal. It was an attempt to deal a solid blow to the skepticism and indifferentism of the Frenchmen. He attempts to alert his countrymen with a direct and painful jab of his pen. In doing this he created some of the finest passages in the *Pensées*, and was the master among masters of the diagnosis of the conditions of human existence.

By *existential shock* we mean Pascal's method of shocking Frenchmen out of their complacency by vivid contrasts, by sharp jabs at frightful inconsistencies, by penetrating analyses of the foolish modes of existence, by pictures of despair placed along side of pictures of grace and redemption. A smug, sophisticated French skeptic must see himself hanging between time and eternity, as a delicate smudge of protoplasm which a piffle of poison could exterminate, as a disposed king miserably remembering his former greatness, and as a discontented wretch who suspects that there really is blessed contentment somewhere. But where?

Pascal points a finger at the calloused heart of an atheist and says that the man's negligence of immortality is monstrous! This is the man who spends so many days and nights in rage and despair over the loss of an office, or over some imaginary insult to his honor, who also knows that someday death will take *all* away and *this* he contemplates without anxiety or emotion. It is, to Pascal, *perfectly monstrous* that in the same heart there is this grotesque sensibility to trifles and such strange insensibility to the greatest items of human destiny. It is an incomprehensible enchantment, a supernatural slumber which strongly suggests a superhuman origin. This indifference is like a man in prison who while awaiting the decree for his death or release occupies his time playing some trivial game. It is not unlike some great judge upon whose decision affairs of the state as well as life hang and who pours out his vital energies in chasing a rabbit during the hunt! For men in this life to refuse to think of the next life is complete irrationality and indescribable ignorance. Criminal negligence in human affairs is absolutely nothing compared to indifferentism about future life.

Pascal has a new cannon ball he wishes to fire at this fortress of indifferentism: *the new astronomy!* Pascal was the first modern thinker to see the frightening "existential" character of the new theories of time and space. He picks up the smug Frenchman who lives in a smug universe and attempts to frighten him into seriousness with a vision of *the new universe*.

> Let man then contemplate the whole of nature in her full and grand majesty. . . . The whole visible world is only an imperceptible atom in the ample bosom of nature. . . . Let him regard himself as lost in this remote corner of nature; and from the little cell in which he finds himself lodged, I mean the universe, let him estimate at their true value the earth, kingdoms, cities, and himself. What is a man in the infinite? . . . He who regards himself in this light will be afraid of himself, and observing himself sustained in the body given him by nature between two abysses of the Infinite and Nothing, will tremble at the sight of these marvels; and I think that, as his curiosity changes into admiration, he will be more disposed to contemplate them in silence than to examine them with presumption. For in fact what is man in nature? A Nothing in comparison with the Infinite, an All in comparison with the Nothing, a mean between nothing and everything (No. 72, Brunschvicg, edition).

Lost in such greatness, transcending such minutia as propoplasm, ignorant of beginnings and endings, he is confronted with "an impenetrable secret; he is equally incapable of seeing the Nothing from which he was made, and the Infinite in which he is swallowed up" (No. 72). Pascal also has his own dialectic to give man an existential shock—the way *up* and the way *down*. [*Down*]: "Man is but a reed, the most feeble thing in nature, [*up*] but he is a thinking reed. [*Down*] The entire universe need not arm itself to crush him. A vapour, a drop of water suffices to kill him. [*Up*] But, if the universe were to crush him, man would still be more noble than that which killed him, because he knows that he dies and the advantage which the universe has over him; the universe knows nothing of this" (No. 347). [*Down*] "What a chimera then is man! What a novelty! What a monster, what a chaos, what a contradiction, what a prodigy. [*Up*] Judge of all things; [*down*] imbecile worm of the earth; [*up*] depository of truth, [*down*] a sink of uncertainty and error; [*up*] the pride [*down*] and refuse of the universe" (No. 434).

Perhaps the most celebrated instance of Pascal's shock treatment is his famous wager (No. 233). The cool, skeptical, sophisticated Frenchman will not even argue Christianity. He passes by the church with an air of complete indifference on his way to the gambling room. But how foolish he is in the gamble of life! Heaven and hell are the "chips" in this gamble! It is not a routine spin of the wheel upon which we may bet or bide our time. *We must bet!* But a wise Frenchman might say that one does not bet about religion; *one reasons.* No! replies Pascal. Reason can decide nothing here. The game is played at infinite extremities, i.e., eternal destiny and not some matter of business prudence. In this situation reason can neither defend nor argue a thesis. *Therefore we must wager!* We are embarked! Reason fails; to bet is the only resolution of our situation.

The cold, calculating clever gambler makes a bet on life which he would never tolerate in a gambling room! Much to his dismay the religious man whom he considers dumb and credulous makes such a play that no matter how the wheel spins or the dice roll *he wins!* If God is, he wins the reward of eternal life; if God is not, he wins the reward of a good life. The indifferent man is stuck with a hand of cards in the game of life that would scandalize him in a round of gambling! And so Pascal's barb is precisely this: *why gamble so poorly on life when the stakes are so incredibly high?*

By such means Pascal carries on his unrelenting battle against complacency. Man seeks happiness; he ends up with misery. He is a dethroned king restlessly wandering around persecuted by memories of former greatness and present misery. He is infinitely depressed with the weary of weariness and finds release in such a superficial thing as a game of billiards. He launches himself into pleasure which serves as an opiate as he moves relentlessly to death. He struts upon life's stage to play the angel but ends by playing the brute. These are all Pascal's effort to get the knife under the crab's shell.

2. *Reason "debunked."* Pascal's next effort is to dissolve in a powerful acid the current idolatry of reason. If he can destroy "faith in reason," he can restore "faith in faith." He is sturdily opposed to truth made into an idolatrous statue. Truth in and for itself, and separated from the love of God, is an idol and this idol we must neither love nor worship!

(1) *Reason defined.* Reason to Pascal is *Geometric Mind* or *Mathematical Mind.* To Pascal geometry meant not only the spatial character of mathematics, but it included mechanics and arithmetic. In short it was very close to what we mean by "science." The first principles of "science" cannot be matters of demonstration but are self-evident. However, in that they are so abstract and presuppose so much learning they are self-evident only to those capable of the requisite concentration. From these axioms (along with definitions) theorems are deduced. And within its own sphere, the *Geometric Mind* is legitimate.

It was the hope of Descartes and Spinoza that if this method were applied to philosophy the tough problems of philosophy could be solved. So when Pascal attacks reason he is not attacking *Geometric Mind* in its rightful territory, but as carried over by Descartes into the realm of philosophy. *Therefore Pascal is very sharp with Descartes.* Descartes studied science too profoundly! Descartes is not to be forgiven because after invoking God as first cause of motion he dismisses God from his philosophy; Descartes is "useless and uncertain" (No. 78); and if Decartes' analysis of reality is true by mere identification of it with figure and motion then "we do not think all philosophy is worth one hour of pain" (No. 79).

The interesting feature of his reaction to Descartes is that both men were front-ranking mathematicians and men of science. So Pascal is not uttering these words from the cloister! He claims to have studied the abstract sciences and found that "these abstract sciences are not suited to men" (No. 144). There is something untranslatable about the French word *pensée* and the verb, *penser.* Descartes philosophy began with "I think [*je pense*] therefore I am," and Pascal's deepest meditations are called *pensées.* Here were two Frenchmen each with his own profound understanding of *penser* and finding its reality in opposite directions.

The application of the *Geometric Mind* to philosophy of religion inebriates a person into thinking that he has the infallible method of discovering the truth. Such a man arrogantly dispenses with the light of Christianity and sits in his own cubicle and Spinoza-like spins the structure of the universe out of his own mind. If he is provided with a few axioms, some definitions, and some rules, he can write philosophy as veraciously and infallibly as one demonstrates theorems in geometry. But Pascal had learned better than this! From Montaigne he had learned skepticism and from Scripture he had learned of humanity's deep sinfulness, so he knew the truth was not learned in this arid, abstract and uncommitted procedure.

When Pascal decries reason, then, he has in mind *Geometric Mind*. And much of what Pascal says is predicated upon his unique theory of the construction of the human mind, the fine details of which are spelled out for us in Arthur Rich's *Pascals Bild vom Menschen*.

(2) *Attack*. Pascal now moves up his guns to blast out of operation the Cartesian fortress of reason.

(a) The Biblical doctrines of original sin and *Deus absconditus* inform us that man is in sin and God is hidden. In this situation reason is helpless. The blind man does not know which of the three hundred and sixty degrees of the circle to start probing with his stick; and likewise reason does not know which way to turn to find the Hidden God. If the supreme positive doctrine of Christianity is redemption its supreme negative doctrine is the corruption of man. The doctrine of original sin opens the eyes to see man's corruption, and the one who knows *this* doctrine understands the waywardness of the human race. Furthermore, "original sin is foolishness to me. . . . You must not reproach me for want of reason in this doctrine, since I admit it to be without reason. But this foolishness is wiser than all the wisdom of men. . . . For without this, what can we say that man is? And how should it be perceived by reason, since it is a thing against reason, and since reason, far from finding it out by her own eyes, is averse to it when it is presented to her?" (No. 445). A remarkable commentary on this *pensée* is Goethe's reaction to Kant's doctrine of radical evil. Goethe was the fairest flower of German enlightenment; and Kant was its greatest philosopher. Because Kant defended (in his ethics) a doctrine of radical evil Goethe accused him of staining his philosopher's cloak [the ancient philosophers wore a cloak indicating their vocation] with the shameful idea of radical evil so Christians would kiss the hem of his garment (narrated for us by Brunner, *The Mediator*, p. 128).

The doctrine of human corruption is the sand in the machinery of the theistic proofs of Descartes. God happens to be principally the God of redemption and not the God of ontology! The Cartesian may postulate God as The Axiom, but The Axiom is not the God of experience, the God of love, or the God of redemption. At this point Pascal has anticipated what many of the existential and neo-orthodox theologians of the twentieth century shall say.

(b) Pascal shows that the claim to be guided by pure geometric reason is plain stupidity. Here he is like Kierkegaard hazing Hegel. He shows that *imagination* is stronger than reason. There is Descartes walking on a narrow plank across a crevice. *Reason* tells him the plank is wide enough and strong enough; but *imagination* overpowers his reason and he trembles and quakes!

Next he introduces a magistrate who is governed by the strictest canons of law, and dares not let imagination influence the steady tread of justice. But next Sunday the magistrate is in church. Why? Is it not to strengthen reason with *devotion, zeal* and *ardor*? Reason apparently needs considerable bracing even in the court of justice.

Look again at the judge sitting in church with great dignity and composure. Then the preacher appears. But what goes? The preacher's face is so comical! He has had a miserable shave and his garments are covered with the spattering of the lather. As he preaches he utters great truth. Does the judge let his reason sop in these deep truths? No! Imagination gets the best of him and whilst chuckling he loses his judicial gravity!

(c) Pascal shows, further, that no man conducts his life according to the strict rules of Descartes by indicating other means of disturbing the reason. Superstitious or scary things "unhinge the reason" (No. 82). Judges are supposed to be guided by justice informed and guided by reason but in truth they are influenced by hatreds, affections, and bribes calling forth the stinging remark of Pascal: "How ludicrous is reason, blown with a breath in every direction" (No. 82). Furthermore, the greatest judge of the world can be so bothered by a troublesome fly that he no longer can properly reason. "If you wish to be able to reach the truth, chase away that animal which holds its reason in check and disturbs that powerful intellect which rules towns and kingdoms. Here is a comical God! *O most ridiculous hero!*" (No. 366, italics are his).

(d) Love, the choicest of human experiences, does not come from reason but from the heart. How does a man make love? Does he *prove* that he ought to be loved by "enumerating in order the causes of love; that would be ridiculous" (No. 283). God is of love and love is of the heart. "It is the heart which experiences God, and not the reason. This, then is faith: God felt by the heart, not by the reason" (No. 278).

(e) Pascal endeavors to turn the table on reason by claiming that reason is actually dependent upon the heart for its very groundwork of operation. As Rich's work on Pascal shows (*Pascals*

Bild von Menchsen) it is difficult to harmonize or coordinate all of Pascal's remarks about the heart, the spirit, etc., nevertheless the broad outline is clear. The heart is not a blind feeling but it is the intuitive center of the human being which sees things *synoptically*. In another part of his *Pensées*, Pascal calls it the *esprit de finesse* which means the more sensitive, the more intuitive mode of knowing in contrast to reason. Thus the heart knows things intuitively, i.e., directly, and there can be no demonstration of intuitions. The perception of a color is a direct intuition about which there can be no demonstration. With the directness of intuition arises also a feeling of great certainty.

Thus the heart is intuitive and *synoptic*. As synoptic it takes in the whole of a situation rather than a part; it feels the total weight of evidence rather than selecting out certain kinds of evidence. It can thus find a place—because it is *synoptic*—for emotional tones and ethical considerations in knowledge. Being thus at the root of our knowing all other types of knowing are dependent upon it including Descartes' method of deduction. "For the knowledge of first principles, as space, time, motion, number, is as sure as any of those which we get from reasoning. And reason must trust these intuitions of the heart, and must base on them every argument" (No. 282).

He continues by saying that "principles are intuited, propositions are inferred, all with certainty though in different ways" (No. 282). Fundamental notions of philosophy and religion can only rest on an intuitive, direct basis. Propositions rest on a previously established abstract system (e.g., geometric axioms). These axioms of a system are pure inventions or conventions. First principles of the real world can be known only intuitively or synoptically by the heart. This division of cognitive labor was a heritage from his father, Etienne. His father believed that a matter of faith was by its very nature not an object of reason; that a matter of science must be totally divorced from faith. Thus reason has no right to order the maids around in the household of faith; and faith has no right to order the servants around in the household of science.

The conclusion of the matter is that the follower of Descartes is making a fool of himself. He has a very detailed and rationalistic philosophy but none of it really deals with life and faith. The Cartesian philosophy cannot settle the issues of religion nor of the Christian faith. Most detrimental of all, it cannot conduct us to the presence of the living God.

(3) *Skepticism*. If reason is religiously helpless what are we to think of it? Pascal's answer is: *skepticism*. Man is incapable of

both *certain* knowledge and *absolute* ignorance. Man can neither be *dogmatist* nor *agnostic*. If he follows *reason*, that deceives him; if he follows *sense* that deceives him. Man without grace is therefore full of error. He is caught in such strong and conflicting cross-currents that he is rendered helpless. To *this* man Pascal says: "Know then, proud man, what a paradox you are to yourself. Humble yourself, weak reason; be silent, foolish nature. . . . Hear God" (No. 434). Only divine authority and divine revelation can resolve the paradox; reason, helpless and inadequate, can only bow the head and listen to God.

"Skepticism is true," he writes, "for, after all, men before Jesus Christ did not know where they were, nor whether they were great or small" (No. 432). Thus Pascal's apologetics boxes us between the skepticism of reason or the great assurances of the heart. At the same time Pascal is a *convinced* Christian and an *avowed* skeptic. "To make light of philosophy is to be a true philosopher" (No. 4).

The theistic proofs, proofs to show that God exists, come under Pascal's fire because they are functions of reason in an area where only the heart prevails. Our true knowledge of God is to be found only in Jesus Christ: "Thus without the Scripture, which has Jesus Christ alone for its object, we know nothing, and see only darkness and confusion in the nature of God, and in our own nature" (No. 548). The theistic proofs are logically difficult and obtruse! Even when we have satisfied ourselves with a theistic proof within one hour we may be upset for fear that the proof has deceived us. The only sane thing for an apologist is to keep his distance from the theistic proofs: "Therefore I shall not undertake here to prove by natural reasons either the existence of God, or the Trinity, or the immortality of the soul, or anything of that nature; not only because I should not feel myself sufficiently able to find in nature arguments to convince hardened atheists, but also because such knowledge without Jesus Christ is useless and barren" (No. 556).

In verification of this he claims that no canonical writer has ever attempted such a proof. Natural theology has a place for those who already believe in God but natural theology represents no possibility for the unbeliever because God is the *Deus absconditus*. When unbelievers look into nature therefore they only see "obscurity and darkness" (No. 242).

(4) *Place of reason*. Pascal is not a sheer irrationalist. Reason does have a proper function. The number of propositions known by the heart intuitively is rather small and therefore the full range of knowledge must be known through reason. An absolute skepticism is thus rendered impossible. However, reason even has a

critical function in the Christian faith, otherwise we could never distinguish true religion from superstition. Thus he wrote: "Two extremes: to exclude reason, to admit reason only. . . . If we submit everything to reason, our religion will have no mysterious and supernatural element. If we offend the principles of reason, our religion will be absurd and ridiculous" (Nos. 253, 273).

With reference to science Pascal is very clear that this is no place for faith or the heart; this is strictly the area of reason or the scientific method. The religious and authoritarian intrusion of clerics into scientific matters receives severe criticism from Pascal.

To this point Pascal's apologetics has been on the defensive. Those who oppose the Christian faith, Pascal argues, should first learn what they oppose. It is necessary for Pascal to present the essential nature of Christianity so that he might silence the cavillers and encourage the doubtful.

3. *The real nature of Christianity.* By existential shock and in debunking Cartesian reason Pascal prepared the way for his positive approach. We may arbitrarily divide his apologetics at this point into the subjective and the objective phase. In the first he shows the true spirit in which Christianity is believed, and in the other he attempts to deal with the objective verification of Christianity. He makes room for both the heart and reason in religion.

(1) *The Subjective Aspect*

(a) *Pascal's doctrine of the heart.* Pascal divides the human cognitive powers into two divisions: heart and Geometric Mind. Or according to Rich (*op. cit.*) the heart (as the absolute bedrock of *all* knowing) is divided into the heart as *Geist* (spirit-mind) and as will. The heart as *Geist* comes to its fruition in Geometric Mind and the heart as will comes to it fruition as *esprit de finesse* (acute mind, refined mind, the heart in the religious sense). The acute mind, as we have seen, functions *intuitively* and *synoptically* and therefore is the beginning of all our knowing. Without this intuitive and synoptic vision, knowledge could not get started. This intuitive mind differs from reason as ordinarily understood in that the latter usually means *discursive reasoning.* And correspondingly by *heart* Pascal did not mean fogged emotional response but the central, personal, intuitional center of knowing. Thus Pascal can call the heart "instinct," or "sentiment" or "sentiment of the heart" or "inspiration." The heart is, then, the inward, intuitive, synoptic, perhaps even mystical method of knowing. It feels more than it deduces; it is sympathetic more than analytic.

Pascal's doctrine of the heart is therefore at the center of his religious epistemology. If one followed reason (after the Cartesians) one methodologically excluded the possibility of knowing the Christian faith. The *heart* knows God and is found if we seek him with all our heart. The Cartesian method in religion cannot fail but stumble into the problem of *Deus absconditus*.

The order of the heart differs from the order of the reason. Therefore the heart has reasons which are not known to reason. The *heart*, for example, feels God, but the reason does not. How can the reason judge something it does not know? For example Pascal said: "It is the heart which experiences God, and not the reason. This, then, is faith: God felt by the heart, not by the reason" (No. 278). Heart and reason are running along two different tracks. The heart has its direct intuitions which are inaccessible to reason; but reason has its demonstrations which cannot be intuited. Just as the heart must stay out of logic, geometry and science (as far as demonstrations are concerned) so must the reason stay out of religion!

In the realm of the heart the reason has no other recourse but to submit: "Submission is the use of reason in which consists true Christianity" (No. 269); "Reason would never submit, if it did not judge that there are some occasions on which it ought to submit. It is then right for it to submit, when it judges that it ought to submit" (No. 270); and "there is nothing so comfortable as this disavowal of reason" (No. 272).

Speaking in very eloquent words Pascal informs us that God is not a God of geometric truth (which excludes automatically the possibility of a natural theology); nor a God of the elements (and so excludes paganism); nor a God of providence (and so excludes Judaism). Rather "the God of Abraham, the God of Isaac, the God of Jacob, the God of Christians, is a God of love and of comfort, a God who fills the soul and heart of those whom He possesses, a God who makes them conscious of their inward wretchedness, and His infinite mercy, who unites Himself to their inmost soul, who fills it with humility and joy, with confidence and love, who renders them incapable of any other end than Himself" (No. 556).

According to Pascal three different sorts of things lead us to faith: reason, custom, inspiration. When we believe things because they are beliefs accepted within our society we believe by custom. Christian faith is belief from reason and inspiration, *but never reason without inspiration*. "It is not that [Christianity] excludes reason and custom," he writes. "On the contrary, the mind must be opened to proofs, must be confirmed by custom, and offer itself in humbleness to inspiration, which alone can produce a true and saving effect" (No. 245).

Religious epistemology is here divided from the epistemology of science and much of philosophy. The latter two are externally oriented and are interested in establishing objectivity; the former is inward, spiritual and intuitive. Further, Pascal strongly states that there are no connecting links between reason and intuition until sin is removed. They represent two very different modes of knowing although it is the one person or the one "heart" which knows. Nothing is more foolish than to apply the wrong kind of knowing to a given subject matter. Reason in the area of religion is such an example, and reason will never find God.

(b) *Pascal's doctrine of faith*. Faith is a gift of God, and is a function of the heart: "It is the heart which experiences God, and not the reason. This, then, is faith: God felt by the heart, not by the reason. . . . Faith is a gift of God; do not believe that we said it was a gift of reasoning" (Nos. 278, 279). Of course the function of faith in the heart is not without the function of the mind. Faith is not of itself anti-intellectual nor anti-volitional. Whenever God puts grace in the heart he also puts reason in the mind. But if we attempt to put religion in the heart by force we do not put faith there but terror.

If faith is a gift of God how do we come by it? Man may attempt to *reason* his way to God but we have already seen how futile this is according to Pascal's presuppositions. Such a procedure is useless and barren for God gives his truth to the one who loves him. In connection with this there is a very interesting passage in a work outside of the *Pensées*:

> For He departs from the secrets of nature, which hide Him, only in order to stimulate our faith to serve Him with all the more ardor when we know Him with greater certainty. If God revealed Himself continually to men, there would be no merit at all in believing Him; if He never revealed Himself, there would be no faith. But ordinarily He conceals Himself, and He reveals Himself but rarely to those who He wishes to engage in His service. This strange secrecy into which God has withdrawn and which is impenetrable to the eyes of man, is a great lesson to lead us into solitude far from the eyes of man (*Great Shorter Works of Pascal*, p. 146).

It is clear from this passage that faith and revelation are closely conjoined; that faith is not possible without a profound inward movement of the heart; and that faith is not a mere movement of the assenting mind. That which generates faith is humiliation, submission, and inspiration. But what does *submission* involve? In a most disputed passage (No. 233) Pascal says that a man is to imitate the faithful and from this imitation, this going through the motions, faith will come. But when faith comes there will also come stupification (*cela vous abêtira*). Faith by mechanical imitation? What does *abêtira* mean in this connection? However we interpret the verb (*abêtira*) Pascal's movement of thought is clear. *Faith comes by submitting, imitating, listening!*

This, then, is the inward or subject part of his apologetics. In a word, true knowledge of God and true fellowship with God is of the heart, of faith, of feeling. It is a glorious experience in which God makes us unforgettably his own. Reason or Geometric Mind is utterly incapable of functioning in this experience.

(2) *Objective aspect.* One of the emphases that modern students of Pascal agree upon is that Pascal was a serious and accomplished student of Sacred Scripture. Certainly his attempt was to formulate a Scriptural apologetic. Pascal read his Scriptures in the Latin, Greek, and Hebrew and made his own translations and paraphrases. His sister Gilberte said that he practically knew the Bible by heart and could readily tell if a verse were cited correctly or not. It is in respect to the character of biblical religion which Pascal knew by his detailed knowledge of Scripture which forms the impetus behind the objective aspect of his apologetics.

(a) *Pascal's doctrine of authority.* Pascal was nominally a Roman Catholic but many scholars believe that his thought is virtually Protestant. However, in agreement with Roman Catholicism and a strong Protestant orthodoxy, he was emphatically pledged to a strong principle of authority in religon. In the area of science the *only* method is the scientific method and authority must be excluded here; but in Christian faith matters are determined by authority (*Scriptures* and the *fathers*) and reason or the scientific method must be excluded. Pascal addresses man's reason and cries, "Hear God!" (No. 434). Truth is brought into the human heart *by the authority of him who speaks* and not by reason. To resort to reason and not Scripture is to resort to feeble reason. Faith, to the contrary, submits herself to Scripture!

(b) *Divine initiative.* Although Pascal says that faith comes by submission or inspiration, he also teaches very strongly that it is God who bestows it. For example he says, "Therefore, those to whom God has imparted religion by intuition are very fortunate, and justly convinced. But to those who do not have it, we can give it only by reasoning, waiting for God to give them spiritual insight, without which faith is only human, and useless for salvation" (No. 282). It was Pascal's exposure to Calvinism, Jansenism, and the Scriptures which contributed to this aspect of his thought.

There is even some evidence that Pascal had a copy of the famous Geneva Bible.

Very important for Pascal's doctrine of faith is *pensée* number 248: "Faith is different from proof; the one is human, the other is the gift of God. *Justus ex fide vivit* ["The just shall live by faith," Rom. 1:17]. It is this faith that God himself puts into the heart, of which the proof is often the instrument, *fides ex auditu* [faith from hearing, Rom. 10:17]; but this faith is in the heart, and makes us not say *scio* [I know], but *credo* [I believe]."

According to Pascal faith is concerned with the divine verities and their establishment in the heart is not by reasoning but by the operation of God himself. Of course we do *know* these verities but God does not give them to the mind and then to the heart, but he gives them to the heart and then to the mind. In this order of knowing the proud reason must learn its proper humility! This is the order of love. For by coming *first* into the heart we love them, *then* we know them. This is the reverse of ordinary human experience in which we first know in order to then love.

God gives faith by sentiment in the heart. When he does that we are Christians. Therefore the most fervent prayer we can pray is "O Lord incline my heart to Thee!" For unless God inclines the heart, men will never believe; but they will believe as soon as he does. We have here the Reformers' doctrine of the internal witness of the Holy Spirit but Pascal does not seem to be able to put his finger precisely on the theological structure of this doctrine.

The heart has no need for proofs if it is inclined towards faith by God. Humble people who never read learned books and never even heard of theistic proofs are believers with full assurance for "God Himself inclines them to believe, and thus they are effectively convinced" (No. 287).

(c) *Proofs.* Pascal can hardly defend a Christian faith which is completely subjective for he knows if nothing else the Christian faith contacts history. Furthermore, he is aware that religions compete for the truth and therefore he must say something about resolving this competition.

(i) Pascal demands that if a religion claims to be the true one it should cure pride and sin; it should have a correct doctrine of human nature both in its greatness and in its littleness; it should teach that there is one God who created all things, and that this God *should be loved*; it should teach us our duties, our sins and their cures; it should teach us our greatness and our misery which will lead us to both esteem and despise the self, to love and hate the self. Pascal finds that only Christianity meets such tests.

(ii) Pascal has a strong Christological element in his apologetics. Christ alone is really the proof of Christianity! Only in Christ do

we have the full knowledge of God and all proofs of God apart
from Christ are weak. Without "a necessary Mediator promised
and come, we cannot absolutely prove God, nor teach right doctrine and right morality. But through Jesus Christ, and in Jesus
Christ, we prove God, and teach morality and doctrine. Jesus
Christ is then the true God of men" (No. 547). Without
Jesus Christ and Scripture nature is "darkness and confusion"
(No. 548). "It is not only impossible but useless to know God
without Jesus Christ" (No. 549). In his most famous passage of
all, *The Mystery of Jesus* (No. 553), he gives us one of the greatest
meditations on the person of Christ in Christian literature and
thus sets forth the only true religion as that religion incarnate in
Jesus Christ.

He also makes appeal to routine matters of Christian evidences
as he becomes more and more aware of the contact of Christianity
with history as well as with the heart. He sees the remarkable
providence of God in the history of the Jews. He sees the validation of the faith in fulfilled prophecy with Jesus Christ as the
supreme fulfilment of prophecy and proof from prophecy. He appeals to miracles and asserts that "men owe it to God to accept
the religion which He sends. God owes it to men not to lead them
into error" (No. 843).

In keeping with his subjectivistic method Pascal has no great
hope in the evangelistic use of the proofs. Miracles and prophecy
are not absolutely convincing. God "so regulates the knowledge of
Himself that He has given signs of Himself, visible to those who
seek Him, and not to those who seek Him not. There is enough
light for those who only desire to see, and enough obscurity for
those who have a contrary disposition" (No. 144); "the prophecies,
the very miracles and proofs of our religion, are not of such a nature that they can be said to be absolutely convincing. But they
are also of such a kind that it cannot be said that it is unreasonable to believe them. Thus there is both evidence and obscurity
to enlighten some and confuse others" (No. 564). Perhaps the
best way to sum up Pascal's apology is with his own words: "None
is so happy as a true Christian, nor so reasonable, virtuous, or
amiable" (No. 541).

BIBLIOGRAPHY

Cailliet, E., *Pascal, Genius in the Light of Scripture*
_____, *The Clue to Pascal*
_____, and Blanknagel, J., editors, *Great Shorter Works of Pascal*
Clark, William, *Pascal and the Port Royalists*
Durand, A., "Mind and Heart in Pascal," *The Month*, new series, Vol. 6, November, 1951
Eastwood, D. M., *The Revival of Pascal*
Jordan, H. R., *Blaise Pascal, A Study in Religious Psychology*
Knight, H., "The Relevance of Pascal," *Hibbert Journal*, Vol. 48, April, 1950
Morris, Bishop, *Pascal, The Life of Genius*
Oman, John, *The Problem of Faith and Freedom in the Last Two Centuries.* Lecture II, "Jesuitism and Pascal's Pensées."
Pascal, Blaise, *Thoughts, Letters, Minor Works*
Patrick, D., *Pascal and Kierkegaard* (2 vols.)
Rich, Emil, *Pascals Bild vom Menschen*

Chapter III

SOREN KIERKEGAARD (1813-1855)

This one man, Soren Kierkegaard, is at the same time Denmark's greatest theologian, man of letters, religious psychologist, and apologist. Kierkegaard is recognized as the founder of existentialist philosophies and the inspiration at many points behind such great thinkers as Brunner, Barth, and Niebuhr. Although the influence of his life and works were not appreciably felt by his own generation he represents one of the very few great turning points in western intellectual life in the areas of philosophy and theology.

But is Kierkegaard an apologist? Did he not scorn proofs for God's existence? Did he not call the intellectual approach to Christianity *paganism*? yes *blasphemy*? Did he not castigate apologetics itself? The answer to all these questions is *yes*. Kierkegaard is not an apologist if apologetics is equivalent to natural theology or Christian evidences or philosophical verifications. In the sense that Butler and Paley are apologists, Kierkegaard is not! But if apologetics has as its central concern the problem of truth and knowledge then Kierkegaard is an apologist for he certainly has spoken on these two issues. Kierkegaard does repeatedly discuss the truthfulness of the Christian faith or the truth of the faith and this is apologetical territory.

I. KIERKEGAARD'S DIAGNOSIS OF HIS TIMES

To understand Kierkegaard one must understand his enemies. Whom was he bombarding? attacking? sniping? barraging? What evoked such a torrent of words and books and eventually a premature death? Certainly there have been attempts to explain Kierkegaard from a number of considerations. Rudolph Friedmann interprets Kierkegaard from a psychoanalytic viewpoint. T. Haeker (supported by A. Dru) argues that Kierkegaard was a hunchback. However our concern is not with these psychoanalytic or physical nor even biographical features of Kierkegaard, but with the Christian situation in Denmark during his lifetime.

1. One of the leading philosophies of Denmark was Hegelianism having been introduced by Heiberg and Martensen. However, we must not think that Hegel took over Danish scholarship as the impression is sometimes given in treatments of Kierkegaard. But

Danish Hegelianism was one of the principle things Kierkegaard reacted against. Hegel pictured Reality as being structured by a well-knit logical system. From an original abstract category of *being* he proposed to deduce all the categories of Reality. Hence to be a Hegelian one must be a marvelous logician and system builder!

Into this system Hegel incorporated Christianity but not as it is found *in situ* in the New Testament. Hegel considered that the theology of the New Testament was the *symbolic* version of his philosophical metaphysics. The incarnation did not mean that God truly entered into humanity through the person of Jesus Christ, but that God and man are metaphysically continuous, that God and man are of the same essence. By such a retooling of Christianity, philosophy and Christian theology could be harmonized into one great system. This was truly *the* apologetic of Christianity according to many scholars of the time of Hegel and thereafter. Hegel had given Christianity royal philosophical respectability. Christianity was now in accord with the noblest of philosophies. A philosopher need not be ashamed of confessing Christian faith, and a Christian theologian need not feel embarrassment from philosophy.

Against this synthesis Kierkegaard waged unrelenting war. He was one of the few men in the hey-day of Hegelianism who offered a real criticism of the system. "The System," as Kierkegaard represents this synthesis, comes in for very rough treatment and sarcasm. Undoubtedly some of the extreme emphasis of Kierkegaard on inwardness and subjectivity is due to his reaction to Hegel. However, just as Pascal's devil was Descartes, Kierkegaard's is Hegel.

2. The second foe of Kierkegaard was *Romanticism*. Although Romanticism was in concord with Kierkegaard in believing that the way to happiness was not by speculative philosophy, nonetheless, Kierkegaard felt that it took too easy a view of the problems of human existence. Part of the mood of Romanticism was to feel at home in nature. In Kierkegaard's diagnosis it represented the *aesthetic* stage of existence. It means the life lived for the pleasure it yields with boredom as its only fear. It is the *unrevealed* life—the life with no decision, no inwardness, no pain, and no suffering.

In *Stages on Life's Way* Kierkegaard describes the Romanticists (the aesthetes) as being on the lowest stage of life and who never pass beyond immediacy or pleasure. The intermediatory stage is the ethical, and the highest is the religious which is itself divided into two stages. It is an inward crisis which causes a person to pass from the one stage to the next. But passage from the ethical to the religious, and the passage from the lower religious to the higher religious are more profound than passing from the aesthetic to the ethical. It is not our purpose to sketch out each of these stages but to stress that *real existence* is religious existence which is characterized by pain and suffering and not by pleasure.

3. Next Kierkegaard turns his heavy guns towards Danish Christendom. To be born in Denmark meant automatically to be a Christian. All Danes are baptized and so all Danes are thereby Christians! Orthodoxy filled the land of Denmark. But what kind of orthodoxy is it? It is the orthodoxy of playing the game of Christianity. Orthodoxy and superficiality are accordingly synonymous. A Dane becomes a Christian with no effort, no pain, no suffering, no cross-bearing, no discipleship.

Instead of using the universal acceptance of Christianity in Denmark as a proof of the truthfulness of Christianity, Kierkegaard in scathing irony uses it as a disproof of the New Testament! The New Testament represents faith as the way of the narrow gate and the narrow path. Few find this gate of suffering and cross-bearing. But in Denmark the gate is ever so wide and the path ever so broad and all the Danes are upon it. Obviously the Danes are correct so the New Testament must be false.

It was while carrying on a violent combat with the State Church that Kierkegaard collapsed on the streets of Copenhagen. He was taken to a hospital where he subsequently died. To his last moment he would receive communion from none but a layman. His farewell conversations with his friend Boesen are some of the most touching in religious biography. His friend Lund reported that on his death bed he looked sublime, transfigured, and seemed to light up the entire room. His niece reported that his spirit seemed to shine through his body as if already the body were entering the dawn of the resurrection.

Although his *Attack on Christendom* is taken by some to be a piece of anti-clericalism, it cannot be denied that it was written from a heart of Christian compassion, not Voltaire-like skepticism. And no real minister of Christ can read it without a desire to be chastened of the Lord. It remains as one of the greatest pieces of religious irony in the history of Christian literature.

II. WHAT IS GOD?

With more than thirty works to his credit Kierkegaard obviously worked with some sort of system of thought. And it certainly was a radical one. In fact Kierkegaard is one of the few men in the history of the Christian Church who has been able to offer a very unique and very different interpretation of the Christian faith. In this regard he stands within the inmost circle of those few great geniuses. In order to grasp the spirit of this reinterpretation we shall ask certain questions about the more fundamental aspects of his system. Of course Kierkegaard does not have a Hegelian system, but he does have an existential system. He does set forth in *Philosophical Fragments* a cluster of fundamental convictions which form the inner core of existentialism and this cluster of fundamental convictions and the basic interpretations of Christian faith he makes from these convictions form Kierkegaard's system.

We turn first to Kierkegaard's understanding of God. In this regard we find Kierkegaard taking a very unique position. He does not accept any natural theology which infers the existence of God from creation nor does he accept any mystical or pantheistic doctrine which finds the concept of God imprinted upon the soul.

1. Kierkegaard stresses the *transcendence* of God in a most radical way. The transcendence of God is not "spatial" but existential. It describes the *absolute difference* between God and man, a difference of such a character that God cannot be known by any rational or objective or empirical way. There is an endless yawning chasm between God and man. There is an infinite difference of *quality* between God and man. God is the eternal—man is the temporal; God is holy—man is that one thing which is utterly inconceivable about God, sinful. God encounters man not as the Friend but as the Unknown! Man does not reach up like a child searching for his father's warm hand, but God sovereignly sets before man the conditions for knowing him.

2. In full agreement with Pascal, Kierkegaard affirms that God is *Deus absconditus*. God is not writ with large print in creation. God is unnoticeable, invisible, and *secretly* present in His works. Kierkegaard says that a man could live the routine of his entire life from "womb to tomb" and never discover God in his works. Man may go through many experiences which raise the ethical issue and never get the impression of the *infinity* of God. The assertion that God is known directly Kierkegaard calls *paganism*. God would be known under such conditions without any prior irruption or shattering of the ego or inwardness or passion. There would be no *transformation* of the knower. God is hidden and elusive and there is *nothing* obvious about him. True, creation is his work but man is confronted with the handiwork of God but not with God.

3. God is Subject and never Object. This is a bit of existentially colored theology. Of course Kierkegaard believed in the "objectivity" of God in the sense that God is not just my thoughts about him. But God is not known as objects are known but as a person is known. If God were known as objects are known one could know God and remain the same sinful, selfish creature. Unless *knowing* transforms it is irreligious. To try to prove God's existence by objective, i.e., rational means, is impossible because God is Subject and is known only by our *subjectivity*. If God is Subject, he is Person, and therefore is known by "subjectivity in inwardness," or in more prosaic language, existentially. Subjects are known by self-communication whereas objects are known by their properties. And that which corresponds to God's self-communication (which a Subject and not an Object does) is our inwardness or subjectivity. With this inwardness or subjectivity *there is transformation*!

The transcendence of God, the hiddenness of God, and the subjectivity of God means that all traditional philosophical approaches to God fall flat on their faces. Neither in rationalism nor idealism nor empiricism can God be known. God is known only as Subject, i.e., inwardly, subjectively (however, not *subjectivism*!), existentially. *This is a knowing which also transforms.*

It must be said in fairness to Kierkegaard that by *subjectivity* he means the mode whereby we believe in God, and not *subjectivism* which is a bad word in philosophy and theology implying that all we really know (when we claim to know something) is ourselves.

III. WHAT IS MAN?

The *theology* of Kierkegaard determines his *anthropology*! His doctrine of God is the framework for his doctrine of man.

1. *The divine aspect of man.* Man is spirit. Unregenerate man is potential spirit; regenerate man is realized spirit. This inward potentiality when awakened is man's God-relationship. It is this relationship which in turn makes man truly man. Man as spirit, of course, also has a body and a soul, but the essential and existential thing about man is spirit. Spirit enables man to mediate time and eternity, and man is therefore only truly man when as spirit he mediates time and eternity. This mediation of time and eternity must await further exposition.

The goal of man is eternal happiness. The function of Christianity is to give man an eternal happiness. Possessing potential spirit man is a free creature who can have face-to-face communion

with God. This is the cross which philosophies cannot carry, remarks Kierkegaard. Philosophers outline the universe in circles of
generalities or categories. Particulars become lost to general classes.
The individual man is lost to the class of humanity. Kierkegaard
vigorously protests this.

If man is spirit, man is free and has a divine side. Man as spirit,
man as free is thus capable of *a certain inward action. This sets
man above the general class of humanity.* Faith is the paradox that
the individul human being is really higher than the class, humanity. Thus Kierkegaard protests against man being buried under
heavy philosophical timbers. In particular he protests against
Hegel's system which swallows up the individual man. *Concrete
human life is higher than any philosophical category.* This is, of
course, one of the fundamentals of existential philosophy and
theology.

2. *Human aspect.* The divine aspect of Kierkegaard's anthropology provides the *basis* for man's religious experiences; the
human suggests the *necessity.* Kierkegaard has a very strong doctrine of sin. His own inward experiences and his existential philosophy led him to recast the doctrine of sin into a psychological
form rather than an exegetical or historical one, but nevertheless
it does have a certain biblical ring to it. The total *otherness* of
God is matched (at the extremity!) by the *sinfulness* of man. The
parallelism between the thought of Pascal and Kierkegaard at
this point is very close.

This psychological reinterpretation of the Fall and original sin
is contained in Kierkegaard's work, *The Concept of Dread.* It
anticipates certain features of "depth-psychology" and has had
an important influence on twentieth century concepts of sin. Although Kierkegaard himself used the word "psychological" in the
sub-title of *The Concept of Dread* recent theologians would prefer
the adjectives "mythical" and "existential" for the Kierkegaardian
formulation of the Fall and original sin.

Besides man's *otherness* from God and his *sinfulness* man is involved in *existence.* Kierkegaard raises many protests against the
detached observer whom he finds best exemplified in the philosopher. The detached observer claims to see the universe from a
place of superior vision, from some philosophical vantage point
denied the peon and peasant. This detached observer, this Privat-
docent, Kierkegaard attacks with great scorn, wit, sarcasm and
irony. This gentleman can sketch out the universal system of truth
but he cannot account *within the terms of his system of universal
truth* (which should explain *all* facts) why the professor's coat has
a patch on the elbow, why the professor must pick up his pay

check, why he should have a feeling of derision or contempt about
some matter. Such a man makes a great intellectual castle of truth
and then lives in a miserable shack nearby! Here Kierkegaard's
attack on the Hegelian professor parallels Pascal's attack upon
the Descartes.

According to Kierkegaard the position of pure, isolated, detached thinker is impossible. Every man is an *existent*! He lives
caught in the meshes of life, in the relativity of knowledge, in an
intellectual helplessness. The task of man is not to create The
System—Kierkegaard's polite slander for Hegel's philosophy, nor
is it to be a scientist. A man may be a philosopher or a scientist
but this is not *the task* of man. Kierkegaard says that the great
merit of Socrates was to see that *the task* of man was his existence.
Kierkegaard's university thesis was on Socrates and he found in
him his spiritual godfather.

Man is an *existent*; this much Socrates saw. Kierkegaard would
add that he is a *religious* existent. And therefore *the task* of man
is to find the true form of religious existence. Kierkegaard sees
that man as sinner needs a Savior, and as an existent he needs the
Truth, and this he finds resolved in the incarnation, in the God-
Man, Jesus Christ, who is both man's Savior and the resolution of
the problem of religious existence.

IV. WHAT IS TRUTH?

The fundamental problem of Christian apologetics is the problem of truth and knowledge. Kierkegaard is an apologist in the
very specific and undeniable meaning of the term because he says
a great deal about truth and knowledge. In fact, his little work,
Philosophical Fragments, is one of the greatest works in the history
of theory of knowledge because it lays the groundwork for the
epistemology of existentialism.

1. *The nature of real truth*

(1) The first qualification of truth is that it must be *essential*
truth, better yet, *existential* truth, i.e., *personal* and *religious*.
Kierkegaard said in his *Journals* that the great passion of his life
was to find the truth, the truth *for him*! *The truth he can die for*!
Typical philosophical, scientific, or rationalistic definitions of truth
will not do here. Truth that is truth for me produces trusting devotion, not mere assent; it must be, as Kierkegaard so emphatically
said, *for me and for my life*!

Kierkegaard has no quarrel with the sciences or any other
knowledge which is the product of research, investigation, critical
analysis or experimentation. He would only demur and say the

knowledge such investigations produce is barren of existential worth. The criticism of science and research would only be at that point in which somebody should substitute this kind of knowledge for existential knowledge. Kierkegaard is interested in *existential truth*. Existential truth has to do with *the task of man as existent*. It is that kind of truth which corresponds to man's condition as an existent.

Man as an existent, i.e., as living in the meshes of space and time and events, cannot see the universe as a whole. He, therefore, denies the possibility of any universal system of truth. But in defending existential philosophy neither can he defend the possibility of an existential universal system for that would be denying the very essence of existentialism (expressed in the famous existentialist dictum that existence is *before* essence). But if no system of truth exists as such then the universe itself might appear irrational. Kierkegaard prevents this by saying that to God there is an existential system.

Hegel and Kierkegaard differed at a most fundamental point, namely, *the status of logic*. According to Hegel *the principles of logic were also the principles of Reality*. This is known in philosophy as *logical realism*. To be sure Hegel had a particular kind of logic called *triadic* (because it was composed of a thesis, antithesis, and synthesis), and *dialectic* (because the oppositions in Reality were reconciled in a new synthesis). But the point is that the structure of logic is also the structure of Reality. But Kierkegaard's view of logic is very similar to that of recent logical positivism or analytic philosophy, namely, that the rules of logic or the principles of logic are completely free from any metaphysical or ontological significance. In the terms of recent philosophical jargon the rules of logic are but the rules for the proper manipulation of symbols.

If thought (principles of logic) and being (Reality) are separate (i.e., existence is prior to essence) then—and this is what Kierkegaard is aiming at—*a new and different method of contacting Reality is mandatory*. Man as an existent does separate thought and being. The doorway to reality by any sort of procedure (philosophical or religious) which presumes that rational thought can achieve a system of Reality *is slammed shut*.

(2) The second characteristic of essential truth is that it is *paradoxical*. If man is an existent, if the principles of logic are not the principles of Reality, if existence is prior to essence, if man is the totally other from God, *then* the truth of this holy, transcendent God must appear to man the existent as a paradox. For the three-term dialectic of Hegel (thesis, antithesis, synthesis) Kierkegaard substitutes the two-term dialectic of the paradox. And

so to Kierkegaard the paradox is no logical conundrum, no game of mathematical tricks, *but an ontological principle*. The paradox expresses the logical form of the truth of God (the infinite Spirit) as it is received and heard by man (the finite spirit).

Here again we find a great divergence with Hegel. When Hegel found a tension or paradox or opposition in reality he attempted to resolve it with a synthesis. The mind feels tense, for example, in the opposition between Greek art and Egyptian Art. But the intellectual tension is eased when it sees the synthesis of Greek art and Egyptian art in Western art. This easing of intellectual contrasts by an act of *intellectual synthesis* Kierkegaard calls *mediation*. But this sort of mediation is not possible within existentialist thought. Therefore a harmonizing out of the *contrieties* of existence is not possible.

Three things must be said about Kierkegaard and *reason* as we reflect upon his doctrine of paradox: (i) in the sense that formal logic is sometimes identified with reason it must be said that there is no Reality in logic (i.e., logic is not ontology!). (ii) That reason as exemplified by Hegel's philosophy is to be rejected because it presumes that reason can decode the riddle of existence which it cannot. (iii) *But reason is right and proper in that it sets up the paradoxes of faith*. The two terms of the paradox are not chosen willy-nilly but are the result of intense rational thought. Otherwise we would have no true paradox but sheer irrationality. But once the reason has established the paradox it cannot relieve (i.e., mediate) the paradox. Only the passion of faith can do this.

Of course in science and research reason has its rights, but in these matters we are free from existential concern. The structure of paradox Kierkegaard reserves for existential problems. Thus great care must be exercised in assessing Kierkegaard's proposed "irrationality."

(3) The supreme test for truth is *inwardness* or *subjectivity*. In a word this means the manner in which man the *existent* appropriates the *existential truth*. Put another way it means that man's potential as *spirit* (i.e., man's unique ability to mediate eternity in time) becomes actual. This inward movement of the spirit, this *existential activity* of man is what is meant by *subjectivity* or *inwardness*.

Kierkegaard makes the unusual statement that Christianity as *objectivity* does not exist. If Christianity confronts us with an existential experience (inwardness, subjectivity), then its reality is known only in this existential experience; therefore, its reality remains unknown (i.e., it does not exist) if it is approached by ordinary methods of thought and reason (i.e., dispassionately). Thus Christianity as an existential confrontation *exists* whenever

an existent existentially responds to it. This existential confrontation and existential response Kierkegaard opposes to Hegel's system
which may be appropriated by the sheer use of one's intellectual
powers which *involves no transformation of the self.*

According to Kierkegaard's thought statements about God,
Christ, and the gospel are *possibilities.* They are not truths in and
of themselves. One might call them *prescripts*, or *formulas* for
action. The existential truth rests in the person, not in the sentences or prescripts or formulas. These possibilities call for *decision* (which here stands in existential thought in contrast to
mere *assent* to rational truth). When the existent properly responds to these existential possibilities then he (the subject) *is in
truth.* Thus, whereas Hegel was interested in true theses, Kierkegaard is concerned with subjects (persons) *in truth.*

Kierkegaard, however, is not a mystic. He does not believe that
the mind loses itself in ecstasy, nor that its powers are paralyzed
or suspended. There is an intellectual or cognitive element in the
existential encounter and Kierkegaard calls this *an objective uncertainty.* An objective uncertainty speaks to the *logical status*
of a theological sentence. The sentences about God, or immorality,
or Christ are not *logically compelling.* They are not free from
ambiguity in form or in argument. Nor are they mere surmizes,
hunches or guesses. From the standpoint of scientific or objective
criteria the "existential sentences" are objective uncertainties, and
the existent can have no *higher* certitude than this.

But in that these theological sentences are also *existential possibilities* they do excite us. We do *decide* for them. We do *embrace*
them. But we do not embrace them with a rational act, but with
the inwardness of faith, with the passion of faith, with subjectivity.
Thus the *maximum* truth we can have is the passionate and inwardness embracing of these existential possibilities which for
the mind (i.e., as objective) are uncertainties. This *decision*, this
venture is absolutely crucial to the structure of an existential experience. Take this away and the passion of subjectivity would be
lost and with that the whole essence of an existential experience.

(4) Having made the venture of faith how does the existent
know it is the correct one? Perhaps the Mohammedans have their
ventures of faith too?

Kierkegaard's defense at this point is very simple: the experience
is so absolutely unique that it is incapable of being doubted, and
incapable of being imitated. No other religion offers the experience
of Eternity in Time. For support Kierkegaard appeals to the
structure of love. Supposing a man loves a woman very deeply.
If he is asked, "could you love another woman?" what then? If
he attempts to answer *this* question he does not really love his fair

lady. If he can even contemplate the possibility of loving another he does not truly love. Love is of such intensity and devotedness that it can only love the lover! And so if the Christian be asked if he could be saved another way, what then? If he really tries to answer this question he is—claims Kierkegaard—no longer a believer. A believer in Christ finds the contemplation of the possibility of *another* Savior unthinkable and incredible and impossible!

The subjectivity of faith is totally unique. There are *other* deeply moving experiences of men but they are not to be confounded with the subjectivity of faith. God has his part in this too, for God *directly* gives to believers the full sense of certitude that they have encountered the truth. Truth is truth before God's eyes, by God's help! God is the object of the truth, and the *medium* by which the truth is known.

2. *False approaches to truth*

(1) *Philosophy*. Kierkegaard is opposed to all forms of seeking the truth which are not passionate, i.e., existential. He is for this reason unhappy with those who attempt to find the truth through philosophy. Particularly he is grieved with philosophy because it attempts to eliminate the paradoxical. But existential thought cannot do this and remain true to itself. Philosophy proposes to examine the universe from the vantage point of pure objectivity. But this is impossible for every philosopher is an *existent*. The professional philosopher who is really an *existent* (buried in space, time, history, details of life, etc.) but who pretends to see things *from the aspect of eternity* is truly a fantastic being. The only people we know of are *existents*. We know of no person who abides upon Mount Eternal Perspective.

The very intention of philosophers to be objective disables them from finding existential truth. Philosophy is dedicated to the principle of successive approximation to the truth. It attempts to more and more rationally formulate the truth with increasing precision. But the more accurate it defines the truth the more impossible *faith* becomes. *Assent to a demonstrated proposition is not faith to Kierkegaard*. Acceptance of rationally formulated and demonstrated truth is a passion*less* act of assent; faith is a venture which is directed towards a paradox and is passion*ful*. The former has no power of spiritual transformation; the latter does.

Supposing Herr Professor is going to become a Christian but he wishes to protect his flank so that he is not caught performing some irrational act. This Kierkegaard calls a comedy! The professor starts the comedy with the usual approximation process of philosophers. He attempts to come closer and closer to the truth.

The philosopher will not believe like shoemakers, tailors, and simple folk but he will believe like a rational expert.

But the professor forgets that the hall-mark of existential truth is the paradoxical or absurd. And his method of successive approximation to the truth slowly eliminates the absurd. Thus when the Faith it trimmed of all its absurdity the professor is ready to believe. He now *emphatically* knows Christianity is true. But at that moment faith eludes him. Faith is not an emphatic knowing! The absurd is the object of faith, and faith can only *believe* the absurd (or paradoxical).

(2) Kierkegaard has no patience with *natural theology* and *theistic proofs*. To approach God via the theistic proofs is both paganism and blasphemy. To attempt to *think* one's way to God is the supreme case of *thoughtlessness!* This is paganism, for the pagan thinks that he can approach God without any inwardness or subjectivity in the seeker. But there can be no Christianity until there is a sense of guilt, an irruption, an infinite resignation, a breach!

The approach of the theistic proofs ignores the drastic separation of God from man. It assumes a spiritual continuity which simply does not exist. It calls for no shattering of self, and no infinite act of resignation both of which are demanded in the true subjectivity approach to God. Infinite resignation is to resign one's self from finding happiness in some typical creaturely formula for happiness. It is a surrender to finding happiness only in Eternity and not in Time. It must be remembered that Kierkegaard uses the word "eternity" to mean a dimension of the present life (hence a qualitative definition) and not the endless duration of time (a quantitative definition).

It is true, affirms Kierkegaard, that nature is the work of God but when we look at nature we see nature and not God. *God is elusive!* He does not reveal himself with big letters in nature. God is *elusive* so that he might protect the truth. If God were directly presented in nature man would know God with none of the marks of a real existential religious experience. There would be no pain, no suffering, no guilt and no resignation.

In that God is elusive man must seek God. If God must be sought man must reflect *why* he must be sought. In this reflecting it might occur to man that his depravity might be the cause of the elusiveness of God. If he attains to this he has attained to the first step of his inwardness.

Therefore God keeps himself elusive. He is so elusive in his works that a man may live a hundred years and never see God in his works nor be overwhelmed with the infinity of God from ethical considerations suggested within life. Therefore, Kierkegaard says, it cannot occur to any one that God exists! Nature is his work yet he is not there! God is found by the pilgrim only as the pilgrim commences the inward road of existential religious subjectivity. The elusiveness of God is designed to excite that possibility.

V. WHAT IS FAITH?

1. Faith is *a solitary act*. There is a great list of theologians who have classified faith as primarily an act of the mind in response to truth. Faith is based upon clear, unequivocal knowledge. Kierkegaard breaks with this honorable tradition. *Faith is a passion, in fact, the most intense passion.*

Faith is a pathway each man treads alone. No man can counsel the man in the act of faith and no man can understand him. This does not mean that faith is for just the few people capable of such an intense passion or capable of such necessary solitude. Faith is every man's *potentiality*. The way to faith is described in *Stages on Life's Way* and in *Fear and Trembling*. When a man is led to see the emptiness of the aesthetic life through *boredom* he makes a transition to the ethical stage. In the ethical stage he eventually faces the problem of *guilt*. In that ethics itself has no remedy for guilt the man may well turn to despair, but it may also direct him towards the religious stage. Thus guilt may lead the man to the experience of *infinite resignation,* i.e., repentance.

However, according to Kierkegaard resignation and faith are not once-for-all experiences but are the constant elements of Christian experience. As an *existent*, as possessing *spirit*, man does not exist in some solidly established spiritual condition, but in a state of perpetual tension or suspension between Time and Eternity. Thus man must be always mediating Eternity in Time with resignation and faith. *This is the existentialist new man!* Resignation is to lose all things, faith is to gain all things. This faith which follows on resignation is not—as already suggested—an act of the mind or better yet an act of intellection, but a passion. *It is the highest passion of our inwardness*. Thus when an existent is confronted with the gospel message (especially in the paradoxical form in which Kierkegaard framed it) he responds with faith. This means he responds with the highest passion of his subjectivity. And this infinite passion *transforms* man—and it is this transformation that Kierkegaard perpetually has in mind as he writes for he is strongly reacting against an *untransformed* Christianity.

2. *Faith is prompted by paradox*. Just as faith is not an act of

the mind as such (i.e., intellection) its object is not rational truth. Faith is aroused only as it is stung, offended, or shocked. It is the paradox which stings, offends, and shocks. And in this stinging, offending, and shocking, faith is aroused. Rational truth does not shock and is therefore existentially powerless.

Kierkegaard has a particular paradox in mind for faith: Jesus Christ as the God-Man is the Supreme Paradox. That God should appear as humble man, as humble teacher is the Absolute Paradox and the Absolute Break. What is this Absolute Break?

The ancient skeptics developed their *Canons of Discord.* They attempted to show that all attempts to prove anything whatsoever were self-refuting in that they all involved an infinite regress. To prove that P is true one must assume that O is true; to prove O is true in order to prove that P is true, one must prove N is true . . . and so on endlessly. There simply is no absolute starting point in the quest for truth. Now according to Kierkegaard Christ as the Absolute Paradox is also the Absolute Break and therefore the interruption of this infinite regress. Christ as the God-Man provides the original, absolute starting point for truth.

The supreme example of faith is Abraham offering up Isaac, for this event more than any other in Scripture reveals the existential structure of faith. Abraham is the solitary individual going up the mountainside. Nobody understands him and nobody can counsel him and he in turn cannot communicate with anybody. If he attempts to communicate the divine word which he has received it will sound as if God is tempting him. The command he has received is *absolutely unique*; it pertains to Abraham and to his existential situation *alone.* If Abraham attempts to communicate it, he must express himself in language with its universal concepts. But as soon as his *unique situation* is expressed in *universal concepts* the express existential character of it is lost.

Faith simply cannot be communicated! Abraham is asked to slay his son. On the level of universal ethical principles this is wrong. But God suspends the ethics of the situation for a religious purpose, and Abraham is not confronted with an ethical decision but a religious one. Here Abraham squarely faces a paradox: he must *slay* the son of *promise.* He risks the venture of faith and is willing to slay the son of promise. This is the word of God to him. But he believes that the son is also the son of promise. Thus he believes both in the passion of faith, and receives his son back again.

Analyzed ethically and objectively Abraham's actions are incomprehensible. But the man of faith understands, for the way of Abraham is the way of faith—inwardness, subjectivity, passion, paradox, the absurd, but above all, *transformation.*

True to its existential nature, faith is always venture, leap, risk.

If there is no risk there simply is no faith. To risk is to venture all upon an objective uncertainty. To demand objective certainty is to put an end of faith. To accept an objective uncertainty as the final truth *for me* is, in the language of logic, a risk or venture or leap. Kierkegaard presses even harder. The greater the uncertainty, the greater the faith; the bigger the risk the larger the faith; the less objective uncertainty the more subjectivity.

It must accordingly be underscored that Kierkegaard opposes *knowing* and *believing*. To know is to accept something on rational and objective grounds; to believe is to risk all on an objective uncertainty. Therefore knowing and believing are two different things. Knowing seeks mediated truth; believing seeks the absurd. Knowing leaves the knower unchanged; believing transforms the believer.

3. *Faith is in a Person*, the Person of the Teacher, namely, Jesus Christ as God-incarnate in his humility. Faith is then not in doctrines. If faith were in a doctrine then we would have the hybrid-situation of faith in objective truth (doctrine) and faith as a passion (in the God-Man). Faith is not doctrinal but existential, existential communication. The object of faith is not a truth to be communicated but a Person to be chosen. Of course Kierkegaard does not rule out the doctrinal. But the *sentences* which we use in preaching and teaching must never be viewed as the end itself, as the goal or object of faith, but as *existential possibilities*.

If faith were primarily faith in a doctrine then we would have to examine the doctrine to be sure that we did not botch it. But to ascertain the precise accurate form of the doctrine we would have to call upon the approximation-process of objective knowledge. But faith cannot be so grounded or it would violate the entire existential nature of faith. Faith is in the reality of the Teacher. Certainly this cannot mean faith in any teacher or a human teacher. It must be faith in the Teacher who is the God-Man.

If we are not interested in doctrine we might be candidates for an asylum, remarks Kierkegaard. Are we not wallowing in the nonsense of the paradoxical? Kierkegaard answers with a very firm No! Faith is the *highest* passion, and it is directed towards the *Supreme Paradox*. And therefore the highest passion in the supreme paradox cannot be deceived nor deluded nor can the existential structure be imitated.

VI. WHAT IS A CHRISTIAN?

Kierkegaard felt that his greatest task was to define a Christian. The Christian was certainly not the conventional churchman! A

Christian is a person transformed by faith; a person who has passed along the stages of life till he has attained the religious stage. What are the marks of such a man?

1. The surest test of a real Christian is *suffering*. An *existent* can only suffer as he approaches God and the nearer he gets the greater the suffering. Suffering is the infinite dissatisfaction we have with ourselves as we approach God. We become so desperately aware of what we should be in our existence and of what we truly are. This is one point in particular in which Kierkegaard distances himself from mysticism in its ecstatic interpretation of nearness to God.

2. Another test is that the Christian is *lonely*. Christians enter the kingdom one by one in Abrahamic solitude. We stand as the The Single One before The Other. Faith is essentially entering into a *private relationship* with deity and therefore *loneliness* is a sure mark of faith.

3. The third mark of a true Christian man is *subjectivity,* or *inwardness*. Faith is a form of inwardness. But there are a number of different forms of inwardness. However faith is the supreme form of inwardness in that it is our subjectivity raised to its highest power. Therefore faith is unique from all other forms of inwardness. The formula of faith is holding to an objective uncertainty with an infinite subjectivity or inwardness. This formula fits *only* the believer. It does not fit the lover, nor the enthusiast, nor the thinker. Only the believer has infinite subjectivity and only the believer is responding to the absolute Paradox.

4. The Christian is *the contemporary of Christ*. This notion is set forth in *Training in Christianity*. From one perspective Christ is a person of history. *Can he be recovered for faith by historical methods?* Impossible! Historical method is part of *objective* investigation, or *rational* truth, or the *approximation process*. Historical truth is therefore passionless truth. To assert that Christ is available to us by mere historical research is nonsense and unChristian confusion. There is no Christ nor true Christianity (as inwardness) available to historians.

God knows but one tense, the present. If man knows God he knows God in God's time, the present. The same holds true for Christ. If we would know Christ we must enter his "time belt," i.e., eternity. *We must become contemporary with Christ.* Thus a Christian is defined by Kierkegaard as *one who is contemporary with Christ*. From the abstract existential sense this is the same as mediating Eternity in Time.

The passage of centuries does not concern Christian faith. One of the hotly disputed philosophical questions of his times was the relevance of history to metaphysics. How can facts of history which are *past, contingent,* and *obscure* be the grounds for a faith which is *certain* and *absolute?* Christianity gets caught in this dilemma because it presents a gospel which is about a historical Person and the most dramatic incidents of his life. Kierkegaard's contention is that the (i) the sheer passage of time does not alter the reality of Christ, and (ii) that Christ is not recovered by history but by faith which makes one a contemporary with Christ. Christ is historical in that he did live, but in that he is the Supreme Paradox, the God-Man, he is *very unhistorical.*

If we would be Christians we must "enter" Eternity. The past has no existence for an existent. The future is not yet here. Only the contemporary is the real to the existent. Kierkegaard spells it out that a man is contemporary with two things: (i) his own age, and (ii) Jesus Christ! This event which occurred in history is also out of history, i.e., in "Eternity," and therefore Christ can be contemporary with believers of all ages.

BIBLIOGRAPHY

For a list of the translated works of Kierkegaard (as of 1953) see Minear and Morimoto, *Kierkegaard and the Bible, An Index. Princeton Pamphlets,* No. 9

Bretall, R., *A Kierkegaard Anthology*

Carnell, E. J., "The Problem of Verification in Soren Kierkegaard," (unpublished doctoral dissertation, Boston University, 1949)

Chaning-Pierce, A., "Soren Kierkegaard," in *Modern Christian Revolutionaries,* Donald Attwater, editor

Collins, J., *The Mind of Kierkegaard*

DeWolf, L., *The Religious Revolt against Reason*

Diem, H., *Kierkegaard's Dialectic of Existence*

Gates, J., *The Life and Thought of Kierkegaard for Everyman*

Geismar, E., *Lectures on the Religious Thought of Sören Kierkegaard*

Holmer, P., "Kierkegaard and Religious Propositions," *The Journal of Religion,* 25:135-146, July, 1955

Macintosh, H. R., *Types of Modern Theology*

Patrick, D. G. M., *Pascal and Kierkegaard,* 2 vols.

Pratt, J. B., *Religious Liberals Reply*

Swenson, D., *Kierkegaardian Philosophy in the Faith of a Scholar*

——————, *Something about Kierkegaard*

Theology Today, issue of October 1955, Vol. XII

Thomas, J., *Subjectivity and Paradox*

Thomte, R., *Kierkegaard's Philosophy of Religion*

Chapter IV

EMIL BRUNNER (1889–   )

In Emil Brunner's *Revelation* and *Reason* is contained one of the most trenchant treatises on apologetics of the first part of the twentieth century. It is marked with vigor of style, clarity of thought, and depth of scholarship. It represents the summary of his thought as it has grown through the years. There are apologetic elements in his work *The Philosophy of Religion from the Standpoint of Protestant Theology*. In our exposition *Revelation* shall stand for the first book and *Philosophy* for the second.

I. INTRODUCTION

Brunner writes from the standpoint of neo-orthodox theology. His thought and that of Karl Barth have more in common than they have in difference. However, many other thinkers have influenced Brunner besides Barth as indicated by both Jewett (*Emil Brunner's Concept of Revelation*) and Schrotenboer (*A New Apologetics: An Analysis and Appraisal of the Eristic Theology of Emil Brunner*). Principally among these are Buber, Ebner, Overbeck and Kierkegaard. In his little work, *Faith, Hope and Love*, Brunner says that his method in theology is that of an "existential exposition of the Biblical Word, in which indeed the Word is to be understood not so much in the Bultmann-Heidegger connotation as in that of Kierkegaard" (p. 7). The similarities between Brunner and Kierkegaard are very great but Brunner tones down the extremes of Kierkegaard, and represents a more sustained theological exposition. Further, Brunner perhaps has a healthier regard for the nature and life of the Christian Church. Also to Brunner's credit is his recognition of the role of the Holy Spirit, particularly the witness of the Spirit, in our apprehension of the Christian faith. "The doctrine of the Holy Spirit is the Christian answer to the truth in subjectivism, the doctrine of that inwardness which is not in the least degree our own" (*Philosophy*, p. 113).

II. BRUNNER'S DIAGNOSIS OF HIS TIMES

Brunner like Pascal and Kierkegaard before him believes that there are disposing cultural and religious factors working against true faith. The two chief purposes of his apologetics are (i) to show the proper relationship between revelation and reason, and (ii) to alleviate the current improper conceptions of Christianity.

1. Misconceptions of the Christian religion

(1) *Philosophical.* Science, philosophy, and religion are interested in the truth. Each has devised its own methods for the ascertaining of the truth. The subject matter determines the methodology. A proposition in geometry is not settled by chemical analysis of the ink and paper, nor is a problem in theology settled by recourse to physics. It is the contention of Brunner that there is a specific methodology for theology but that philosophers have subjected theology to an alien methodology. The inevitable result is the damaging of the Christian faith.

Philosophers do talk about God, but he is always a philosophical type of God. He is the Unmoved Mover or the First Cause or The Whole or the Absolute. He is usually the object of philosophical analysis or synthesis. At both points philosophy has been wrong. God is the Living God, the forgiving God, the saving God. He is the God who is *Subject*! Such a God is not the product of philosophical thought. He is the Redeemer! He is the *Subject* who can be approached only in faith. His chief blessing is not to provide us with the major premise of our metaphysics but to save our souls. Only harm results when the God of philosophy is substituted for the God of our Savior, Jesus Christ.

(2) *Catholicism.* Another source of harm for the true gospel has come from the Roman Catholic Church. The first evil it has fostered is *authoritarianism* in Christianity. The second is that it has attempted *a systematic rationalization* of Christian dogmas. The first two produce the third: faith is defined as theological, i.e., as *assent to authority and dogma.* Authoritarianism degenerates the conscience and produces religious serfs and not free men in Jesus Christ. The grafting of Aristotelian Thomism on to Roman Catholic theology has brought all the evils of the philosophical approach directly into the heart of Roman Catholic theology. Faith, rather than being the inward transforming I-Thou relationship, is defined as intellectual *assensus* to dogma which is free from encounter, and therefore free from the spiritual transformation of the self.

(3) *Fundamentalism.* If warmth of words and intensity of expression are indicative of depth of conviction then (according to Brunner) the chief cause of the present-day rejection of the gospel is traceable to the Fundamentalists' misrepresentation of it. According to Brunner Fundamentalists are guilty of the following serious errors: (a) altering the true concept of revelation; (b) with the Catholics defining faith as assent; (c) imposing on the

Scriptures a spurious post-Reformation doctrine of mechanical inspiration; (d) ignoring the progress of biblical criticism; and (e) in their pre-critical method of biblical interpretation they force the Scripture and modern science into a head-on collision. Its complete misunderstanding of the nature of faith and reason "may be said to have had the most disastrous results" (*Revelation*, p. 8). In even stronger words he asserts that "it is impossible to describe the amount of harm and confusion that has been caused by this fatal perversion of the foundations of faith, both in the Church as a whole and in the hearts of individuals" (*Revelation*, p. 168).

Spelling out these charges in more detail Brunner notes that Fundamentalism defines revelation as the communication of truths unavailable to man. The main burden of revelation is therefore *doctrinal disclosures*. Paralleling this is the Fundamentalist's definition of faith as the acceptance of a creed. The theological confusion at this point is that it sets faith in Christ on the same level as faith in Old Testament mythologies (e.g., the long day of Joshua).

Fundamentalism has defended the verbal inspiration of Scripture and the inerrancy of all its statements. This, Brunner considers as idolatry and bibliolatry. Verbal inspiration is a fiction imposed on the Bible by post-Reformation dogmaticians who were attempting to effectively combat the Roman Catholic system. It bequeaths to the Church the unfortunate and impossible task of attempting to resolve all the contradictions in Scripture and to alleviate all the difficulties of Scripture.

Fundamentalists carry on as if Wellhausen had never been born! In spite of all the work done in modifying Wellhausen's theses Brunner believes that his fundamental position remains intact. "Wellhausen's view as a whole has been victorious," he claims (*Revelation*, p. 287 fn.). Neither have the Fundamentalists faced the problems of the synoptic study of the Gospels. Variations in style, order, and material details would show them how impossible it is to hold the theory of verbal inspiration.

Fundamentalism has fought a losing battle with modern science. Brunner picks out three areas of conflict in which the Fundamentalists have been defeated. Modern astronomy has demonstrated the immensity of space shattering the "cozy" picture of the universe found in Scripture; geology and astronomy have demonstrated that there have been immense epochs of time through which our world has passed making it impossible to appeal to creation in the year 4004 B.C. Finally, anthropological science has destroyed any doctrine of a literal Eden and Fall, and any descent from an original pair. This spirited attack on Funda-

mentalism (and somewhat on orthodoxy) is found in both the
work of *Revelation* and *Philosophy*.

2. *Misconceptions of religion in its essence.* Besides those who
have willfully or ignorantly changed the nature of the Christian
faith there are those who have improperly defined the essence of
religion.

(1) The *anthropologists* through a comparative study of religions have tried to assert that religion is the outgrowth of some
basic human reaction as fear or that it is the product of some sort
of sociological development. In either case the relativity of religious truth is affirmed and Christianity is deprived of its uniqueness.

(2) The *religious liberals*, casting themselves loose from a substantial doctrine of revelation, have tried to ground Christianity
in some basic structure of all mankind. Thus the religious root in
man according to Schleiermacher is the feeling of dependence
and in Ritschl it is a valuational judgment. This represents a
serious misconception of the very character of the Christian faith.

3. *The arrogance of science.* Brunner has a good word for science
whenever he can say it and certainly to science in its own right
he has no quarrel. But when science becomes arrogant and pa-
rades itself as metaphysics he sternly opposes it. He makes it very
clear in both *Philosophy* and *Revelation* that arrogant science,
and philosophies based narrowly upon science are great evils.
Scientism (a philosophy narrowly based on science) is never
friendly to religion to say nothing of the Christian revelation. The
notion that science can solve our problems, that science alone
provides relevant answers to significant questions, is one of the
leading factors in the current disrepute of Christian faith and the
alleviation of this difficulty is one of the major purposes of Brunner's work.

III. THE CONCEPT OF REVELATION

The heart of Brunner's apologetics is his concept of revelation.
Revelation occupies the same place in Brunner's system that inwardness does in Kierkegaard's. Brunner's concept is generally
that which passes for neo-orthodoxy. Revelation is the Word of
God and the Word of God is but God speaking. Revelation is
not a sentence, or a doctrine, or a book, or a canon. At this juncture Brunner strongly rejects traditional Roman Catholic and
Protestant interpretations of revelation and seeks (along with
Barth) a redefinition of revelation.

1. *The fundamental notion of revelation*

(1) *Revelation is essentially God's activity in salvation.* Whereas Roman Catholic and Protestant dogmaticians have made salvation and revelation complementary but separate, Brunner organically unites them. Revelation is defined as "the whole of divine activity for the salvation of the world" (*Revelation*, p. 8). Continuing, he says that "Revelation is God Himself in His self-manifestation within history. Revelation is something that *happens*, the living history of God in His dealing with the human race: the history of revelation is the history of salvation, and the history of salvation is the history of revelation" (*loc. cit.*, italics are his).

Revelation is an unveiling, the disclosure of something *absolutely* concealed. This concealing is not man's mere inaccessibility to God but is purposed by God. This disclosure in simplest definition is God Himself for the real content "of the revelation in the Bible is . . . God Himself. Revelation is the self-manifestation of God" (*Revelation*, p. 25). Because God is concealed and known only by his self-willed self-disclosure Brunner repeatedly calls Him *the Mysterious*.

In general terms revelation is "God's mighty acts for man's salvation" (*Revelation*, p. 118). Revelation is saving truth and saving truth is revealed truth. Specifically, revelation comes through the Word of God—partially in the prophets of the Old Testament, and fully in the Christ of the New who deserves unreservedly the title of *The Word of God*. Revelation is not doctrinal communication nor the communication of theological propositions. Rather, it is God acting in salvation, it is God disclosing Himself in Christ the Word of God.

(2) *Truth as encounter (Warheit als Begegnung).* This is a title of one of Brunner's books. It illustrates, in its very naming, one of the cardinal features of Brunner's understanding of revelation. Revelation is never a one-way communication nor a monologue. Nor is it something heard and written down. It is an *encountering*. The divine Person encounters the human person. It has the character of address, God speaks to man! And in an address an answer is expected. It is thus conversation, dialogue, an I-Thou relationship. Revelation is truth as *Person-to-person* encounter. This is its structure as originating in God and proceeding to man. From the human standpoint revelation comes as (and appears as) *illumination*.

In agreement with Kierkegaard Brunner says that this is not a mixed subjective-objective encounter for it has no objective aspect. "Revelation consists in the meeting of two subjects" (*Revelation*,

p. 33) . Revelation is that *event* in which God speaking through His Word, Jesus Christ, meets and carries on a conversation with man.

(3) *The nature of revelation.* Brunner calls this event of revelation transcendent, irrepeatable, unique, absolute, and personal. It is *absolute* truth and is not therefore verifiable by the reason or by experience. It is an event which cannot be grasped by ordinary categories of thought because it is a sudden incursion from another dimension, and because it is unique, mysterious, and irrepeatable. It is placed above and beyond all that men call truth in common talk or in scientific research or in philosophical discourse. Revelation has a signature of its own; it is *personal* and *absolute.*

Being such a unique event revelation has no proof for itself in the customary sense of proof. It has its own logic, its own rationality. Revelation simply cannot be proved if we mean by proof here the same thing we mean, in law or science. When the apologists have attempted proofs they have played the fool: "A theology that allows itself to be drawn into producing proofs for its claim to revelation has already thrown up the sponge. It is the just punishment for the fact that it does not take its own subject and its own basis seriously. Either faith or proofs; you cannot have both" (*Revelation*, p. 212) .

(4) *The nature of God.* In his doctrine of God Brunner is very close to Kierkegaard. God is not an Object but he is "the absolute Subject, unconditional Person. *He* is absolute Mystery until He reveals Himself" (*Revelation*, p. 24. Italics are his). In agreement with Kierkegaard he believes that if God is Subject then God cannot be known through rational procedures; He can be known only by revelation, by self-manifestation "and in this He shows Himself to be the absolute Mystery, who can be understood only through His own self revelation" (*Revelation*, p. 24) . If this is the nature of God, then God is completely hidden from man's natural faculties and cannot be encountered by philosophical analysis nor natural theology. *God as Subject simply forbids this* for a subject can only be known *through* self-revelation. That which we can think, and therefore know, is always object and not subject and therefore not God.

2. *The place of Christ in salvation.* The most general form of Brunner's conception of revelation is that it is God's self-disclosure on the Person-to-person pattern. The general content of the general pattern is salvation so that God's revelation is God's various acts of salvation. This is sharpened to assert that God's revelation

is Christ, and that the high point of this revelation is the cross.
Thus Christ occupies the center of Brunner's teaching on revelation. "Revelation is God's action in Jesus Christ" (*Revelation*,
p. 10). The dualism of the Old Testament in which God's word
and God's act were separated in the prophetic order is now
abolished in Christ who is at the same time God's word and God's
act. In His *incarnation* Jesus Christ is the unique, irrepeatable,
absolute Event. He is supremely the Word of God, the revelation of God, and the Absolute of religious knowledge. In His death
and atonement the summit of His revelatory work is reached:
"The sacrifice of Christ, as well as His Kingship, is revelation,
and, indeed, it is the center of all revelation. The Cross of Christ
is not only the highest point in the whole history of our redemption, but also the whole history of redemption" (*Revelation*,
p. 106).

This leads immediately to one of the most important parts of
Brunner's theology and apologetics: if Christ is the Word of God
and thereby revelation itself then He is the King and Lord of
Scripture and Scripture is the crib of Christ (concepts he pro-
fessedly borrows from Luther). We do not believe in the Bible
and *then* in Christ; we believe in Christ and *then* in the Bible.
This concept of Christ as the Word of God (and not Scripture!)
and therefore as the Lord of Scripture is the leverage for Brunner's critical treatment of Scripture. Whatever does not bear directly upon Christ as the Word of God is not necessary for faith.
Thus Brunner rejects the virgin birth. He believes it is the way in
which the early Church attempted to explain the incarnation with
some sort of biological theory. We as Christians are bound to the
incarnation for that is the great revealing of the Word of God, but
we are not bound to the Church's explanation of it in the virgin
birth.

3. *The place of the Bible in salvation.* Brunner parts company
with religious liberalism which in principle denudes the Bible of
any great theological significance. Within his own definitional
terms the Bible is the Word of God to Brunner, and it is important to both the Church and to Christian faith. Brunner's thought
goes something like this: Christ is the Word of God whose life
has been recorded in Holy Scripture and all parts of Scripture
which witness to Him can be called the Word of God, but those
parts which do not so witness are human and uninspired.

(1) The Bible is the Word of God in all those places that it is
word-bearing. All those parts of Scripture that are genuine records
of revelation are the Word of God in the sense that they are a

record of God's activity in salvation. The Bible itself is not the Word of God. The Bible is the Word of God in parts. It is so "because in it, so far as He chooses, God makes known the mystery of His will, of His saving purpose in Jesus Christ. The Bible is a special form of divine revelation . . . because in it God Himself reveals to us the meaning of that which He will so say to us, and to give us in the historical revelation, especially in the life, death, and resurrection of the Son of God" (*Revelation*, p. 135).

Brunner is so insistent that the Bible is indispensable he affirms that "no one can come to the Son save through the Holy Scriptures" (*Revelation*, p. 136). Thus the Bible is the Word of God in that it bears witness to the Word of God or in that it is a record of the Word of God.

(2) The *doctrines of the Bible* are trustworthy to the extent that they are word-bearing. Brunner has an extended treatment on doctrine. The Word of God is not a doctrine but is the self-manifestation of Christ "which is accomplished through the instrument of doctrine" (*Revelation*, p. 150). Thus doctrine is essentially a witness. It is the instrument, the means, by which the human heart is turned towards Christ. We cannot present Jesus Christ directly to the world. We can only witness and our witness must be a doctrinal witness for "it is only as we are taught that we can believe in Him" (*Revelation*, p. 151).

Brunner thus defends the necessity of doctrine over against mystical ineffability. God is not present unless there are definite ideas about God which are being pronounced. These ideas are the ideas about Christ which are contained in Holy Scripture, and thus the Scripture is the foundation and norm of doctrine. But having said this we must be cautious for the Word of God can never be fully explicated in human language nor in doctrinal statements. Neither doctrine nor creed can claim infallibility. Doctrine is a reliable although fallible witness. "Doctrine is only a pointer even though it may be a clear and useful pointer" (*Revelation*, p. 156).

There is no formal system of doctrine in Scripture. There is a unity of doctrine but it is a *radial* unity. There are theologies—note the plural—in the Scriptures and these may contradict each other, but there is a center to all the doctrines of the Bible. This center is Jesus Christ and true doctrine radiates out from him, or conversely, true doctrine points inwardly towards him.

Furthermore the witness of the Holy Spirit is restricted to Christ. Really what is not "word-bearing" is not Scripture. Brunner prefers the Revised Version's translation of II Timothy 3:16. The

Holy Spirit did not inspire matters of geography, history, creation, chronology or genealogy. The Bible abounds in errors at these points. The Spirit witnesses to Christ and in that sense alone has the Spirit inspired Scripture. The testimony of the Spirit is limited to the Father and the Son and does not pertain to all kinds of matters. We are called upon to believe in Christ, not in geography, history, genealogy, or chronology.

(3) *Brunner's attitude towards inspiration and criticism*

(a) Brunner is very severe with the doctrine of verbal inspiration. We cannot equate the Scriptures outright with the Word of God. He says very strongly that this is "actually a breach of the Second Commandment: it is the deification of a creature, bibliolatry" (*Revelation*, p. 120). In *The Philosophy of Religion* he says that this view makes the Bible "a holy object, a fetish" (p. 35). However, in *The Mediator* Brunner is willing to make one concession: if one can accept the Scriptures only under the thesis of their verbal inspiration he had best do this than reject the Scriptures altogether and so lose the true Word of God (p. 326).

(b) For radical biblical criticism of both Testaments he has a good word. Wellhausen's views have been modified in details but in their essentials they have won the day. Brunner has great admiration for Bultmann and sees no disparity between faith and radical criticism. He thus clearly puts himself on the side of Wellhausen with reference to the Old Testament (*Revelation*, p. 287) and Bultmann with reference to the New (*Revelation*, p. 285 fn). Of course this does not represent a total approval of all these men have said or stand for.

Strangely enough he is not agnostic with regard to the general credibility of the Gospel records. The Gospels are substantially correct even though various accretions and myths have grown on the essential record like mould on bread.

On the basis of such conceptions of the Word of God and the role of criticism Brunner declares that all debates between critics and theologians are meaningless. It is only when the critic assumes that the Bible is the Word of God *per se* or when the theologian affirms that it is such that there is conflict.

(c) One feature of his view of the Bible that he leaves somewhat undeveloped in *Revelation and Reason* is the mythological interpretation of Scripture which he discusses elsewhere, such as in *The Philosophy of Religion*. Theological statements are essentially "parabolic" (*The Mediator*, p. 455) and "mythological" (*The Mediator*, p. 378 ff.). Orthodoxy takes too much of the theology of Scripture as starkly literal and historical. However such concepts as original revelation, original righteousness, original sin are not to be given this stark literal and historical interpretation. They are not so much "historical facts" but "conditions" or "presuppositions" of all historical existence. Thus the Fall is not so much an event which took place with one man, at one spot, and at one time; but original sin is *always* at work, in *every* man at *all* places and in this sense is profoundly historical.

Summary: Revelation is the self-disclosure of the Mysterious One, the One who through His anger for sin withdraws Himself. But now He reveals Himself in love and through Jesus Christ. Thus the Word of God in particular is Jesus Christ. The Bible is only *indirectly* and *partially* the Word of God as it is the dependable witness of revelation and of Jesus Christ the Word of God. Its assertions are pointers, witnesses, directives which are reliable but not infallible. Revelation is a two-term concept and only exists properly when both terms are present. This is expressed in its definition as *encounter*. It is a divine-human dialogue, meeting, confrontation, Subject-to-subject. As such it is mysterious, unique, and absolute. It is truth in the personal and divine dimensions, and is therefore radically different from philosophical and scientific knowledge.

IV. BRUNNER'S CONCEPTION OF FAITH

Brunner is very sure of two things: orthodoxy—whether Catholic or Protestant—has misconstrued both revelation and faith. Orthodoxy teaches that faith is assent to doctrine and this is "the greatest tragedy in Church history" (*Revelation*, p. 39). The damage here is that faith is intellectualized and thereby drained of all its existential vitality.

1. *Birth of faith*. Faith is a gift of God's grace. It is not earned nor self-evoked. Although faith is the response to the preaching of the Word of God its actual emergence is mysterious. "How the heart of man opens to receive the Word of God, and how the reason receives and understands the Word, is as mysterious as the incarnation of the Son of God" (*Revelation*, p. 415).

The leverage of the Word of God on the human heart is the sense of guilt. Brunner really hedges man in on two grounds. He comes at him with *critical idealism* to show the limits of human knowledge. This establishes the fact that man cannot resolve his own problems of existence for his knowledge is too restricted. Then switching to the matter of guilt he establishes the religious need for a word from beyond man. This sense of guilt is the critical point of contact of divine revelation with man. It represents the *universal* confrontation of man by God.

Of the bad conscience of man Brunner has some pointed remarks. In the sense of a bad conscience man is aware (dimly of course) that he is before a tribunal other than himself. The person with a sense of having done something good is apt to confuse his own goodness with the divine goodness; but the person under the pain of a bad conscience never identifies himself with God. Therefore the sense of guilt is the point of contact for the gospel, and when the guilty one believes the gospel he experiences the forgiveness of sins.

2. *Faith defined.* Faith is the act in which the human person realizes divine revelation. Revelation intends faith; faith is the response to revelation. Thus faith and revelation are very strong correlates. Faith is encounter, faith is decision, faith is obedience, faith is the response of the human person to the divine Person.

True faith *transforms* the individual and this is what faith as assent fails to do. However faith as Person-to-person encounter does transform. Faith transforms because it is *obedience* to the Word of God, because it is a *shattering* of the ego which involves a dying and a rising with Christ, because it is *a living by the strength* of God and not by personal religious striving, and because it is *sharing* the light which shines on the face of Jesus Christ who is the God-man.

Faith is seeing what I could not see in my natural state; faith is becoming contemporary with Christ so that the "sense of spatial and temporal remoteness, all external objectivity has disappeared" (*Revelation,* p. 170) ; faith is God Himself assuring me that I have encountered the Truth for "it is not the apostle who assures me that Jesus is the Christ, but God Himself" (*Revelation,* p. 171); faith causes the scandal and the folly of the gospel to cease; faith means "being gripped by the Word of God; it means that the person submits in the very center of his being, in his heart, to Him to whom he belongs because He has created him for Himself" (*Revelation,* p. 421) . Thus in faith the gospel becomes as true and clear to the believer as any truth of mathematics and yet it is true in a very different way from such truth because it is truth which takes captive. It is truth which totally possesses the believer.

3. *The offensive of the cross.* The cross is an offense to unregenerate human reason. The cross cannot be rendered inoffensive by historical imagination nor by sympathy nor by deep human

understanding nor by the human point of view. To the natural reason it is a scandal, an absurdity, an unintelligibility. Because the cross is God's act and God's revelation it is unique and irrepeatable and "therefore [is] above all human analogies; it can never be understood along lines of intellectual argument" (*Revelation*, p. 166). The root of the cause for our antipathy for the cross is that it goes counter to our own sinful struggle for independence. Faith is the obverse of this struggle and therefore it can turn the scandal of the cross into the power of God and the wisdom of God.

4. *Uniqueness of faith.* Brunner makes faith completely unique so as not to be confounded with any other human action. It is "the deepest instinct of the human heart" (*Revelation*, p. 35). It is in a class of its own and can be reduced to nothing else. It has no counterpart in the objective I-it world but prevails only in the subjective I-Thou world. It is the kind of knowing which stands over against all knowing of objects. Being so unique and different it cannot be imitated nor can it be deceived.

V. THE RELATIONSHIP OF THE GOSPEL TO EVIDENCE AND TO REASON

1. *Type of evidence Christianity presents.* In brief Brunner teaches that there are two kinds of truth: (i) truth by typical methods of rational investigation, and (ii) truth by encounter. All conflicts of faith and reason are due to the extension of one domain into the other. The pattern is similar to the one in which Brunner harmonizes criticism of Scripture and theology. The scientist who illegally converts his science into materialism conflicts with revelation; and the theologian who interprets Genesis I literally causes Genesis I to conflict with geology. But if the theologian and the scientist remain within their respective spheres there is no conflict.

If this is true faith cannot have rational or scientific evidence and rational investigation cannot refute revelation. Brunner is very clear in separating his two spheres of reason and science, and, revelation and faith. Christianity then does not belong to the sphere of rational knowledge but to the sphere of revelation and faith. Attempts to rationalize the Christian faith are then absurd. Too much of traditional Christian apologetics and Christian evidences were guilty of this fault. If revelation belongs to the sphere of the supermundane then revelation would cease to be revelation if it could be rationalized in terms of the mundane. But faith lives in the sphere of divine truth and not rational truth.

This means a sharp division of labor. To be a Christian is not to suspend one's rational faculties. In the sphere of mundane matters these faculties must do the work. But man must not try "to exercise [his rational faculty] in a sphere where it has no function" (*Revelation*, p. 76).

We thus have two categories: rational knowledge and revealed knowledge. They are poles apart. Rational knowledge cannot supply the evidence for revelation. Revelation has its own kind of evidence. The evidence for faith is the experience of faith. Brunner writes: "It is the experience of the evidence for faith which is no whit inferior to rational knowledge though it is different. It is the evidence of the God who here and now reveals His presence, the presence of the Holy Spirit, in and beyond His Word" (*Revelation*, p. 172).

We cannot have it both ways for "we must decide either for proof or for trust, either for rational evidence or for the evidence of personal encounter" (*Revelation*, p. 179) . If asked if we have evidence for our faith we must say that we do. We have the evidence of personal encounter, the evidence of divine disclosure, the evidence of the Word of God, the evidence brought by personal decision. The verification of Christianity is the peculiar *qualia*, the *uniqueness*, the *irreducibility*, the transforming *inwardness* of the act of faith.

2. *Relation of revelation and reason*

(1) It is evident from the preceeding discussion that Brunner believes that faith is above reason but not contrary to reason. Faith and reason are not competitive nor contradictory. Nor does faith proceed from reason nor does revealed theology graft itself upon natural theology (not to be confused with general revelation) . At three points rational knowledge and revealed knowledge contrast: (a) In natural knowledge we are masters of what we know; in revelation God masters us. (b) In natural knowledge the knower is enlarged in virtue of the acquisition of more truth; but in revelation the knower is transformed by the truth. (c) In natural knowledge the knower knows an impersonal something, an "it," an object; but in revelation God makes Himself known to us and draws us into a community, the community of the I-Thou relationship.

(2) Revelation is in full agreement with all that natural knowledge claims and if there is disagreement it is due to the arrogance of reason. (a) The gospel comes in human language and therefore

the rational faculty must grasp the meaning of the words and sentences used. Revelation could not come to an irrational creature. (b) The gospel does not destroy human reason nor does it deny its proper function. To the contrary, faith liberates reason. There is no crucifixion of the intellect in faith. (c) By observing these distinctions it will be seen that all conflicts of faith and reason are sham battles. "There is no conflict between science and faith, but only between pseudo-science and faith, and pseudo-faith and science" (*Revelation*, p. 217). Therefore, Christians do not deny the valid truth of the sciences. Whatever is true according to the rules of natural knowledge is accepted by Christians. (d) When conflict does occur it occurs because the boundaries have been crossed. Revelation conflicts with rationalistic and positivistic metaphysics; it also conflicts with the irrational arrogance of those who pride themselves on their intellect, and of irrational self-sufficiency of reason.

3. *Relationship of Christianity to natural theology, science, philosophy, and comparative religions*

(1) In the area of natural theology Brunner's position is not essentially different from Pascal's or Kierkegaard's. (a) However, he is not as radical as Barth. Barth's contention is that the only kind of revelation there is, is saving revelation. Brunner agrees that only saving revelation saves but there can be revelation which does not have the gospel as its content. Nature is a revelation of God but in agreement with the Reformers he does not believe that out of this general revelation a natural theology can be constructed. Although general revelation and special revelation exist together in harmony this is not so with natural theology. "In short, Biblical and natural theology will never agree; they are bitterly and fundamentally opposed" (*Revelation*, p. 61). Only Christians, whose eyes have been opened, really see God in Nature and have the only genuine natural theology. The non-Christian converts Nature's revelation into idolatry. Brunner sums up his position in the following words: "We do not teach the revelation in the Creation by any process of rational argument; this truth is based upon the divine revelation of salvation. We do not teach 'natural theology,' but in the context of Christian theology, we teach revelation in this particular form which is communicated to all men, but is not rightly received by all, because all men are sinners" (*Revelation*, p. 77).

(b) Accordingly Brunner is very testy about proofs for the existence of God. These proofs have some value *after* revelation has enlightened the heart. For no "proof of the existence of God leads me to the Lord God; by this I do not mean that such 'proofs' have no value, but that they do not lead to the knowledge of the Living God" (*Revelation*, p. 45). Hence they cannot lead to the *encountering* of God without which there is no salvation. "God can never be found along any way of thought," he writes. "For indeed this idea of God bursts through and destroys all the fundamental categories of thought: the absolutely antithetical character of the basic logical principles of contradiction and identity. To want to *think* this God for oneself would mean insanity" (*Revelation*, p. 46, italics his). Here we have flouted two of the standard pillars of logic—the law of contradiction and the principle of identity.

The proofs as such are plagued with diseases! Only a small portion of the human race can evaluate them so if God is known in this manner he is known by a pitifully small group. And if only a few of those who are capable of following such philosophical reasoning are impressed, their logical structure must be weak. The amount of religious certainty derived from the proofs is hardly anything compared with the joy and certitude which comes from the knowledge of God in revelation.

Even more damaging is the kind of knowledge the proofs present to us. Proofs move in the area of First Cause or the Highest but not with that which faith needs, namely, the Living God. But even so the proofs are marred by divergencies among the philosophers. In fact, the entire history of philosophy is marked by the *numerous* and *enormous* differences among philosophers. Yet all of this is in the name of reason! Therefore Brunner asks: "In view of this state of affairs what becomes of the proofs for the existence of God? For these proofs are *one* kind of rational metaphysics, no better and no worse than others in so far as the criterion is strictly rational thought" (*Revelation*, p. 342, italics his).

(2) With regard to science Brunner asserts that his notion of revelation is miraculous and is therefore offensive to modern scientific mentality. Thinking men have striven for a uniformitarian view of Nature and revelation contradicts this ideal. How shall the supernatural be defended in view of this modern spirit? Brunner insists that we must commence with the correct notion of miracle by centering our attention on The Miracle—God incarnate in Christ. We must not get lost sniping back and forth about any or every miracle but we must realize that the miracles of the Gospels are dependent upon The Miracle for their validity.

On the other hand there is no justification for resorting to recent developments in physics to bolster up our faith in miracles.

Heisenberg's principle of indeterminacy is neither here nor there with regard to the credibility of the miraculous.

The scholar is guided by two criteria in any investigation: *economy* and *adequacy*. "Economy" means that the scholar does not use any more factors in an explanation than are absolutely necessary; "adequacy" means that the phenomenon under consideration is truly and sufficiently explained. Currently the scientists have so concentrated on *economy* that they are failing to be *adequate*. If they enlarge their principles so that they would be adequate for all possible phenomena then they could conceivably make room for the supernatural.

Whether the scholar knows it or not he is working with miracle all the time. Viewed from the categories of physics, a living organism is a miracle, and viewed from the standpoint of strict physiology or biology a rational creature must appear as miraculous. Is this not sufficient analogy to justify another miracle, the miracle of revelation?

This is no simply-minded analogy, however, for it merely justifies the space in which a miracle of revelation may take place. The uniqueness of the incarnation, The Miracle, is very different from the uniqueness of biology to physics. It is the Idea which man cannot control; it is the action of the pure freedom of God. However when Christ did become a man he did not become a monstrosity but lived out his life within the terms of nature.

We do not believe in miracles and then in Christ. We believe in Christ and then in miracles. He is the object of faith and He stands as the one unique and absolute event. To Him science can say neither yes nor no. "The truth of the claim of Christ is not a problem of science, but it is the problem of personal decision" (*Revelation*, p. 308).

(3) Philosophy has a place in Brunner's method, but not such a place that it dominates theology. The real God or the living God is known through revelation and not through philosophy. The point of contact between God and man is not in philosophical ideas but in human guilt. Speculative philosophy follows such a different path than revelation that it is hardly serviceable to the cause of revelation.

Brunner does engage in some evaluations of philosophy. The virtue of *atheism* is that it protests the humanization of theology and its vice is that it is an exaltation of the freedom of man at the expense of the freedom of God. *Pantheism* has the virtue of recognizing the sovereignty and greatness of God but the vice of extending this to the point of eliminating genuine human individuality and freedom. "Pantheism is a danger to strong minds and weak consciences" (*Revelation*, p. 352). The virtue of *subjective idealism* is to see the testimony of God in the human spirit (i.e., the true, the beautiful, and the good), the vice is to lose the identity of the individual in the Divine Mind or the Divine Spirit. *Deism, Agnosticism,* and *Positivism* are movements in the opposite direction from pantheism and idealism. They represent the modern reaction against metaphysics and are fundamentally skeptical. Their virtue is that they show the bankruptcy of purely rational thought in religion.

Theism (with proper qualifications) is Christian philosophy. Its central truth is that it does make God the central concept for all thinking. Its vice is that it is usually diluted with pantheism or idealism and so competes with revelation.

Having said all of this Brunner nevertheless maintains that there is a Christian philosophy. He writes: "Christian philosophy is a fact" (*Revelation*, p. 374). The Christian philosopher is given his stance by revelation and from that stance he writes philosophy. The history of the Church and the history of philosophy proves that there is a Christian philosophy for the philosophers use concepts and discuss problems originating in Christian. theology, and the theologian uses the topics and concepts developed in philosophy. Even though men like Pascal and Kierkegaard were extreme in their disavowal of philosophy they are healthy checks on a tendency to overuse philosophy in theology and so prevent damage to the Christian faith.

Barth states that a Christian philosophy is not necessary because the Word of God has an answer to *everything*. Brunner takes the word "everything" with an exacting literalism and says that it is foolish to look in the Scriptures for answers to problems in mathematics and physics. The activity of Biblical interpretation itself involves certain rational faculties. The interpreter needs training in logic and the use of ideas. Barth's highhanded dismissal of Christian philosophy is not to be countenanced.

The situation may be described as follows: at one end of a continuum is mathematics and at the other end is divine revelation. In mathematics pure reason is sufficient; in revelation only faith will do. As the pointer moves from mathematics towards revelation the more existential the subject matter becomes and the use of pure reason diminishes as the necessity for faith increases. A Christian philosophy is not identical with revelation so it represents a mixture (and a happy one!) of faith and rational thought. Thus the rule is that the more personal and existential a subject matter is the more faith enters; and the more abstract and impersonal it becomes the more it can be treated adequately by rational thought. Thus metaphysics has a large existential factor in it whereas physics has a minimal existential factor. The relation of faith and reason in most subject matters is therefore not disjunctive (faith or reason) but proportional (faith and reason).

In another example he states that God created the universe and in understanding creation reason using the methods of science is competent. But if we wish to tell the entire story we must also deal with the Creator as well as the creation and the Creator is known only by faith. But why is reason so competent and yet so incompetent? In original creation reason was competent but as soon as sin entered the *imago Dei* is distorted and the way back to God can now be only by faith. The explanation for this is that faith is a Declaration of Dependence whereas sin is man's Declaration of Independence. The distortion of sin does not affect purely objective and technical problems; but once the focus of attention is upon the problem of the heart the influence and power of sin is such that it fogs over the rational powers. The closer we approach the center of existence the more radical is the influence of sin, and the more abstract and formal the issue is the less it is influenced by our sinfulness.

If something of natural knowledge lies in this maximum existential zone then it is the role of Christian philosophy to offer a corrective. The scope of this Christian philosophy must be carefully delimited. The *encounter* is not a philosophical affair but is radically different, and therefore philosophy can never have the same concern for Christians as theology. The duty of the Christian philosopher is not that of preacher or theologian but that of the mediator. He deals with those problems which radiate out from the encounter, especially those problems in which both theology and philosophy have a common interest (e.g., time, history). The Christian philosopher works with the Christian theologian but he speaks a different language. The theologian makes explicit the great vocabulary of the Bible whereas the Christian philosopher relates that vocabulary to philosophical thought.

Therefore, a Christian philosophy is possible. A Christian does not cease to think and his thinking comprises Christian philosophy. The Christian philosopher realizes that the root of all trouble in philosophy is the autonomy of the human reason, and that the sole cure is the *encounter*. Therefore he alone is the truly critical philosopher: "The Christian philosopher alone is in a position to see man as a creature, as finite, not absolute reason and as a fallen creature as 'man in revolt'" (*Revelation*, p. 393).

(4) *With reference to comparative religions* Brunner makes a survey of the leading contenders for revelation or for religious

truth. Of course they all claim to be religions of revelation. Brunner makes three assertions with regard to them: (a) the fact of counterfeiting does not mean that there is *no* genuine coin nor do competing revelations mean that *all* are false. (b) The full force of Christian revelation has been obscured by the misconception of revelation by Roman Catholics and Fundamentalists. (c) Competing views may be eliminated by showing that none of them have the unique, absolute, and universal doctrine of revelation contained in Christianity.

BIBLIOGRAPHY

Brunner, Emil, *Dogmatics*, Vol. I and II
_____, *Faith, Hope and Love.*
_____, *I Believe in God*
_____, *Man in Revolt*
_____, *Philosophie und Offenbarung*
_____, *Revelation and Reason*
_____, *The Divine Imperative*
_____, *The Mediator*
_____, *The Philosophy of Religion*
Jewett, Paul, *Emil Brunner's Concept of Revelation*
Schrotenboer, P. G., *A New Apologetics: An Analysis and Appraisal of the Eristic Theology of Emil Brunner*

Part II

Systems Stressing Natural Theology

I. AQUINAS AND ARISTOTELIAN EMPIRICISM

II. BUTLER AND LOCKIAN EMPIRICISM

III. TENNANT AND SCIENTIFIC EMPIRICISM

Chapter V

THOMAS AQUINAS (1225[?]-1274)

I. INTRODUCTION

St. Thomas had a large round face, was heavy-set, and had a quiet disposition. His fellow students, who were together studying under Albertus Magnus, dubbed him "the dumb ox." Upon his concluding a very brilliant recitation one day much to the surprise of all, the learned Albertus Magnus said: "We call this young man a dumb ox, but his bellowing in doctrine will one day resound through out the world." This prophetic word has certainly been fulfilled for Thomas is not only studied wherever the history of philosophy is taught but wherever the philosophy of religion is taught and wherever Roman Catholic theology is taught. Both Protestant and Roman Catholic scholars agree that the *Summa Theologica* is one of the greatest of all treatments of Christian theology. And wherever natural theology is seriously studied attention will be given to Thomas's famous *Summa contra gentiles*.

He was not only a great thinker but a man with a great spiritual heart. He never began study without prayer and when wrestling with obscure passages he added fasting to his prayers. He finally stopped penning his *Summa* when he had such mystical experiences that he claimed that what he had written paled in significance in comparison to these experiences.

1. *His sources*

Like other geniuses Thomas was able to use the work of the past and yet not let it dominate him, and from older materials, adding his own genius, create a new tradition in Christian thought that bears strong influence even into the twentieth century.

The first great source for Thomas was the Holy Bible. He had a profound knowledge of it and although he was in harmony with the traditional mystical interpretation of the times he had a profound respect for its historical and literal meaning. In the *Migne* edition of the *Summa Theologica* the enumeration of scriptural citations runs to eighty columns of small print!

His second source was the traditions and writings of the Roman Catholic Church. He quotes fifty-six Greek fathers, twenty-two Latin fathers in which he reveals a first hand knowledge of them. He cites nineteen councils, forty-one popes, fifty-two fathers, and forty-six philosophers in his *Summa*.

His third source was Augustine. To Thomas, Augustine was the summit of theological learning and wisdom. The greatest single theological influence upon Thomas is certainly that of Augustine. He learned from Augustine that natural knowledge is instilled in us by God because God is the author of nature and he learned that this natural knowledge needed the supplementation of revealed religion.

The fourth source was Aristotle. Just as Scripture was the supreme source of revealed truth so Aristotle was the supreme source of our natural knowledge. Thomas repeatedly calls him "The Philosopher," and cites him as possessing full authority. To be with Aristotle was to be with the truth, and to be against Aristotle was to be against the truth.

This turning to Aristotle marked a great shift in the apologetics of the scholastic period. The Platonic, neo-Platonic, and Augustinian traditions dominated Roman Catholic thought up to the time of Albertus Magnus. It was at this time that Aristotle was being rediscovered by Mohammedan, Jew and Christian alike. Thomas made a systematic substitution of Aristotle for Plato all the way through his philosophy and theology. He Christianized Aristotle, and Aristotelianized Christianity! Although Thomas is unabashed Aristotelian he was not an uncritical follower of the Greek master. In the realm of faith and revelation, Aristotle was as any other pagan in need of divine revelation. And what Thomas took from Aristotle he took from the perspective of a theologian enlightened by the Christian revelation.

The other sources of Thomas are minor compared to these. Of Plato's dialogues he knows the *Timaeus* best. He does cite the *Phaedo* and other Platonists. Of the Latin philosophers he cites Boethius, Cicero, Macrobius and Seneca. He also had important interactions with the Islamic philosophers and some Jewish philosophers. He borrowed from Maimonides the thesis that some truths need to be known by both reason and revelation. His arch foe was the Arabian, Averroes, and although he combatted his doctrine of *two truths* (what is true in philosophy or theology, may be false in theology or philosophy) he did find in him a model for his own commentaries on Aristotle. However whatever sources and materials Thomas did use, he used within the scope of his own creative powers.

The protrait of Thomas in the church of St. Catherine in Pisa sums him up pictorially. The figure of St. Thomas is colossal in size. He has on his knees four volumes which are the four parts of his *Summa contra gentiles*. In his hands is the Holy Bible which is painted larger than the *contra gentiles*. Over him is Christ surrounded by Cherubim. From Christ's mouth comes a ray of light to each of the six figures prostrate at His feet. These six figures are the great Biblical teachers—Moses, John, Mark, Paul, Matthew, and Luke. From each of these teachers proceeds a ray to the head of Thomas, and three rays come from Christ directly to the head of Thomas. To the right of Thomas is Aristotle holding his *Ethics,* and to the left is Plato holding his *Timaeus.* Rays come from each of these to Thomas. Rays also proceed from the books of Aquinas illuminating the believers grouped on the sides. His enemy, Averroes, is at his feet smitten by the light. At his side lies his *Great Commentary* penetrated by a ray proceeding from the books on St. Thomas' knees.

2. *His basic philosophy*

In order to understand the apology proper of Aquinas it is necessary to have a minimum grasp of his basic philosophical principles which are essentially Aristotelian.

(1) *Matter and form.* A given object is composed of matter and form. The essence of matter is that it has the power or potential to become something, i.e., to receive a form. The essence of form is to act, i.e., to concretely bestow form upon matter. Thus matter and form are parallel to potency and act. Now this sounds highly abstract (which of course it is) but it concretely says that a tree is the combination of a certain substratum stuff (matter) which has received a definite pattern (oakness), and both make the oak tree.

Thomas sets out a continuum which commences at one end with pure matter which is pure potency, and at the other end with God who is pure actuality. To be pure matter does not exist but pure act (God) does. Between these points is strung the whole universe (physical, moral, spiritual). Thus the key for the resolution of most explanations with Thomas is this form/matter, potency/act structure.

Thomas has a complex doctrine of causation which is reflected in so much of Roman Catholic dogmatics but one aspect of that complex doctrine must be mentioned here, namely, that *forms* do function as dynamic causes. Thus the oak tree is not only produced by wind, rain, snow, sun, and chemicals but by the dynamic function of the form of oakness.

(2) Thomas' *doctrine of knowledge* (epistemology) is essentially Aristotelian. First of all it is intensely *empirical.* At this point he breaks with the traditional epistemology of Plato as reinterpreted by Plotinus and then by Augustine. Plato's epistemology is rationalistic, that is to say, the criteria for truthfulness are essentially

those of the *mind*. In the duality of sense and mind the criteria
of the mind have priority. Thus in Plato's theory of knowledge
truth is essentially composed of ideas, or forms, or eternal concepts.
Aristotle was not a pure empiricist, for the mind did have a structure for him also, but he gave a precedence to our sensory experience which Plato did not. The mind does come upon ideas or
forms but only *after* they have been abstracted from the delivery
of the senses, and are never found *independently from* sensory experience (at least as far as men are concerned). In a word Thomas
simply substitutes the perspectives of Aristotle for those of Plato.

The human mind, says Thomas, is a blank at birth. In contradiction to both Plato and Augustine he finds that it is not
staffed with innate ideas. Thomas himself says that "it is natural
to man to attain the intellectual truths through sensible things,
because all our knowledge originates from sense" (*Summa Theologica*, I, 1, 9—from now on just cited with the numerals). *There is
nothing in the mind which is not first in senses.* Plato's position
is that unless there is something *first* in the mind we would not
be able to decode what the senses reported. There is a concession
here, however, to Platonism in that the mind is recognized as having a *potential structure* and so Thomas does not teach that the
mind is a simple blank disc upon which experience writes its record
willy-nilly. However it must be emphatically stated that *all the
fundamental concepts of philosophy are extracted from the senses.*
There is no mixing here in which the mind contributes *some*
forms.

Secondly, Thomas' theory of knowledge is *inferential*. Augustine
believed that he had a *direct* experience of both God and the self.
Thomas counters this by saying that the nature of man determines
the manner of his knowing. Man is soul and body, intellect and
matter. Therefore, what the soul and the intellect know they
know through the body and matter, and this can, therefore, only
be *indirectly* or *inferentially*. Our knowledge of God and of the
self accordingly is inferential. This is another way of rejecting
the doctrine of innate ideas.

Thomas argues that although man's knowledge is indispensably
rooted in the senses it is not confined to the senses. The senses
occasion knowledge but the knowledge itself is not a collection
of sensations but is *intellectual*. The mind abstracts essences and
relationships from the sensory material presented to it. It therefore can penetrate to reality, i.e., become metaphysical, whereas
most empiricisms degenerate to skepticism. Man's knowledge is
fundamentally sensory only in the sense that it takes its rise from
the senses. But knowledge transcends the senses. First of all the

objects in the senses are not dumb or mute objects but carry metphysical materials within themselves (i.e., they are created entities, they do possess forms) ; and secondly the mind itself acts reflectively and therefore intellectually in knowing an object. Man's knowledge is never without a sensory basis, never without a sensory relationship, but it is not constituted exclusively or exhaustively by this relationship. Thomas attempts to avoid the pitfalls thereby of a pure empiricism.

Thirdly, knowledge is *abstractive*. Man's sensory equipment is such that he can perceive objects. The object as a sensory report comes before the intellect via the consciousness of man. At this point the mind does some fast and clever footwork. It lifts the "phantasm" or "sensible species" out of the sensory report. The active intellect then lifts, i.e., *abstracts*, the universal from the sensible species.

Here we see concretely how the transition is made from a purely sensory report of knowledge to the intellectual side of knowing. The mind at birth is a potentiality; it is the *intellectus possibilis*. If this mind were never sensorily stimulated it would remain a complete blank, i.e., it would know nothing. But when the senses stimulate the mind, the mind goes into action! Working with the powers of memory, of imagination, of cogitation, and of unification (the so-called common sense) it forms concepts which are the stuff of true knowledge.

It might be surmised from this that the mind does not really know objects, but only has pictures or ideas or representations of objects. But contemporary Thomists insist that Thomas taught that we know the object itself, and not just ideas about the object. That is to say Thomas is *an epistemological realist*. Objects do not exist only in virtue of their being perceived, and what is perceived is not a copy of the object but the object itself. Thus Thomas advances beyond the position of representationalism (i.e., that our senses only give us representations of objects) and of phenomenalism (which restricts knowledge only to sensations). Opponents of Thomas insist that all of this is belated fence-patching. Once having given the radical priority to the senses he cannot on principle save himself but must go all the way to skepticism.

With reference to the doctrine of universals he is a moderate realist. One of the most vexing problems of the scholastic period was the status of universals. In the sense that universals existed in the mind of God as archetypes (i.e., models) for creation they are *ante rem* (before the concrete object or particular object); in that universals enform objects they are *in rem* (in the particu-

lar); and in that they can be abstracted from the particular by the
mind they are *post rem* (after the particular). This differs from
realism proper (of the Platonic type) which affirms that universals
have a unique existence of their own. The universal embedded
in the particular *reminds* the mind of the truth of the universal
which it already possesses. In contrast to this Aristotle and then
Thomas taught that the mind *abstracts* the universal from the
particular.

(3) In *the concept of being* Thomas is again with Aristotle
against Plato. The Platonist is interested in the concepts, i.e., in
essences for this is the stuff of knowledge. Thus "structure" is
before "stuff." But Thomas is interested first in the "stuff," in the
doctrine of being, i.e., in ontology. Ontology is the study of "being
as such." Thus philosophy is first concerned with being, then with
concepts. The mind first grasps being and *then* essences. That is to
say, although we cannot separate the two, the important thing is
that the mind grasps being as determined by essences.

The direct outcome of this may be seen in the theistic proofs.
That God is (ontology) Thomas believes is capable of rather
direct demonstration; but the attributes of God (essences) present
a more complex and difficult problem. The being of God as such
is more fundamental than the essence of God and the former is
capable of a readier logical treatment than the latter. Some contemporary Thomists affirm that this is Thomas' most enduring
contribution to philosophy, and others say in his giving priority
to existence over essence he has anticipated modern existentialism.

II. NATURE AND FUNCTION OF HUMAN REASON (*ratio naturalis*)

Reason is a fundamental endowment of the human soul bestowed upon him by God at creation and continued until now.
There is a strong optimism of human reason which permeates the
thought of Thomas and which to some of his critics looks far more
Greek than biblical. One of the great issues of the Protestant
Reformation was an attempt to reassess the damage done to man's
rational powers by sin. However Thomas' robust "faith in reason"
expresses itself throughout his philosophy, apologetics, and theology.

1. As far as *philosophy* is concerned the natural light of God
within man constitutes a reliable intellectual tool. It can construct
a valid metaphysical system. It is thus *philosophically competent*.
Philosophy exists within its own right because the human reason as

such can attain the truth, and does not need the props of grace or special revelation.

This is a strong repudiation of the scholastic Augustinian position. Augustine (and Erigena) considered philosophy to be the ancillary of theology. Philosophy really had no independent life of its own for sin had too doleful effects upon the human person. Unless the mind were lightened with the light of God it remained in darkness!

However the introduction of the major writings of Aristotle into scholastic thought changed this. The ancillary role of philosophy was replaced by a philosophy which stood in its own rights. Thomistic enthusiasts trace the founding of modern philosophy to Thomas. In the tradition from Augustine to Anselm philosophy does not exist in its own right. It was but the humble servant of theology. But Thomas deserves the credit of wrenching philosophy away from the lordship of theology and giving it a status of its own. Thus the academic dignity of modern philosophy existing as an independent unity within the life of a university can be traced to Thomas.

This philosophy which the competent human reason can determine turns out to be a refined and "Christianized" Aristotelianism. Thomas sincerely believed that if the human mind followed the truth without prejudice it would arrive at the general outlines of Aristotelian philosophy and this is still very much Roman Catholic conviction. And it must be emphatically specified that the mind can arrive at this valid philosophy without the illumination of the Holy Spirit.

The philosophy of Aristotle as Thomas incorporates it into Christian thought becomes the basis of common ground for argumentation with the heathen. Natural reason is common to pagan and Christian alike and forms the court of appeal in religious debate. Thomas can then press upon the heathen his claim that natural reason leads to the existence of God, angels, and the soul. But there is something more. When the conclusions of natural reason are compared with the truths of revelation there is a congruence. Two credits accrue at this point: (a) It reveals that human reason is competent if it comes to some of the same truths as special revelation; and (b) it reveals the truth of revelation because in some areas it is congruent with the truths of philosophy. It might be said from this perspective that the essentially apologetic of Thomas is *showing and demonstrating this congruence.*

2. Thomas admits that reason cannot attain to all the truths of Christian faith. This is seen in Aristotle himself who lacking divine

revelation blundered in his theology. However Aristotle was not deceived by his reason (as Tertullian would argue) but he was limited by the limitations of reason. There is a world of difference between reason as deceptive and reason as limited. If reason can be deceived it is incompetent, but if it is only faced with limitations it is valid up to the boundary of its limitations.

Thomas takes his stand within the limitations of reason not the deception of reason. Within its boundaries reason is metaphysically competent, i.e., it is capable of arriving at the truth in metaphysics. It can be made even stronger. Reason can vigorously demonstrate propositions. Reason can achieve absolute truth with full certainity. Let us assess the implications of this claim. Most modern philosophers believe that only in formal systems (logic, mathematics, geometry) can theorems be demonstrated. In the area of science, laws of science are probability sentences. And in the area of philosophy we are confined to discursive reasoning which can hardly close in and prove, verify, or confirm anything. According to the old philosophical dictum, metaphysical systems are matters of responsible and learned choices, but not demonstrations. But Thomas claims to *demonstrate* philosophical theses with the same precision and finality as theorems in formal systems are demonstrated!

Having described the powers of reason Thomas then gives us its *functions*. It is the function of natural reason to demonstrate the *praeambula fidei*. This means those things which are the presuppositions of revelation and Roman Catholic dogma. Natural reason can demonstrate the existence of God, the existence of the soul, the details of natural law, and the divine origin of the Roman Catholic Church. Natural reasons can make the teachings of revelation more lucid by illustrating them from the created world. Natural reason can dispose of arguments against the Christian revelation. Natural reason can show the necessity of transferring from natural theology to revealed theology. These certainly are very strong claims in the area of religious truth, and Roman Catholic theology reflecting Thomism represents along side its strong authoritarianism a very pronounced rationalism.

3. Certainly the greatest achievement of any apologetics would be that of proving *the existence of God*. This topic then will bring us into the heart of the Thomistic apologetic.

Thomas rejected—as already mentioned—the Platonic and Augustinian tradition. Against Augustine he does not believe that the knowledge of God or the idea of God is innate. There is something innate in man and that is the intellectual potentialities of the mind. The mind has powers, potentialities, but it does not have specific innate ideas or concepts.

However Thomas backs up and admits, in a certain sense, the knowledge of God is innate. We all have a knowledge of God but it is a confused knowledge. He writes: "To know that God exists in a general and confused way is implanted in us by nature, inasmuch as God is man's beatitude. For man naturally desires happiness, and what is naturally desired by man is naturally known by him. This is, however, not to know absolutely that God exists" (I, 2, 1).

One is tempted to say that this is stolen from the first page of Augustine's *Confessions*! What Thomas apparently means is that the restlessness of man for happiness is really a restlessness for God. But no proof can be derived from such poorly defined feelings.

Thomas also rejects the Augustinian thesis that from the knowledge of truth we can eventually proceed to God the author of all truth. Thomas argues that the existence of one truth simply argues that truth in general is possible. The famous ontological argument, rooted in Augustine and developed by Anselm, is likewise rejected. The Aristotelian position of Thomas makes him reject all the Platonism in Augustine and Anselm. Therefore Thomas rejects innate ideas, illuminationism, "ontologism," and the ontological argument. The basic logical flaw with the argument is that it deals with mental possibility and not with existence (I, 2, 1).

If the Platonic, Augustinian, and Anselmic tradition is rejected then our knowledge of God is necessarily *inferential*. Because man is a body-soul creature he cannot have direct knowledge of God who is pure spirit. The only being man can know is being as mediated through matter. Therefore God's existence is not self-evident (*ibid*) but must be proved from the effects of God in creation.

Metaphysical being can only be known in matter and this includes the being of God. Being is first grasped by the senses, as we have seen in Thomas' doctrine of knowledge. The being of God must then be known at the foundation by a perception of the effects of God in creation. If the most debated problem of scholastic philosophy was that of universals, the most frequently cited verse of the scholastics was Romans 1:20. And Thomas uses it to prove that the existence of God may be known from the things created. Although the material for the proofs is founded in the senses, the proofs themselves are the achievement of the intellect. The intellect can prove the existence of God by inferring the existence of God from His effects in creation, (I, 2, 2).

This proof is a demonstration. He writes that "The existence of God . . . can be known by natural reason" and that by arguing from effect to cause "we can demonstrate the existence of God from His effects" (I, 2, 2). We refer the reader back to our discussion of the significance of demonstration. This demonstration consists of five theistic proofs. They have been called the Five Ways, or the One Way in five forms. In the broadest sense they follow the general metaphysical thought of Thomas. (i) From the existence of motion we can reckon back to the Prime Mover; (ii) from the existence of causation we can deduce the First Cause; (iii) from the contingent character of objects we can calculate the Absolute God; (iv) from the gradation of life from the very simple to the very complex we can properly postulate God as the Capstone of being; and (v) from the governance of the world we can deduce the great Designer.

The structure of each proof is somewhat the same. The data are provided by the senses; they are subjected to the cause-effect schema in its various forms; and the conclusion is that the supreme Being exists. Thus the proofs are strictly inferential and *a posteriori*. At root is the negative assertion that an infinite regress is repugnant to the intellect, and the positive evaluation that the created thing can only be properly acounted for by a Creator.

But Aquinas can hardly rest with the demonstration of the existence of God as great a philosophical achievement as this is. Something must be said of the character or nature of this God and this leads on to the doctrine of the attributes. The logical structure of proving the existence of God is the cause-effect schema. Given the effect we can reckon back to the cause. But what schema gives us the divine attributes? What in nature also tells us what God is like?

The first structure which Thomas uses is the so-called *via negotionis* or way of negation. This has its roots in neo-Platonic philosophy in which God is defined in terms of what He is not! Or, it is a method of successive abstractions. God is not in time as we are in time and therefore he is *eternal*. God is not movable as we are movable so God is *immutable*. God is not passive power for passive power is an attribute of matter; therefore God is *spiritual*. God is neither a man nor an object in that he is not composed of parts; therefore He is *simple*.

In justification of this Thomas asserts that God is His own essence and being. He has no *genus* or *differentia*. Therefore we cannot properly and logically define God. This furthermore means that we have no *a priori* or innate knowledge of God. What we know of God's attributes we know by *inference*, and not by deductions from a definition. Hence our knowledge of God is restricted to negative theology and the analogy of being.

The analogy of being brings us to the second structure, the *via analogiae* (I, 13, 5). This is almost the main weapon in the Thomist arsenal. It requires exploration of special terms. A term is used *univocally* when it refers to a directly known and understood object. In the sentence, "A clock tells the time of day," we normally and correctly assume that a clock is a well-known timepiece. A term is used *equivocally* when it refers to something beyond its normal or natural designation. Thus a "bear" may in one sentence mean one of the constellations in the sky, or a type of stock investor in another sentence, or again an aggressive kind of person in a third sentence.

In what sense are there traces of God in creation? In that God is Creator His effects must be there! Just as the artist impresses something of his own self in his paintings or music so God has impressed *something* of Himself in his creation. But is the impression there univocally or equivocally?

The answer is—neither! If God is the *univocal* cause of nature like a father is the univocal cause of his son, then God and nature become identified. This leads to pantheism. But God and man are sufficiently *different* so that we cannot *simply* reason—or reason in a simple fashion—from the son to the father. If we do we virtually make the son *the same as* the father, i.e., we identify God with his effects, or God with nature, and this is pantheism.

Furthermore we cannot say that just as the son is good the father is good, or, just as man is good God is good. God is not good in the same sense in which man is good due to the significant differences between God and man.

On the other hand we cannot say that the knowledge of God within his creation is equivocal, i.e., ambiguous. If that is so there would be a drastic separation of God from his works. It would also call for a separation of cause and effect which would violate a fundamental thesis of metaphysics.

If God is not known in nature univocally and yet he is still known in nature, how is he known? He is known by the means of the structure of *proportionality*. The relationship between God and his effects is not direct (pantheism) but proportional (theism). If we say, "man is good, and therefore God is good" what we really mean to say is: "just as man is good with references to manhood, God is good with reference to Godhood." This proportionality between the effects and perfections of God in creation and Himself is called *the analogy of being*.

God's being is different from creation, yet it is reflected in cre-

ation. The relationship between the being of God and the creation
is thus analogical. It is this analogical relationship which is the
basis of the entire Thomistic philosophy, apologetics, and natural
theology and without it the Thomistic system would collapse.

The relationship of the watchmaker to his work is analogical.
We do not make a direct deduction from the watch to the watchmaker! For example, if the case of the watch is beautifully etched
we do not reckon that the watchmaker's skin is covered with
elaborate tattoos. We reckon *indirectly*, i.e., analogically. We deduce the cleverness of the watchmaker from the watch case. So
from creation we indirectly and analogously deduce the attributes
of God, namely, his perfection, goodness, uniqueness, infinity, intelligence, and will.

III. HIS CONCEPTION OF FAITH AND REVELATION

1. *The need for revelation.* Although Thomas had a profound
respect for the powers of the human mind he realized its limitations. The purpose of man is more than that of adjustment to his
environment for although born on this earth he is a super-terrestial
being. And as such he is in need of eternal truth, heavenly truth,
saving truth in order that he might attain to certain happiness.

Salvation pertains, then, to things *above* nature and reason.
Thomas writes: "Hence, in order that a man arrive at the perfect
vision of heavenly happiness, he must first of all believe God, as
a disciple believes the master who is teaching him. . . . For the
things which are of faith surpass human reason, and hence they do
not come to man's knowledge unless God reveals them" (II, II, 2,
3, and, II, II, 6, 1) . This citation reveals the double-layer structure
of Thomas' apologetics. Natural reason creates a philosophy; the
philosophy creates a natural theology and an ethic of natural
law; the natural theology and ethic create the presupposition for a
revealed religion. But there it ends. We can begin the second
chapter only if a revelation occurs, and this revelation will be
about man's supreme destiny, namely, his salvation.

2. *Definition of revelation.* Being a Roman Catholic Thomas
includes the revelation deposited within the Church as well as
Scripture. But this revelation yields a theology which differs from
natural theology even though at some points there is overlap. It
is the science whose particular genus is that it is "inspired of God,"
(I, 1, 1) . Even though it is revelation it is also science and this on
two grounds: (i) it constitutes a valid knowledge of salvation, and

(ii) it reduces to higher principles which take the place of the customary axioms (I, 1, 2).

This divine revelation is especially important in three areas of our knowledge of God: (i) we know by revelation that God created the world, for on Aristotelian premises we assume the eternality of the world; (ii) we know the plan of redemption by revelation and this includes the doctrine of the Incarnation and the gift of the Holy Spirit; and (iii) by revelation we know that God is triune, (I, 32, 1). From the effects of God in nature we are allowed only to deduce the being of God; we are not allowed to make distinctions among the persons of the trinity.

The *proof* for this revelation is to be found in the traditional arguments for the supernatural work of God in the two Testaments (miracles, prophecy, and the beneficial influence of Christianity upon humanity). To this he adds other considerations. The Scriptures *plainly* state that they are a revelation from God. *Natural reason* does not give us enough truth and therefore the race needs a special revelation. And if God is a good and gracious God He must inform us of his triune nature (I, 12, 12).

3. *Definition of faith.* Thomas' definition of faith alternates between a psychological analysis of it and an authoritarian interpretation of it. The first is generated by his philosophy and the second by his Roman Catholic heritage.

(1) Faith *psychologically* considered is an act of the intellect and of the will. Of the two the intellect is the more important. Thomas writes that faith resides in the intellect for "to believe is an act of the intellect, inasmuch as the will moves it to assent. Faith resides in the speculative intellect as is clear from its objects" (II, II, 4, 3). If faith is fundamentally an act of the intellect then *to believe is to think with assent* (II, II, 2, 1—a definition derived from Augustine). But this act of believing with assent is not the same act as accepting as that of accepting scientific knowledge. It is an act with reference to things the vision of which is not clear. Faith is not the inquiry into things demonstrated by natural reason but an inquiry into those things "whereby a man is induced to believe, for instance, that such things have been uttered by God and confirmed by miracles" (II, II, 2, 1).

However Thomas believes that there is an opaqueness to faith that natural reason does not have. In natural reason we have a clear and distinct notion of our terms and how they are achieved and demonstrated; but the knowledge of faith is a *given* and so we do not have this clear vision of it (I, 12, 12). Faith is half-way between scientific knowledge and opinion. In scientific knowledge we

know by clear demonstration the intellect assenting in virtue of the
necessity of the evidence. In opinion we assent to the provisional
truthfulness of something because the evidence is incomplete.
Faith is *like* science in that it assents with firmness which a demonstrated truth deserves, and it is *like* opinion in that its object is
not a matter of scientific demonstration.

Therefore, although faith is in the intellect, however in view
of the opacity of the object of faith the intellect is moved by the
will. First, the act of faith is an act of the intellect for there cannot
be blind faith. Secondly, the will which moves the intellect to faith
has been previously supplied by the intellect with information
which forms the basis of the motivation. Thirdly, faith is always
made on some credible grounds, i.e., it is not an irrational act.
There are credible, extrinsic reasons for the act of faith.

(2) There are two facets to the *theological* aspect of faith. First,
faith is a divine virtue and therefore can occur in the human heart
only by God's grace. The second is that faith is response to the
voice of authority. The first speaks to the "light of faith" which
is similar to the Reformers' doctrine of the illumination of the
Holy Spirit, and the second refers to the supernatural origin of
revelation. Revelation is God-given and must be accepted as the
authoritative word of the divine Teacher. "Hence, in order that
a man arrive at the perfect vision of heavenly happiness, he must
first of all believe God, as a disciple believes the master who is
teaching him" (II, II, 2, 3). On another occasion he affirms that
what God has revealed man must accept by faith (I, 1, 1), and yet
again he writes that "Therefore, we must not attempt to prove
what is of faith, except by authority alone, to those who receive
authority; while as regards others, it suffices to prove that what faith
teaches is not impossible" (I, 32, 1).

(3) It is evident from any study of Thomas that some things
taught in natural theology also are found in revealed theology.
In the first instance they are received as reasonable and in the
second instance they are received by faith. Why does this over-
lapping exist? Here Thomas borrows from Moses Maimonides
who faced the same problem in his Jewish apologetics. The reasons
why some truths of reason are repeated in revelation are: (a) Because ordinary men with no philosophical training could not
demonstrate such technical theses they are thereby repeated in
revelation that they may be received by faith; (b) because such
theses are necessary for the spiritual life of all Christians, and in
that all Christians cannot demonstrate them, they occur in revelation; (c) because these theses depend upon such a vast erudition
which ordinary men do not have—for they are based on the scien-

tific constitution of things—they are repeated in revelation; (d) because many men do not have the intelligence necessary to make the demonstrations the theses are repeated in revelation; and (e) because most men are too busy with matters of business, farming, etc., they do not have the leisure to make such demonstrations, and therefore these truths are repeated in revelation. However, such a procedure as this has the unhappy overtone of restricting real religious certainty to professors.

4. *Certainty*. Thomas faces a distinct problem with reference to religious certainty. In that only reason can have clear vision (by which Thomas means logical demonstration), faith is restricted because it deals with *opaque* objects, i.e., matters which are not directly accessible but revealed. But in that faith is faith in revelation it must have a point of superiority. Thomas' resolution is that faith in things demonstrated by natural reason is superior to faith in things received by revelation *at the point of evidence*. The natural reason makes its objects clear and therefore its knowledge is superior to that of revelation. But in that faith puts men in contact with a supernatural realm it is superior to natural reason due to the intrinsic worth of its object. Faith as a divine grace is thus superior to natural reason. Reason is superior in the clarity of the mode of attaining its knowledge; faith is superior in the character of the knowledge it knows. Reason's certitude depends upon internal evidence, i.e., that which is rationally demonstrable; faith's certitude depends on external evidence, i.e., the evidences of revelation whereby God attests revelation. Thomas protects his flank very carefully at this point and affirms that faith is more certain than science and other intellectual virtues. He cites I Thessalonians 2:15 and then reasons that "nothing is more certain than the word of God. Therefore science is not more certain than faith, nor is anything else" (II, II, 4, 8).

IV. THE RELATIONSHIP BETWEEN NATURAL REASON OR PHILOSOPHY AND THEOLOGY OR REVELATION OR FAITH

Thomas adopts the solution suggested by Hugo St. Victor who divided knowledge into the *mundane* and the *divine,* the former known by natural reason and the latter by faith in divine revelation. God is the author of both the mundane and the divine; truth is the goal of both; and therefore they can never be in conflict. A dictum which Thomas uses again and again is that only the false can contradict the true. Therefore, reason and revelation can never contradict each other. If there is a contradiction there must be a mistake somewhere. Only a false theology can contradict true philosophy, and only false philosophy can contradict true theology. Here then is virtually full and equal weight given to both natural reason and revelation. Although we might not be able to formally harmonize one with the other at all points we can rest assured that at whatever points they do approach each other only harmony with prevail.

But again with a strong theological instinct Thomas wishes to protect the sanctity of the theological system which he defends and he makes revelation the highest science and affirms that anything which contradicts it must be false. Revelation is the noblest science because: (a) it has God as its subject matter and therefore its subject matter possesses the highest dignity; (b) it has the greatest certitude seeing that it comes from God; and (c) its practical value is the greatest for it aims at the "eternal beatitude" (I, 1, 5).

Reason and revelation have a supporting relationship to each other. The basis for this, in addition to what has been mentioned before, is that reason or nature anticipates grace or revelation and nature is not contradicted by grace but is perfected by grace. This thesis (*gratia non tollit naturam sed peficit*) pervades and colors the entire Thomistic apologetic. Accordingly, reason does not do violence to faith and faith does not do violence to reason. Thomas argues that the necessary implication of I Peter 3:15 is that reasons in support of faith do not lessen the merit of faith. He writes: "Now the Apostle would not give this advice, if it would imply a diminuation in the merit of faith. Therefore reason does not diminish the merit of faith" (II, II, 2, 10).

Furthermore, reason may be used in theology for purposes of clarification. It should be mentioned here that although reason may show that faith is not absurd nor deceived, reason cannot *prove* the truths of faith for to prove the truths of faith would end the merit of faith (I, 1, 8). There must be a certain *venture* in faith for only then is there merit. There is no merit in trusting one's self to a heavy stone bridge crossing a small stream; but there would be merit in trusting the character of a friend when some action of his might on the surface of things impugn his character. However theology may draw upon philosophy "in order to make its teaching clearer . . . it does not draw upon the other sciences as upon its superiors, but uses them as its inferiors and handmaidens" (I, 1, 5). In that our intellects are weak it is of great help to be sustained in our faith in revelation by the contributions of natural reason. Thus philosophy serves revelation three ways: (a) it prepares the mind of men to receive by faith the truths of revelation; (b) it develops and delineates the truths of revelation and develops them into scientific form; and (c) it enables reason to defend the truths of revelation.

BIBLIOGRAPHY

Aquinas, Thomas, *Summa Contra Gentiles*
————————, *Summa Theologica*
Baillie, J., *Our Knowledge of God*
Bengignus, B., *Nature, Knowledge and God*
Burtt, E. A., *Types of Religious Philosophy*
D'Arcy, M. C., *Saint Thomas Aquinas*
De Wulf, M., *The System of Thomas Aquinas*
Gilson, E., *The Philosophy of St. Thomas Aquinas* (3rd edition)
Kennedy, D. J., "St. Thomas Aquinas," *The Catholic Encyclopedia*, Vol. 14
Mascal, E. L., *Existence and Analogy*
Meyer, H., *The Philosophy of St. Thomas Aquinas*

Chapter VI

JOSEPH BUTLER (1692-1752)

Joseph Butler was the author of a work considered by many to be the most impressive in the entire history of apologetics. It had the title of *The Analogy of Religion to the Constitution and Course of Nature* (1736). Not many men of such spiritual, moral and intellectual stature of Butler's have graced the rolls of the Christian Church. Here is a man whose entire life was spent in a passionate dedication to finding the *truth*, in theology and ethics. Few men have written a book that has gone through so many editions. In the nineteenth century the British presses produced five editions of the works of Butler and twenty-eight editions of his *Analogy*. In America there were more than twenty printings of the Malcom and Barnes edition. The *Analogy* became one of those choice and honored works placed on the required reading list for graduation from Oxford University.

Butler was raised a Presbyterian but was converted to the Anglican Church and in that Church rose to the position of bishop. He remained within this Church as a thoroughly devoted man. His scholarship was matched by his sincere piety and ethical conviction. Though of some means he gave substantially to charity and never converted his elevated position into occasions for expensive social affairs or banquets. He lived meagerly and even ascetically.

Butler had no patience with *enthusiasm*. The word has a special meaning in religious discourse referring to highly emotional and ecstatic religious experiences. This was exhibited so clearly in Butler's famous interview with Wesley in 1739. Butler heard the report of Wesley's revivalism and branded it as something *very horrid* and ordered Wesley off his diocese. To base religion on religious feelings and experiences ran counter to Butler's theology, ecclesiology, and apologetics.

Butler was a man of great intellectual depth and precision of thought and many of his definitions of terms in ethics and religious psychology are taken as authoritative. In philosophical background he was deeply committed to Locke, whereas in religious disposition he emphasized strict moral behavior and liturgical forms of worship.

His appearance was saintly. He was genuinely modest and sweet of disposition. He had long white hair draping over his shoulders giving him the appearance of a patriarch. It was a spiritually exciting experience to watch him perform the liturgy in his old age where a bright and saintly face radiant with Christian joy was framed by the crown of white hair.

I. HIS TIMES

If it can be judged from Butler's own remarks he lived in a time when Christianity was greatly discredited and judged as fictitious. It is universally admitted that he wrote during the high water season of deism and the age of reason. It was a time when infidel writers were in abundance. Men everywhere were discrediting the major theses of the Christian faith. By attempting to show the irrationality of these doctrines they were claiming the right to assess the Christian system as such as false.

It was the age of a religion of reason. There was a great distaste for anything that smelled of superstition and a reaction to anything which attempted to pass itself off as mystery. The religious was the reasonable and the reasonable was religious. The final arbiter in all matters of religion was intellectual clarity judged by the court of human reason. The ideal of the religion of reason was the so-called "natural religion" which existed among men prior to their corruption of it.

Many of the critics of Christianity admitted the existence of God and the sufficiency of natural religion, but denied both the necessity of, and the claim for, special revelation. The authenticity of the Scriptures was denied and man's moral accountability and immortality were skeptically regarded. In the area of ethics hedonism was defended graced with a spirit of moderation. The righteous were taunted with Tertullian's (supposed) dictum: "I believe because it is absurd," and often rephrased it for their purposes to read, "I believe because it is not absurd."

Deism moved along a broad front but it is generally recognized that if it had an official creed it was that of Lord Herbert. He affirmed that there is a God; that He should be worshipped; that virtue and piety are the chief parts of worship; that we ought to be sorry for our sins and repent; and that God does reward and punish in this life and in the life to come. Deism was a strange mixture of flippancy, skepticism, and serious religion. As such it included a mixed multitude of independent thinkers whose platform was basically composed of denials rather than affirmations. They denied special revelation; they denied any uniqueness to Scripture and demanded that it be treated as an other book; they frequently denied the deity of Christ; and they ruled out of religion the mystical, the emotional, and the mysterious. Their religion was a *natural religion.*

This *natural religion* posited a belief in God who ruled the world as its Moral Governor. It found unnecessary the doctrines of the Trinity, traditional Christology, and divine atonement. The virtue in Christianity was that it *republished* the basic elements of *natural religion.*

In the early days of deism it defended this natural religion with a rationalistic theory of knowledge but under the influence of John Locke (1632-1704) it became empirical. Locke was famous for his attack on the notion of innate ideas. According to the theory of innate ideas the mind at birth was stocked with certain moral, ethical, intellectual and perhaps even aesthetic ideas which experience did not create but brought to the surface of consciousness. Dynamically these ideas made the process of acquiring knowledge possible, for unless there was some sort of formation of the intellect itself nothing could be grasped by the intellect. Locke countered by saying that apart from a very general power of the mind to form associations the mind was a blank sheet at birth. Upon this blank sheet in conjunction with the associational power of the mind experience wrote its transcript. Locke thus exerted an enormous influence on religious thought including such greats as Toland, Collins, and Tindal as well as Butler.

Butler's attack on deism was then a sort of within-the-camp attack. Traditional apologists were bombing deism from some distant position but by accepting this Lockian epistemology and the deists' theory of analogy Butler enters within their camp and by hand spikes their guns. So capable, so thorough, so devastating was Butler's attack upon deism that no real formal answer was ever made.

There were two other features of the intellectual climate of Butler's time which need some comment. First, religion was interpreted by some as being nothing more or less than morality. Furthermore, religion was interpreted as being a product exclusively of the reason. Both of these features colored Butler's own understanding of the Christian faith. Poetry, gratitude, joy, and beauty were hardly religious categories. One could deduce from Butler that the universe was ordered but never that it was beautiful. One could assume that the religious man was thoughtful but never that he was emotional.

The second feature was that Newton had demonstrated that one universal system of law governed the entire physical universe. Butler took his cue from Newton and in terms of the natural, moral and religious aspects of the universe maintained that all was governed by one universal system, or scheme of laws including all creatures in its comprehensiveness. *The same general laws* are exhibited in all domains of God's governance.

II. EVALUATIONS OF BUTLER

Opinions of Butler range from that of Bishop Hoag who said he could never look into the *Analogy* without getting a headache to the men who consider the *Analogy* the greatest defense of Christianity in its entire history.

Tholuck, a great German theological scholar felt that reading the *Analogy* was like going through sand on foot. Others claimed rather than freeing the soul it weighed down on the soul like a lead weight or that it was a book written from a narrow legalistic standpoint. William Pitt claimed that the book pushed him into atheism rather than Christianity and the great Unitarian theologian, James Martineau, concurred in this in the sense that Butler so treated the irresolvable problems of Christianity that his book becomes a case for atheism rather than for Christianity.

Added to the charges against the nature of the argument are the invectives aimed at the style. The *Analogy* took twenty years to write and it was condensed and recondensed until it reached a maximum of logical concentration. Thus Butler is charged with being a great thinker but an equally bad writer. So crabbed, so logical, so choppy is the style that it has been declared an honor to even understand Butler! To follow line after line of closely stated, minutely guarded, properly qualified exposition is itself a very serious intellectual undertaking. The punction is a grammarians nightmare with colons, semicolons, and commas used in novel ways and this is complicated by the fact that so many sentences have qualifying clauses to be sure not too much or too little is said. However, for all of this, if the energy is spent in tracing out Butler's thought, it will be found always to be clear. There is no ambiguity here.

On the credit side we note that the Scottish philosopher Hume thought the *Analogy* the best defense of Christianity that he had ever read. Cardinal Newman was also much impressed with the *Analogy* and believed Butler to be the most authoritarian voice in Anglican theology. Sir James Mackintosh thought the *Analogy* was the most original and profound work ever composed by man. There is no need to extend the list of laudatory opinions but one other item deserves recognition. Butler's sermons on ethical topics are considered masterpieces of ethical precision and argumentation. The odd situation in the twentieth century is that while the

Analogy never gets more than a passing reference in philosophy Butler's few sermons on ethics are still being read and cited as one of the major contributions to ethical thought in the total history of philosophical ethics.

III. THE FOUNDATIONS OF HIS SYSTEM OF APOLOGETICS

Although it is claimed that the *Analogy* is strictly an apology and not an apologetics this is really not the case. Butler's apology grows out of an apologetics. Butler took the proving of Christianity very seriously. The very supposition that Christianity might be true demands that it be treated with great seriousness and to treat it lightly is presumptuous rashness. He professes that he does not know a "higher and more important obligation which we are under, than that of examining most seriously into its evidence, supposing its credibility; and of embracing it, upon supposition of its truth" (p. 197, Malcom edition) .

1. *Lockian empiricism.* Modern philosophy began on the high road of rationalism .(i.e., that the truth is determined by the reason and not by the senses) of Descartes, Spinoza and Leibniz. It was made mundane and empirical by Locke. He postulated (for he had no empirical evidence for such an assertion) that the mind of the infant at birth was like a clean slate. By reason of the sense organs a steady stream of impressions pour into the mind. By an innate power of reflection these impressions are organized and schematized. Thus from the primeval data of our impressions, reworked and compounded by the reflective or associational power of the mind, there emerges such notions as God, infinite space, endless time and substance. If such a system is thoroughly carried out it is known as *sensationalism* for the origin of knowledge and the adjudication of knowledge is in the senses. It is also called an *empiricism* for although an organizing power is granted the mind the critical test of truth is in the sensory information supplied by the senses. It stands in radical contrast to *idealism* which affirms that knowledge is composed of trans-temporal, trans-spatial concepts or universals. And it also contrasts with *rationalism* which claims in the relationship of sense and thought that the final word is with thought and not with sensation.

Butler placed himself within this Lockian empirical tradition with its emphasis upon the limitation of knowledge. It must be remembered that although Butler read widely and wisely he very infrequently cites his authorities which makes it difficult to give chapter and verse on these matters. However the influence of John

Locke is unmistakable. Butler renounced both rationalism and idealism and cites Descartes as an example of a philosopher resting his case upon hypotheses, i.e., upon inverifiable contentions (p. 70). Neither is there any mysticism or apriorism in Butler's system. He defends a strict empiricism, and a strict inductionism. It is a system which attempts to make both theology and apologetics vigorously empirical and deductive contrasting sharply with any speculative approach to these two areas.

When Butler appeals to experience (e.g., 79, 83, 176, 211) he means *sensory* experience. Butler means by experience what modern philosophers have at times called *sensa,* i.e., the reports to the mind of the sense organs. As apologists, then, we may employ only what the senses reveal and this pertains to the highest type of knowledge, even of God himself. Whatever the function of reason might be it is circumscribed by the deliveries of the senses.

Butler follows the pathway of common sense, a reserved agnosticism, and a rejection of speculative metaphysics. He seeks to ground religion—to use a recent expression—in brute fact. He is against Plato, Augustine and Thomas in so far as Thomas represents a speculative metaphysics. The ultimate data of religion must be of the same stuff as the ultimate data of science. It must be that sort of stuff which has unquestionable authority to the man of common sense. Involved in such an earthly, sensory and restricted notion of the origin and limits of knowledge must be a certain agnosticism or skepticism. Therefore, when in some exposition Butler runs into complications or into some labyrinth of thought he freely admits it and moves on. He never calls a problem anything but a problem. He makes no existential leaps and if he cannot thread his way out of some vexed problem he does not resort to the cutting of Gordian knots nor to leaps of faith nor the *Deus ex machina.* The system of Christianity is not a completely revealed system but a revelation of a number of discrete facts and therefore in the conditions of this life we cannot prove complete coherence.

Butler never argues the case for Christianity beyond its strength. He never underestimates the force of an objection. He does not avoid saying that in some instances the Christian position is vague and inconclusive. His emphasis upon human ignorance is unrelenting. He fights no straw men, and he discusses the world as he finds it, not as it is remade by a Leibniz with his best of all possible worlds.

Butler is telling the world that there is no *a priori* knowledge of God that is coercive. God's existence and ways are to be deciphered from His handiwork, and our conclusions are not absolutes but probability statements.

2. *His appeal to reason.* Our senses provide our reason with the data for religious thought. Reason at Butler's time was considered more or less the same in every man. Mankind was envisioned as a sort of intellectual democracy. Reason was an innate power of man and his sovereign court of appeal. Its deliveries were considered trustworthy to an eminent degree. Hence Butler is always appealing to the reasonable man or to reasonable men. He calls reason "natural reason," "the light of nature," and in one interesting paragraph he uses synonymously the expressions "by reason," "by light of nature," and "by experience" (p. 260). This means that the reasons employed in apologetics, and the mind to which these reasons appeal, is a common human possession and trait.

In congruence with his trust in reason Butler constructs his entire apologetics. The assumption is that if the evidences satisfy the canons of reason *the prudential man must grant assent.* The only alternative to being prudential is to be foolhardy and if faith is prudence, unbelief is foolhardiness. However, no prudential man demands *absolute* proof. According to Butler no absolute proof for anything exists. The prudential man acts on the slope of the evidence, and when he detects the direction towards which the evidence slopes he acts accordingly.

The most important function of reason is to judge a revelation. Butler states that reason "is indeed the only faculty we have wherewith to judge concerning anything, even revelation itself. . . . For [revelation] may contain clear immoralities or contradictions [i.e., may be tested *ethically* or *logically*]; and either of these would prove it false" (p. 210). He emphasizes this again when he writes that "reason can, and it ought to judge, not only the meaning, but also the morality and evidence of revelation" (p. 221). Of course what Butler is saying (in his language) is that the "light of revelation" is judged by the "light of nature."

In another connection Butler writes: "Let reason be kept to: and if any part of the Scripture account of the redemption of the world by Christ can be shown to be really contrary to it, let the Scripture, in the name of God, be given up" (p. 245). Having said that he does caution us by saying that we must be careful as we are such limited creatures and God is great and His universal scheme so great. It is not reasonable to object to revelation or religion because we do not understand all the connections and relationships within the divine scheme.

IV. HIS THEOLOGICAL APPROACH

Butler is not directly arguing with the atheist but with that person who admits the existence of God, admits a known course of nature, and admits the prudential principle for the guide of action. Whereas in theory of knowledge he followed empiricism and common sense in theology he was Arminian, moralistic, and probationary.

1. *Arminian and probationary.* A certain young scholar at Oxford named Laud had a tutor named Buckeridge. This tutor was vigorously opposed to Calvinism and steeped in Arminian theology. Impressed by Buckeridge, Laud adopted his views. Later this William Laud became Archbishop Laud! He gave the Church a strong, vigorous leadership and was much in favor of Anglican High Church liturgy. Under his strong-willed leadership the Anglo-Catholic party (of which he was the leader) took a decided Arminian position in theology. Butler alined himself with the High Church movement and was in thorough agreement with its Arminian theology. The entire overtone of his thought is characterized by the probationary spirit which is the root of Arminianism. He had little regard for the views of Augustine, Luther or Calvin which saw the probation of a race in the fall of one man, but emphasized the unsharable responsibility of each individual. This theme is constantly intruded in the *Analogy*. Life's pains, life's sicknesses, and life's perplexities are all part of our probation. If we could see the truth with unquestioned certainty life would lose its probationary qualities (p. 252). Thus man's limitation of knowledge which is judged aversely by some apologists is given a positive twist by Butler as part of man's probation.

2. *A universal scheme partially understood.* Another feature of his theological approach is that Butler sees the human race under one great universal scheme. Within this universal scheme the same sort of general laws obtain. *This is the metaphysical ground for Butler's doctrine of analogy.* The Governor of nature and the Lord of religion and the Giver of revelation has used similar laws in governing all three of his domains. The three domains stand or fall together. It is impossible to lodge an objection in one without by implication lodging it in the other two. If one objects to *redemption* in grace, he thereby objects to *medicine* in nature!

Furthermore, to admit that a certain law holds in one domain (e.g., transformation or life) demands that it be admitted in another (immortality). Admit that certain laws pertain to every realm God administers, admit that there is one universal scheme administered by the one God, then Butler is difficult to refute. This is God's creation according to Butler, and if it is God's creation the moral domain is served by the material domain. Thus in principle we must see the universe from the apex down and not from the base up, even though in our order of knowing we must work from the base to the apex.

However, Butler is careful to maintain that this universal scheme is not perfectly known. If our knowledge is imperfect then it does not consist of absolute statements but of probability statements. But, as also indicated, the very fact that we only know partially is a necessary element of our probationary existence. Besides such admission is a stone thrown at the head of the objector who claims that he cannot believe until he knows the *entire* scheme.

This universal scheme *partially* understood is the heart of Butler's theodicy. It is because we see only a small part of the entire governance of the universe by God that we feel that there are telling injustices. But if we could see the total scheme we would see that the good is victor over the evil (pp. 176-180).

3. *Religion as morality.* Rightly or wrongly, Butler's stern moral interpretation of Christianity has been likened to Kant, famous for his categorical imperative and ethical interpretation of Christianity. At least pressure on Butler from the moralism of Deism must be admitted. Although Butler does believe in Christ and redemption religion appears to him to be essentially a matter of moral behavior. And a strong moralistic interpretation of Christianity readily harmonizes with his probationism and Arminianism. Certainly it cannot be denied that the impact of Butler in the twentieth century is not that of his apologetics (which is really scandalous to Kierkegaardians, Barthians, and existentialists) but that of his ethical sermons.

V. PROBABILITY AND ANALOGY

We confront ourselves now with the direct application of these principles to his apologetics. He states his thesis as follows:

The design then of the following treatise will be to show, that the several parts principally objected against in this moral and Christian dispensation, including its scheme, its publication and the proof which God has afforded us of its truth; that the particular parts principally objected against in this whole dispensation, are analogues to what is experienced in the constitution and course of nature or Providence; that the chief objections themselves which are alleged against the former, are no other than what may be alleged with like justice against the latter, where they are found in fact to be inconclusive; and that this argument from analogy is in general unanswerable, and undoubtedly of weight on the side of religion (pp. 74-75).

1. *Probability.* To this point the general metaphysics and theology of Butler have been set forth. His apologetics proper is built upon the combined principles of probability and analogy, although he does warn us that the proof of Christianity is essentially the *total impact* of the evidence (pp. 66 and 263). Probability provides the *grounds* for action and *analogy* the direction.

With our limited intelligences in a universe of virtually infinite facts how shall we *order* our lives? What shall be our *guide*? Butler has already conceded to Locke that no innate idea is our guide. Further in affirming that reason is given to test a revelation we cannot *immediately* appeal to revelation, but only to a tested and proved revelation. Nor can we appeal to mysticism for that evades the empirical philosophy of Locke. Our only recourse is to experience broadly conceived, i.e., besides our personal experiences the experiences of the race as deposited in history books, etc.

But in saying that experience is our guide we have located the *source* of our wisdom but we have not indicated how this mass of experience is to function. Some organizing and interpreting principle must be introduced. At rock bottom we note that some experiences are *similar to* other experiences. We also note similar runs of events as wind, drop in temperature, clouds, rain, followed by clearing. "Case histories" of moral people or wicked people are also known to us. For similarity in the total range of our knowledge Butler uses the word *likely*. We note similarities in sequence and we then presume that this is a dependable sequence. Every morning we dress according to our years of experience with the weather. With low-hanging clouds with a southwesterly wind in January we prepare for snow before sundown. But in March we would prepare for rain under similar conditions. So whether it is weather, frying eggs, nursing a cold, driving a wagon, or calculating on the actions of a business associate we proceed the same. We spot those experiences which are likely, i.e., similar; we plot their sequence; and then when a similar situation arises in our experience we plan our action accordingly. Thus as every man proceeds through life he collects hundreds of such similarities and forges them into rules of conduct. These rules then are the maxims of his life so that he does have guides in the welter of experiences.

To phrase it another way it may be said that if man has no innate ideas, if he has no perfect nor absolute knowledge, if he cannot *immediately* appeal to a revelation, then the only way to ·

act prudently or wisely is to discover the *trends* within experience and act according to them. *The reasonable man without perfect knowledge guides his life by the trends ascertainable within experience.* In Butler's much quoted formula," probability is the very guide of life" (p. 68). The emphasis properly falls on *guide,* not *probability.*

Probability admits of degrees. A statement in logic, for example, is true or false. The evidence for or against the statement is "airtight" because we are working within a closed system. In empirical matters we attempt to show that a proposition is true by stacking up the evidence in its favor. But any such stack of evidence is only evidence to a certain degree, and this is what is meant by probability. For Butler probability has to do with the uncertain and unpredictable routine of life which while not yielding absolute knowledge does yield trends which are reliable guides for conduct. These trends may be faint at first and upon many repetitions they may achieve practical certainty.

Butler wants to settle for the world as he finds it. It is a world of dim lights, of twilight. But man must walk in this world. And he opens his eyes as wide as he can and attempts to discern the shapes the best he can. And by doing this a man can even walk in twilight!

Butler has been criticized from two points. First, sometimes it does snow in July! That is to say the trends we detect do not always run off the same way. The sky may glower for a week without shedding a drop of rain and for one week we carry a raincoat to no advantage. Second, sometimes a hunch pays off far more royally than prudential decision.

Butler's rejoinder would be that probability is the *guide* of life. It usually rains when the clouds glower so we carry a raincoat. Our past experience *guides* us to this. The man who leaves his raincoat at home will come home more times drenched than dry. And no man can guide his entire life by hunches without running into disaster. For the routine of life, day in and day out, year in and year out, the only prudential guide is probability. No question we will be fooled or disappointed in some instances. Furthermore, some trends (as in business or economics) might be very difficult to determine. But when the prudential man is confronted with a new situation the only compass he has is the organized total of his past experience, and he acts on this experience as trends have organized it into maxims whose logical status is that of probability statements.

Although this kind of knowledge is neither certain nor infallible, it is the only kind we have. Sunk in the thousands of contingencies of life we have no *a priori* rule. Only probability can guide us here. By probability we thread our way through our political life, economic life, practical life, *and religious life.* This is the compass of the prudential man and he will follow it wherever it leads. A man denies his prudence if he conducts his ordinary life by probability *but refuses to do so in religion!* If he denies that probability reaches into religion and makes his religious decision on some other grounds he is no longer a prudent man.

Furthermore, man is under *moral obligation* to conduct his life prudently. He is under moral obligation to follow the dictates of probability. *He is therefore under moral obligation to accept Christianity even if its evidence is only probable.* (It is of some interest to note that Butler rarely uses the word "faith," and it does not occur in Malcom's index).

2. *Analogy.* If probability is the ground for action, then *analogy is the means of transferring the prudence gained in one realm to that of another.* According to Butler from the *known course of nature* we determine our likelies, our probabilities. Here is the rootage in the great ordering of creation. The second source of *analogies* is to be found in the cumulative cultural history of the human race, which in conjunction with our own personal experience, we form maxims of prudential principles. Many of these, Butler reasons, are God's way of directing our lives. It is a part of the known course of nature that pain is a means of saving us from misfortune. We have also discovered that pleasurable things are usually good things. Thus pleasure and pain are God's methods of directing our own biological welfare. Society with its punishments and rewards is also the rule of God but in this instance in regulating human society.

If the function of probability is to detect trends within a range of experience, analogy permits us to cross from one universe of discourse to another. Thus Butler moves from the known course of nature, to natural theology, and then to revealed theology using the same principle. Consider the question of immortality. In the known course of nature we see that life has a way of manifesting itself in different levels and that it has a certain momentum. By transferring this *trend* to man we presume that the soul has its momentum, and that having lived on this earth in one form it may well exist in a next world in another form. *The metaphysical basis is that God governs all domains by the same general laws.* The levels of life and the momentum of life on the biological level become evidence for immortality in the territory of natural religion. There are frequent examples among peoples of mediation and these are sufficient justification for the one Mediator, Jesus Christ. In revealed theology we have the doctrine of the atonement; in nature we have medicines which counteract diseases; in social experiences we have acts of mercy by the courts in view of the special condition of the guilty; and all of these constitute analogies of the atonement.

Butler is here facing the opposition of men to both natural and revealed theology. If men grant the facts observed in the general course of nature and the existence of God, then it is to be expected that difficulties encountered in nature will be reflected in natural and revealed theology. This is a dictum he derived from Origen who said that "he who believes the Scripture to have proceeded from Him who is the Author of nature, may well expect to find the same sort of difficulties in it, as are found in nature." On the other hand, granted the general course of nature and the existence of God, it can be shown that the same scheme of similar laws pertains to both natural and revealed theology. Thus the basic data are the known facts of nature; the problematic data are the proposed truths of natural and revealed religion; and the justification of the problematic data is to show that the principles they embody will be found by use of the analogy in the known course of nature.

Butler insists that "this general way of arguing is evidently natural, just and conclusive" (p. 69). Following this he clearly indicates how the method of analogical reasoning proceeds. It commences with the observation of facts and then moves on to others "that are like them," from that part of the divine government which we already know (i.e., the known course of nature) to "that larger and more general government of God" (i.e., religion), and "from what is present to collect what is likely, credible or not credible, will be hereafter" (pp. 70, 71).

The conclusion that Butler comes to from this analysis is that "both [nature and religion] may be traced to the same general laws, and resolved into the same principles of divine conduct" (p. 73). In fact, the two are so parallel that "both could naturally be expresssed in the very same words, and manner of description" (p. 103). The order of religion is exemplified by the order of nature; the moral scheme of the universe is not a fiction, but it is "natural for it is suggested to our thoughts by the constitution and course of nature" (p. 127). Therefore religion is "rendered credible" because it is in its principle and laws "of a piece with general conduct of Providence . . . in all respects within the compass of our knowledge" (p. 133).

3. *Illustrations of Butler's theses.*

(1) An excellent revelation of Butler's apologetic method is to be found in the manner in which he treats immortality. What are the probabilities that we shall survive our death? *First* we note that in the known course of nature many creatures of nature exist in different states of perfection. Thus worms become flies and eggs hatch into birds. We also note the radical changes in existence in the human being especially in his embryonic life in contrast to his post-natal life. The doctrine that we shall live beyond our physical death in some altered form has its many analogies in the known course of nature.

Secondly, we know that our human powers have a momentum to them. We have enduring capacities to love, to suffer, to act, powers which endure our entire lifetime. At root we have in nature the laws of physical momentum which show how a body commencing a certain course persists in it. It is a law wider than just momentum for we may observe that most things once existing persist in existence. Therefore we have analogical evidence for the persistence of the powers of our personality after our death.

Thirdly, there is no reason to believe that death ends all for this is neither apparent from the nature of death nor from the data of analogy. All we know about death is its immediate physical characteristics, but from this we cannot deduce that the powers of the self suddenly vanish into nothing. There are many analogies in life to the contrary. In a sleep or a coma our powers are inactive but still there.

Furthermore, we must carefully note that the body is not the locus of the powers of the self, but the *medium* of these powers. For example, one does not see *with* his glasses, but *through* them. The glasses are the *medium* of sight. The eye bears the same relationship to the soul. It is the lens of the soul, and therefore the destruction of the body is only the destruction of the medium and not the power.

Appealing to logic Butler argues that there is no logical connection between the end of the body and the end of the self. Of course we have no empirical evidence of the soul carrying on after death, but the known course of nature favors it. Our powers carry their momentum right up to the moment of death and we have every analogical reason to believe they carry on after our death. Impressive at this point is the realization that each of us has gone through a number of changes in his own life—babyhood to youth, youth to adult, adult to old age—and yet our powers have persisted throughout these changes. The survival of our powers through death is therefore in harmony with the known course of nature.

(2) Supposing somebody wishes to turn the tables on Butler and argue that death is the analogy of the death of the self! Here is analogy used against Butler! How does Butler handle this rather shrewd objection?

First, he argues that death could destroy us on the grounds that we are materially composed and so can disintegrate. But souls are not materially composed and so cannot come apart. Furthermore consciousness is one single, indivisible power. The soul, which is the subject of the consciousness, is therefore one single, indivisible entity. The unity of the soul is also seen in our dismemberment. We may lose fingers, arms, legs, eyes, hair and teeth and we are still the same self for all the loss of bodily parts.

Secondly, although we cannot prove experimentally the simplicity of the soul the evidence is all in its favor. We have already mentioned that loss of bodily parts does not effect the soul. Further the body changes in size radically from childhood to adulthood and the personality persists through this radical transition. However even if it be granted that the soul has parts we only need remark that the human body remains the same general constant in its loss of members. So the soul could undergo a change or a loss and remain the same essential soul.

Thirdly, By careful attention given to the relationship of sense to personal existence we come to realize that the body is only the medium of perception for much can happen to the body which does not effect the self. Sense organs are not the locus of perception. In dreams we are physically asleep yet we have perception! Therefore, perception is not dependent upon the body. Even if limbs are severed we retain the power of manipulation as seen by the skillful use of artificial legs and arms. Therefore, the loss of bodily parts is not the same as the loss of the powers of the self.

(3) Another objection can be made to Butler's analogical reasoning. Why cannot the same arguments be applied to brutes? Do not animals dream? In reply to this Butler says *first* that this may well be the case. Who knows? Certainly we expect to see infants in heaven as adults not infants. Could not brutes undergo some similar transformation? *Secondly,* all such an argument could prove would be the abstract possibility of the immortality of the brute but not that the brute is a moral creature. However, such creatures are necessary to round out creation and their status is shrouded in mystery. Therefore, they neither add to nor detract from the argument.

(4) But, says the critic attempting to press Butler even harder, is not the soul so *dependent* upon the body that the loss of the body entails the loss of the soul? Butler replies to this *first* that perception may be dependent upon the body, but certainly reason and memory are not. Death may destroy perception, but it may not destroy reason and memory. There is no such dependence upon the body with reference to these two powers.

Secondly, experience is composed of sensation and reflection [after Locke] and although death ends sensation it certainly does not end the power of reflection. In our own experience we know that once sensation has reached the mind it is freed from the sense organ and there they may be [according to Locke again] manipulated free from the senses.

Thirdly, Various diseases have attacked the human body crippling it, wasting it, enervating it, and yet the intellect remains unimpaired. This is a clear demonstration of its independence from the body.

These then are sufficient examples to show how Butler shuttles back and forth from the known course of nature to natural theology. He moves from the governance of God known to all in nature, to the controversial governance of God in religion. With the use of the bridge of analogy he attempts to render the controversial credible.

(5) An example of his argumentation in revealed religion centers around the concept of *mediation*. Of course a strong deism would challenge this element of New Testament revelation. In reply Butler argues *first* that our own social experience constantly witnesses mediation. Do we not all help each other? Are we not individually helped by other people? If this is true of social experience why not of religion? If one objects to mediation of Jesus Christ is he not in principle objecting to all mediation?

Secondly, in our social experiences we have ways of recovering from a very unfortunate circumstance. Good friends give us a hand; the judge tenders mercy instead of penalty; the creditor kindly extends his patience and does not force collection. Therefore, God's alleviation of the straits of our sinnerhood is perfectly analogous to our own social experiences.

Thirdly, nature contains diseases and remedies. To counter the diseases mankind has developed the science of medicine. The analogy to medicine in religion is redemption. Thus the Scriptures present Christ as Mediator, as Redeemer, and as the Alleviator of our sins. Such mediation is of one piece with mediation among humans, and the mediation of medicine in case of diseases (cf. Part II, Chapter V).

VI. REVEALED RELIGION

The *Analogy* is neatly divided by Butler into two distinct parts, the first treating natural religion and the second revealed. It is important to sample some of his more important notions about revealed religion.

1. There are two *needs* for a revealed religion. The *first* is that mankind needs to learn afresh the moral government of God. So, Butler says that Christianity is a *re-publication* of natural religion. This concept was borrowed from the famous work of Tindal, *Christianity as Old as Creation; or the Gospel, a Republication of the Law of Nature* (1730). Moral religion, which Butler called the most important part of Christianity, needs the reënforcement and reiteration of revelation. The *second* need is to provide man with truths inaccessible to reason which are necesary for man's salvation. Reason is concerned with the relation in which God the Father stands to us. But in "Scripture are revealed the relations, which the Son and the Spirit stand to us" (p. 194). Revelation has the special topic of mediation for its content, and the work of Son and the Spirit as its special operations.

2. The *proof* of this special revelation is treated very traditionally by Butler. Miracles and prophecy are given "to prove a particular dispensation of Providence, i.e., the redemption of the world by the Messiah" (p. 189). Although these matters may be challenged on philosophical grounds considered *practically* there is no better means of convincing the average person. As practical proofs they are the strongest kind of evidence "which human creatures are capable of having given them" (p. 189). Butler's defense of miracles and prophecy follows worn paths and is the least original part of his apologetics.

The important matters to be noticed here is that Butler is faithfully carrying out his program, namely, that of testing a revelation with reason. Reason examines the claim to revelation by the standards derived from natural religion, and of testing the evidence for it by the principles of knowledge. There can be no *a priori* objection to revelation for we cannot know whether God will or will not reveal himself. But once a revelation is claimed, it must be tested by reason. Reason satisfies itself with Christianity because it is in accordance with the *moral standards* of natural theology, and is rendered credible to our knowledge by miracle and prophecy. The one bright point in his treatment of miracle is that the analogy of miracle in ordinary providence is the *unusual* event. A miraculous escape from danger, or an unusual natural phenomenon form the analogy of miracle in the known course of nature. Thus *natural religion* is rendered credible by *analogy;* whereas *revealed religion* is rendered credible by *analogy* and the *evidences* of miracle and prophecy. Of course all the way through Butler's arguments there is an appeal to consistency of thought and also a bit of anticipation of modern analytic thought. For Butler is quite sensitive to what is deducible from an axiom or proposition and what is merely presumed to be deducible.

With reference to Biblical criticism Butler makes an observation of unusual merit. He says that no dispute about the obscurity of the style of Scripture or about the authorship of a book or related problems or about variant readings of the text can overthrow the authority of Scriptures unless "'the prophets, apostles or our Lord had promised, that the book containing the divine revelation should be exempt from those things" (p. 214). Framed another way Butler is saying that in textual and literary criticism the Christian is bound only to that which the Scriptures binds him to. Thus the critic has no right to ask more from the Scripture than the Scripture promises and the Christian scholar is not to commit the Christian faith to that which the Scripures are not committed.

With reference to Biblical interpretation he insists that in our exegesis we should let the Bible speak for itself. We should have an inductive and not a dogmatic spirit in approaching the Scriptures.

The conclusion that Butler comes to, near the end of his *Analogy,* is: *"The whole of religion is then throughout credible"* and this is both the spirit and the goal of his apologetics (p. 312, italics are ours).

BIBLIOGRAPHY

Adamson and Grieve, "Joseph Butler," *The Encyclopedia Britannica,* (11th edition), Vol. IV

Baker, A. E., *Bishop Butler*

Bernard, J. H., "Butler," *Hastings Encyclopedia of Religion and Ethics,* Vol. III

Butler, Joseph, *The Analogy of Religion to the Constitution and Course of Nature*

Collins, W. L., *Butler*

Knox, R. A., *Enthusiasm*

Mossner, E. C., *Bishop Butler and the Age of Reason*

Stephens, Sir Leslie, "Joseph Butler," *Dictionary of National Biography,* Vol. III

Chapter VII

F. R. TENNANT (1866-1957)

One of the great intellectual giants of British theology in the first half of the twentieth century was F. R. Tennant. Although not completely unknown in America (J. O. Buswell, *The Philosophies of F. R. Tennant and John Dewey;* P. Bertocci, *The Empirical Argument for God in Late British Theology;* D. Scudder, *Tennant's Philosophical Theology*) he nevertheless has had a limited hearing.

Tennant commenced his career as a scientist, particularly as a chemist. He was also trained in biology, physics, and psychology. The attacks on Christianity by Huxley aroused the interest of Tennant—at the time a typical orthodox Anglican—in the problem of the verification of Christianity. He returned to Cambridge to study theology, philosophy, and logic. He spent the remainder of his active career with that institution. He has an earned D.D. from Cambridge and an honorary D.D. from Oxford. The standard whereby Oxford grants an honorary D.D. (as apocryphally reported) is that it withholds the degree until it is a disgrace not to grant it!

In the specific area of theology he made contributions in the doctrine of sin (*The Concept of Sin, The Origin and Propagation of Sin, The Sources of the Doctrines of the Fall and Original Sin*) and miracles (*Miracle and Its Philosophical Presuppositions*). He also contributed articles for the fourteenth edition of the *Encyclopedia Britannica* and *Hastings Encyclopedia of Religion and Ethics*. His articles in this latter work are for the most part in the complex area of philosophy of science. He was invited to give the Tarner Lectures at Cambridge which was an unusual honor for a theologian for usually these lectures are given by experts in the philosophy of science (*Philosophy of the Sciences*). Other lecturers were such eminent philosophers as Whitehead, Broad, Russell and Moore. Tennant's teachers were men of outstanding academic reputation—James Ward, W. Johnson (famous logician), McTaggart and Sidgwick. Among his colleagues were Russell, Hobson, Barnes, and Broad. He was also elected as a fellow of the British Academy, a supplement to the Royal Academy and limited to one hundred and fifty members. His greatest work and the product of a life time of intensive scholarly research and lecturing is his *Philosophical Theology* in two volumes.

The general concensus of opinion among theologians and philosophers is that Tennant's *Philosophical Theology* is the greatest apologetics for Christian faith which has yet appeared in the twentieth century and which is grounded upon *an empirical basis.* Tennant writes against the background of dominant British empiricism, realism, and phenomenalism. In an early essay in *The Cambridge Theological Essays* he defends theses which are in rather close agreement to those of Ernst Mach and Karl Pearson's *The Grammer of Science.* From reading Tennant one would not know that Kierkegaard or Barth ever lived or wrote a line! Nor would one gather that a great revolution in biblical theology had taken place as exemplified for instance by Kittel's famous *Theological Dictionary of the New Testament (Theologisches Woerterbuch zum Neuen Testament,* seven volumes). His world is the world of the traditional problems of epistemology, of the British empirical tradition, of contemporary science, and of an empirically grounded religious liberalism.

I. POSITIONS TENNANT DEEMS INDEFENSIBLE

1. *Rationalism.* In philosophy rationalism is the belief that the mind and its principles is the final umpire in the determination of truth. This is not to be confused with theological rationalism which will allow in religion only that which passes certain hard and usually skeptical criteria of the human evaluator. Philosophical rationalism has been sympathetic to Christian faith in many instances. When Augustine said that "it is evident that none comes nearer to us than the Platonists," (*City of God,* VIII, 5) he was echoing an opinion which found much agreement before him (Alexandrians) and after him.

Tennant proposes to defend a philosophical empiricism and this cannot be done without a refutation of philosophical rationalism and therefore he must indicate its shortcomings. Tennant's mentality is British empiricism in its purest essence. He is a bear for fact, logical order, clarity, precision of exposition, and very hostile to rhetoric which befuddles thought and mysticism which evades the careful craftsmenship of the responsible scholar. He is therefore solidly aligned against the Platonic-Augustine-Anselmic tradition in Christian philosophy. This also lines him against great modern rationalists as Descartes and Spinoza.

Tennant simply does not believe that reason is an inborn, original and unique capacity in man. Nor that reason can function independent from the senses, nor that reason can give us knowledge of reality that is universal and unconditional. He believes that one of the theses of rationalism is that if given enough time it could rationally explain every fact in the universe. Tennant believes to the contrary that there is a great deal in the universe which cannot be so explained and this he calls not the irrational (contrary to reason) but *a-logical,* i.e., not explicable by reason. Further he objects to the thesis of the rationalist that the mind can form propositions which may be applied directly to the universe without the testings of experience. All of these objections boil down to one: *rationalism makes reality an order of pure thought, whereas reality is richer than the order of pure thought.* A reader familiar with the literature of rationalism will detect that there is a bit of the straw man in the manner in which Tennant treats rationalism.

Digging in harder Tennant objects to rationalism on the grounds that it ignores the *impressional* (the data provided by the senses). It presumed to think that all the difficult problems of philosophy could be settled if it be assumed that the order of thought and the order of reality were the same. But, Tennant argues with some justification, that modern studies in theory of knowledge have revealed that the most difficult problem is to determine just what is the relationship between the order of thought and the order of reality. One cannot settle this issue out of court!

The strength of the rationalistic position is its emphasis upon clear thought—thought so clear, so transparent that it strikes the mind with the force of an indisputable axiom. But Tennant confidently believes he can undermine this. Clarity of thought is not the clarity of the sentence as such, but it is a psychological clarity. That is, what is a clear thought to us is the product of a long psychological process. For example, in the Middle Ages certain notions of science were considered true because they seemed so obvious, so axiomatic, so clear! But really the opinions were false and the clarity was simply the clarity of custom or tradition or universal belief. So the clarity of the rationalists is not a logical clarity but the clarity of a psychological process! Therefore, Tennant confidently rejects Plato's doctrine of universals, namely, that universals exist prior to particular objects. Justice (according to Plato) exists prior to, and is superior to, any given instance of justice in human affairs. However, in view of the state of logical theory at the time Tennant wrote, he was not prepared to reject Aristotle's position on universals.

Again depending upon psychology Tennant claims that psychologists cannot locate this inborn reason, nor can they find this mind which functions without the senses. From all that we can discover sensation is absolutely necessary for knowledge to appear. The order of knowing is not that of the universal first and the particular second; but the particulars first and the universals second.

Rationalists set up clarity and distinctness as the criteria of an innate idea. But what is clear and what is distinct to the human mind varies notoriously from century to century. Upon analysis the so-called "self-evident" axioms of logic, science and mathematics are not truly self-evident. They may be *conventions,* i.e., axioms simply stipulated by a scholar or by common consent; or they may be disguised *empirical generalizations.* They are accepted not because of fulfilling any criteria of innateness but in virtue of their pragmatic applicability. By constant use and reference these *conventions and generalizations* become so familiar that they appear to be axioms.

His conclusion is that "the faculty of reason, as invoked by rationalism, has been found to be mythical" (*Philosophical Theology*, I, 213). The human reason has been empirically demonstrated to emerge from "a potentiality innate to the soul, and this faculty cannot function, in its less developed state, apart from sensatio" (*loc. cit.*). The human mind is so imbedded in human nature that all knowledge is, in Tennant's terminology, *anthropic.* Anthropic (in distinction from anthropomorphic) means that all knowledge is human knowledge and is therefore in human symbols and analogies and not in the pure form of eternal verities. *Platonism* is, therefore, no basis for philosophy or Christian apologetics.

2. *Religious a priori.* Another method by which men justify religious faith is by claiming that there is a unique religious structure within man, and that this unique religious structure is the *organ* for mediating the knowledge of God. If this is true then Tennant's vigorous empiricism is by-passed. Tennant must show that there is no distinctively religious act in itself from the empirical and psychological standpoint nor is there any special religious structure within man.

First, Tennant affirms that psychologists can find nothing in the development of knowledge within man which is not ultimately derivable from simple perceptions. They find no additional religious structure in man, nor unique religious experience. Therefore, religious propositions can only "be derived indirectly from the study of the sensible world, man's soul and human history" (I, 306).

Secondly, there is no specific psychological act which can be called religious such as awe, adoration, loyalty, love or joy. All such experiences are part and parcel of every day experiences.

Thirdly, Tennant rejects the theory of the *numinous* as propounded by R. Otto in *The Idea of the Holy.* Otto maintained in this famous work that there is a religious experience which is a primary and immediate datum. It is a datum which cannot be reduced to any other psychological state. Otto calls this the experience of the numinous. Tennant argues that the definition of the numinous is vague. But if it is vague it lacks the essential nature of a true datum. On the other hand the only people who have a clear notion of the Object of religious experience are the people who have clarified the Object by discursive thought. Further, the numinous occurs in such a variety of religious systems that its character must be ever so vague, and if it is capable of serving so many varieties of religion it certainly is too nebulous to serve as a true datum.

Lashing out in another direction Tennant says that there is a difference between the psychological force with which an idea impresses us, and the careful demonstration of its reality. The sleeping man has vivid dreams and the drunkard sees most livid apparitions of serpents. Yet the intense psychological nature of the experience does not prove that dreams or hallucinations exist. We may claim existence for that which survives careful analysis of a competent epistemological nature. Otto's mistake is to think that the profound psychological experience of the religious man actually proves the existence of the proposed Object of this experience.

Fourthly, Tennant inspects the claims of the mystics and finds them inconclusive. Mystics do claim to have *direct* experiences of God and Tennant's dogged empiricism cannot stand if mystics can make their case. Tennant has several reasons which convince him that mystics do not make their case. First there is the repetition of the same error as that of Otto's namely, feeling that the intensity of the experience is its own proof and not realizing that only that which stands up under the epistemological scrutiny may be allowed. The profundity of the experience does not prove the reality of the Object of the experience.

The mystic usually claims that the experience in its very essence is ineffable, i.e., it cannot be put into words. At this point Tennant attempts to deliver a solid body blow. If the experience cannot be put into words it is not knowledge. To say knowledge is to say the truth, *and truth can be cast only into propositional form.* Psychological states are not propositions! If the mystic claims he has truth he must cast it into propositional form and subject it to epistemological analysis. If he claims ineffability he must also renounce the claim to truth.

However, Tennant is willing to concede a point. Suppose men

do have mystical experiences. Men certainly do profess to have strange, occult and incommunicable experiences. Let us not deny them. But even so, that does not entitle these experiences to be called true. The very fact that they are so occult, so supra-normal removes them from serious consideration of being vehicles of the truth.

In a more hard-boiled mood Tennant believes that the experiences of the mystics are not extra-ordinary religious experiences but psychologically ordinary experiences with a religious interpretation. The mystic gives himself away when he reports his experience within the terms of his own local culture. The local color in the experience proves to Tennant that it is not a trans-local experience!

The mystic claims that in his ecstatic experience he loses his identity and unites with the One. However he wants to have his cake and eat it too, and this Tennant will not let him do. If the mystic unites with the One and loses his identity, then he has nothing to say when he comes back to himself. In his union with the One he ceased to be momentarily an individual. But if the mystic insists on saying something he denies that he really united with the One but remained an individual to such a degree that he can give a report of what happened to *him*.

The final rapier thrust at mysticism is that the experiences of the mystics can be acounted for rather adequately by the abnormal psychologists. And if this is adequate there is no need to interpret them as *sui generis* religious experiences.

It might appear from Tennant's attack upon Otto and the mystics that Tennant is no Christian at all! The implication seems to be that there is no religious experience. But Tennant does believe in religious experience. To him that which makes an experience religious in contrast to other experiences *is the Object intended*. Otto and the mystics attempt to make the experience religious because the experience was in itself psychologically religious. He writes: "Religious experience owes its uniqueness to the interpretative concept, by means of which, experiences, that otherwise are not religious in virtue of either their Objective reference or of their affective response, become co-ordinated, explained and endowed with a supernatural aspect: clothed upon with which they now evoke unique emotional reactions" (I, 326). Psychological experience as such is *atheous*—it is neutral being neither for nor against God. For example, there is nothing in a radio set which tunes in religious programs and those alone. The radio transmits all programs alike. It is the *content* of the program which makes it religious, or historical, or philosophical. If psychological experience is *atheous* then no apologetics can be argued from a proposed religious *a priori*.

3. *Revelation.* Having disposed of two of the favorite methods of establishing truth independent from ordinary empirical methods, Tennant now turns to the concept of revelation (II, Chapter VIII). There is an extensive tradition in the history of Christian thought which would ground apologetics in revelation. Is this an option for Tennant?

Tennant is adverse to using revelation for apologetic purposes. Revelation is certainly not in divinely revealed propositions, and, therefore, it is not in itself a genuine principle of knowledge. Therefore, Tennant launches a rather sharp attack on the attempt to use revelation in *apologetics*. His *first* objection is that the seeming revelational character of Old Testament religion is appearance but not reality. Religious thinking in hoary antiquity began with myths. Unless freed from myths religion persists in some crude or grotesque form. But *moralization* does effect a purification in religion and the Old Testament prophets purified Jewish religion by *moralization*. This moralization was possible for *any* people and there is no need to attempt to account for it in Israel by recourse to the thesis of divine revelation. But once moralization began among the Hebrews it developed into the remarkable moral and spiritual insights which made the writings of the prophets so unparalleled in all of religious history. Thus what appears on the surface as revelation is deceiving for at root it is moralization.

Secondly. It is granted that the Hebrew prophets had some unusual religious experiences. But these unusual psychological states need not be referred either to inspiration or revelation for their clarification. Abnormal psychology can not only explain them but indicate parallels in non-religious people. "Such facts as these do not rule out the possibility of divine co-operation," Tennant comments, "but they destroy the evidential value of the prophet's experience itself" (II, 229).

Thirdly, there are a number of serious objections to that view of revelation which affirms that revelation is the communication of truth to the mind of man, truths which are inaccessible by ordinary methods of knowing. This is a *thrust* of truth upon man and does violence to ethical theism's doctrine of the sacredness of human personality. Such truth dropped in upon man could not be understood by man. The knower must be able to assimilate what is known but earthly man cannot assimilate heavenly truths. At best revelation can be defined as help in spiritual insight but it cannot be a sheer thrust of data upon man's consciousness.

Tennant grants the premise of the Roman Catholic position as consistent, namely, that an infallible revelation demands an infallible interpretation. Otherwise any virtue in an infallible communication is lost in the numerous conflicting interpretations. Granting the consistency of this position as a position nevertheless Tennant does not think it is the valid one for revelation is "an enabling of man to get his own insight than as providing him with a substitute for it; as a seeking of free response rather than as a dictation of dogma; as analogous to teaching a person to think for himself rather than to filling a pitcher with water" (II, 232).

Furthermore, the view that revelation is doctrinal communication encounters the same logical difficulty as that of the mystic. Truth comes in the form of propositions which can be first assimilated as to their meaning and then verified or falsified. Anything short of this may well be true but we cannot know it to be such. When revelation comes as a series of great mysteries the human mind simply has no way of managing them. They come as sheer givens; they come from "out there"; and there is no imaginable means of verifying them. Hence we cannot know if they are true or not, and, therefore, we have not the right to call them true. "The name of knowledge . . . must not be bestowed upon propositions which cannot be assimilated by thought and co-ordinated with knowledge, or which assert that reason is unable to comprehend," (II, 232).

Finally, we are not permitted to have two kinds of faith, one for the acceptance of reasonably demonstrated propositions and one for truths above reason. An empirical theism can admit faith only in reasonably demonstrated propositions. This excludes a revelation impinging vertically upon man.

Fourthly, any appeal to Christ as God-incarnate as bearing the full weight of a doctrine of revelation is untenable. The philosophical analysis of the doctrine of the incarnation shows the impossibility of working out any Christological formula which is free from gross contradictions. On the other hand, it is the verdict of scholarship that Jesus Christ was the last and greatest of the Hebrew prophets. Although it may be charged against liberal theologians—and Tennant belonged to "The Modern Churchmen's Union for the Advancement of Liberal Religious Thought"—that they arbitrarily and subjectively strain out the miraculous and theological from the Gospels leaving a very human Christ, nevertheless they do this on the broader basis of the scientific and epistemological convictions of an educated, enlightened, ethical theism. But Christ does have a central place in ethical theism. Christ is "a manifestation of God in the flesh . . . the unique revealer of God.

Christ possessed in the fullest measure insight into the divine purpose in the world and for man, and consequently into the divine
nature, which God would have mankind acquire" (II, 240). One
cannot help but asking at this point, where is the empirical origin
of this kind of assertion?

II. TENNANT'S POSITIVE APOLOGETICS

According to Tennant the three non-empirical efforts (rationalism, religious *a priorism*, revelation) fail to make their case.
Therefore, we are justified in keeping to the empirical procedure.
The task of the apologist is to set forth an empirical, ethical
theism which is constructed in the same general manner as are
laws in science. He realizes that science has its limitations but on
the other hand the only kind of knowledge we can trust (and this
goes for religion!) is that knowledge constructed in harmony with
the methodology of science.

1. The first leg of this empirical journey into religion is Tennant's *psychological empiricism*. All philosophers make some appeal to experience. The difference comes in deciding what territory
the word experience covers. Some philosophers include *value* in
experience and think that value is as real to the perceiver as are
objects. To others experience means *sensory* experience and everything else (like value or ethics) is an imposition upon sensory
experience.

Tennant wishes to commence with experience. However, he
wants the most primitive and ultimate form of experience that
there is. He wants that primeval data from which all metaphysical
systems derive, and to which they must turn back for their justification. He wants an empirical ground so foundational that it can
never be undercut. This ultimate empirical ground is *common,
everyday presumptive knowledge*. It is such knowledge before it is
analyzed or evaluated. It is the common hodge-podge collection
of information, data, and experiences stacked in our minds one
way or another.

However, to this data there must be a method which corresponds to it. This absolutely foundational method which corresponds to the absolutely foundational data is psychology in its
genetic and analytic departments. This combination is the ultimate in empirical procedure and cannot be undercut by a more
empirical one. This is called by Tennant, the *ordo cognoscendi*
(i.e., the order in which things are known).

The foolishness of starting elsewhere is that the philosopher must make presumptions that are too sophisticated and not justifiable. Plato is a good example of the wrong method. He constructs his philosophy out of ideas (or universals or forms or concepts). These ideas have an ontological status. But ideas are not primitive stuff at all! In fact, genetic psychology can trace their growth from the child to the adult. In this growth these concepts become very familiar and this familiarity Plato confuses with axiomaticity. Furthermore, because the mind may manipulate these ideas apart from the impressional (i.e., I do not have to see a horse each time I wish to describe one) Plato drew the false conclusion that they were independent from the impressional. The lowly psychological origin of these ideas or concepts forbids our granting them the heavenly status that Plato gave them.

This common presumptive (i.e., we presume it to be true even though we have not gone through the process of its proper verification) knowledge then enables us to move to a second position, namely *the impressional*. By the impressional Tennant means the sheer thrust of information upon our senses. All concepts and ideas accordingly have their origin in this *impressional*. Another word used in this connection is *sensa*. By *sensa* Tennant means the collection of sense data or sensory information before it is formed into any theory of perception. Sensa are the fundamental of knowledge and philosophy attempts to examine the relations among the sensa, and the concepts which may be validly formed from them. To this point he wrote that: "The presentation, order and nature of impressions, in so far as involuntary or non-selective attention is concerned, are thrust upon us willy-nilly: that is what renders the impressional psychologically ultimate and inexplicable. The analytically simple data of all knowledge to our actual world, are thus posited for us, not by us: they constitute an irrational surd which pure thought cannot eliminate" (I, 36).

In his *Philosophy of the Physical Sciences* Tennant defends at great length the following theses: (i) that the impressional is the ultimate data for all knowledge whether scientific or theological; (ii) that psychology is the first and most basic of sciences; and that (iii) history is second in importance in the classification of sciences. Psychology presents the problem of knowledge as it is posited within us; history, as it is posited for us in the universe.

It would be wrong to think that Tennant ties his hands with the impressional or with the sensa. He believes that from this foundational stuff very complex structures may be elaborated. This process of the elaboration of the simple into the complex is *epigenesis*. *Epigenesis* is to be contrasted with *evolution*. Evolution, in the strict philosophical sense, is unwinding that which is wound in. It means making obvious or explicit what is involved in the beginning. The seed becoming a tree or the egg becoming an organism are examples of evolution. The oak is in the acorn and the creature is in the ovum. Time but unravels what is already there in a hidden form.

In *epigenesis* something new is added. As time unravels something is picked up which was not there at the commencement. Thus Darwin's theory of evolution is really a theory of epigenesis for as life moves through the centuries new organs are added to the forms of life. Applied to the problem of knowledge it means that although the beginning of knowledge is in the impressional or the sensa, knowledge is not merely different combinations of these. Ethics, logic, and aesthetics *epigenetically* grow out of the impressional.

2. *Empirical rationalism.* Tennant is wise enough to know that knowledge is very complex and cannot be explained in terms of the needle of sensation cutting grooves of information in the sensitive stuff of the brain. This is the position of *sensationalism* and this Tennant rejects. In agreement with the Thomists he would say that this would lead to skepticism. A book of pictures, real or in memory, is not the same as a reasoned discourse, and knowledge is more like the latter than the former.

Having rather thoroughly scouted and scotched traditional rationalism (which Tennant did a poor job in sympathetically describing) he must now bring a rationalistic element into his theory of knowledge to save it from *sensationalism* and therefore scepticism. He agrees that the mind must make its contribution or knowledge would not be possible. However he is very careful to always give the priority to the senses in any possible debate between sense and reason!

His philosophical grandfather is Leibniz. Leibniz taught that *perception* is confused *thinking,* and *thinking* is clarified *perception.* He made room in his philosophy for concepts to begin in a very lowly place and gradually working upwards emerge into full clarity. *This means that knowledge and sense have the same root.* This assertion Tennant never wearies in repeating. Thus every perception has "the promise and potency of thought" (I, 37). The notion that perception and thought were two very different things is a heresy of Plato and has dogged philosophy for centuries. Only men like Leibniz and James Ward (and partially Kant) saw through this heresy.

Tennant frequently notes that Leibniz did not follow the rationalism and its dogmatism set out by Descartes and Spinoza.

In contrast to these men he taught that there was a growth and enlargement, or to put it otherwise, an epigenetical psychological development in our knowledge. It was Kant who argued that knowledge cannot be squeezed out of sensations for in themselves they are blind, i.e., just "there"; nor can it be squeezed out of the mind's own abstractions for the mind can create far more entities than actually exist—think just of mythology and fairy stories! Kant therefore argued that in knowledge the senses make their contribution and the mind makes its, and, therefore, a true judgment was always a combination of both. Neither can do the job in itself. The sensations going it alone are *blind*; and the concepts of the mind going it alone are *empty*. The sensations need the interpreting power of the mind, and the mind needs the data of the senses.

So far so good! But this does not quite please Tennant for Kant's notion of the mind is too artificial, too wooden, too compartmentalized, and too much out of touch with genetic psychology. Kant was a good philosopher but a poor psychologist. It was the genius of James Ward to rescue both Kant and Leibniz with the interpreting power and corrective power of modern empirical psychology. Ward was a modified Leibnizian monadologist. Leibniz taught that the ultimate stuff of the universe was composed of "monads" or dynamic little centers of activity which could exist in sleeping form ("matter") or in a highly self-conscious form ("man") with all grades of sleeping and waking between matter and man. Thus Leibniz's universe was a spiritual and dynamic one in contrast to a materialistic and mechanistic one. Ward working with the insights of Leibniz and the best in recent psychology transforms the artificial psychology of Kant with its battery of categories into a psychology of the mind far more in keeping with analytic and genetic psychology.

The greatest single impact upon Tennant was James Ward. Although he changes and modifies Ward's position he does follow Ward in the use of analytic and genetic psychology. Although Tennant frequently hems and haws about the ultimate character of matter (for a really strict empiricism cannot leap over sense data and speculate about what the sense data report) he clearly indicates that he is not opposed to a monadology, e.g., when he wrote that "where, as in plants, there is no macroscopic evidence of psychic behavior, the formative principle, as yet mysterious to science, is further to seek. It may be that only in metaphysics such as spiritualistic monadism, or hylozoism [the theory that in some sense matter is "alive"] of the microscopic order, is a natural explanation to be found" (II, 84).

Being an empirical rationalist Tennant must attribute certain powers to the mind that rightly belong to the mind at birth. These powers must be very general so that room will be made for the epigenetical approach to human nature. The first general character of the mind is *consciousness.* Consciousness is undeniable, i.e., one can only "consciously" deny that there is no such thing as consciousness. It is also underivable, i.e., it cannot be traced to a function of something else. "Consciousness is not given in atoms; its smallest portion is a process, and its simplest portion is complex" (I, 42). He has only devastating scorn for those who would attempt to deny the fact of consciousness. It is a forceful *given* which is too clear, too lucid, and too self-evident to brook any denial.

In our consciousness we are aware of *three irreducible subjective activities of the mind.* The mind has the power of (i) retention, (ii) of differentiation, and (iii) of complication. These are the powers resident in the new-born infant. Tennant's description of the infant is that "save in the merely zoological sense, man is at birth but potentially human. As to the clouds of glory which the infant has been said to trail, psychology discovers nothing that can be so described; no reminiscences of pure-soul life [contra Plato!], no innate ideas of God-given reason [contra Descartes]: nothing but innocent tendencies of the stock, imparted to man by his brute ancestry" (I, 109).

In virtue of these inward powers man is able to take his lowly sensory experience and compound out of it the highly abstract concepts of human thought. Thus man begins with the seeing, hearing, feeling *(perception)*, the mind retains these and juggles them around one way and another *(imagination)*, and finally creates a battery of abstract concepts *(ideation)*. Whether it be the abstract concept of space or the law of identity or the notion of a potential force the root is in sense data. By the process of the general functions of the mind listed above the raw data of the senses is manufactured into the complex concepts of thought. Our notions about science, the external world, the categories, God, religion, metaphysics, ultimately derive from the epigenetic growth of impressions.

3. *Empirical metaphysics.* Whatever metaphysical or religious statements man wishes to make—as philosopher or as theologian—he must make on empirical grounds. Tennant believes that philosophy can be as scientific and objective as science *if all metaphysical statements are controlled by the sense data,* i.e., are empirically grounded. If every philosopher be guided by the

thrust of the external world upon his senses, the brute facts of the impressional, and the *forthcomingness* of empirical data, then philosophy would be purged of all its *individualism* and *personal impressionism.*

Further, the metaphysician must pass all the sciences by in review *before* he may make any assertions. Metaphysics comes *last* in the development of knowledge. Tennant writes: "Metaphysics is a quest which is dependent on the sciences of the historical and phenomenal. Metaphysical knowledge is the last kind to be attained, if it be attainable, and the approach to it is most precarious. Not until we have passed by way of the sciences to metaphysics can we set up a metaphysical system" (*Philosophy of the Physical Sciences*, p. 30).

Tennant desires an objective, reliable *control* over all metaphysical statements, and he finds this on the one hand in that which he calls the impressional, and on the other in scientific knowledge. He claims that any metaphysical scheme which bypasses the sciences is a pastime. Tennant affirms that the facts of presumptive knowledge are "the sole external control; there is nothing else whereby to distinguish opinion and speculation . . . from knowledge and genuine philosophy. . . . Common-sense knowledge, then, shall be used as datum and as touchstone" (I, 4).

A metaphysical assertion, controlled by the impressional and by science is then made *in the same spirit as a scientific statement, has the same type of broad verification that general scientific laws have, and deserves the same assent and respect.* Therefore, a theism built on such principles will command the respect of the enlightened and educated mentality. It will enjoy the same sweet reasonableness as scientific knowledge, and will be an offense to no truly educated person.

It might well be asked how it is that Tennant is so emphatically empirical that he does not become a materialist or a positivist. How is that he can defend Christian theism when he is guided by such empirical theses? Tennant notes many times in his writings that science is guided by the principle of *parsimony* (i.e., Occam's razor). The goal of science is to achieve the *fewest* number of factors or assumptions necessary to explain things. This is sometimes called *reductionism*, i.e., the attempt to explain "higher" things by showing that they are but manifestations of some unusually complex arrangement of "lower" things. Thus the entire scientific mentality is *parsimonious* and *reductive*. It is furthermore *highly selective* for it selects out of the richness of the universe only those aspects which interest it. All of this is unobjectionable as science. The scientist can get his job done no other way.

But the philosopher cannot be guided by parsimony because he is interested in the total universe! The philosopher is guided by *adequacy*. Tennant thus escapes materialism or positivism by moving from *parsimony* in *science* to *adequacy* in *philosophy*. In order to deal with the richness of the universe adequately the philosophy must then employ categories and concepts which are richer and more varied than those in science. For example, he declares that personality is "our highest interpretative concept. For the theist, it is the key to the universe" (I, 127). The scientist must pass up this category for his purposes, but the metaphysician who wishes to be adequate to all the data of the universe cannot afford to pass it up.

III. THE TWO FUNDAMENTAL ASSERTIONS OF THEISM

"The objective determination of religious experience needs . . . to be shown to be other than imaginal or ideal," writes Tennant for "this, indeed, is the fundamental task of philosophical theology" (I, 332). Thus Tennant's great *Philosophical Theology* is his apologetics which he attempts to construct upon the methodological grounds discussed up to this point. The reader might have thought that Tennant is all psychologist and all philosopher judging from the exposition of Tennant so far. But Tennant's theism is built upon such a foundation and it is absolutely necessary to have a minimum grasp of this foundation to understand the apologetic superstructure built upon.

According to Tennant the two fundamental notions upon which all religion rests and without which it would neither be possible nor credible are the *soul* and *God*. Therefore, the Christian apologist must show upon what grounds he believes in both. Tennant's doctrine of the existence of the soul and God is built upon his empirically formulated philosophy and his loyalty to genetic and analytic psychology.

1. *The soul*. The cruciality of the doctrine of the soul is that unless man has a soul there is no meaning in religion. If we are not sure that we have a soul there is no sense in discussing whether there is a God or not. Therefore, the entire case for theism hinges upon whether man has a soul or not (I, 94). Thus the great apologetic purpose of Volume I of his *Philosophical Theology* is to defend the thesis that man has a soul (II, 1).

If the first fact of human experience is that of consciousness

the second fact is that of self-consciousness. This is the first datum
to be reckoned with in discussing the existence of the soul. In
self-consciousness, however, we soon make a certain differentiation.
We classify one set of impressions or one kind of impression as
impinging upon the sense organs from without; we identify a
second set as those arising *within* the body. To this we make another differentiation. We identify those impressions which impinge
upon us with *the order of the external objects* whereas the sensations which arise within the body (feelings of pleasure, pain, joy,
anxiety, etc.) *we identify our personal history. This generates the
first rudimentary idea of a self.*

As noted in our previous discussion the mind has the three
powers of retention, differentiation, and complication. These
three powers come into play at this point and formulate the notion
of *an empirical self.* But these powers do not stop here. As we
become aware of an empirical self *through many years experience*
the question of a pure self, an ego, or a metaphysical self arises.
And the problem of the theist is to prove that this postulated self
or soul does exist.

One of the ways this is done is to take apart the structure of
perception. What happens when a man sees a tree, for example?
Tennant sees a duality here: an object (the tree) is presented to a
subject (the man). This duality is the structure of all perception.
"If consciousness is unique we can now add that it is from the first
to last a duality in unity" (I, 20). This duality is the duality of
the subject-object relationship. It is a duality which is obvious,
clear and undeniable. Efforts to rid consciousness of this dual
nature are distortions of the undeniable data of every man's consciousness. Sensations just do not happen "somewhere." "A sub-
jectless experience is not merely an absurdity: a contradiction in
meaning, it should be a contradiction in terms" (I, 18). There
must be some sort of self or ego or soul for the very structure of
perception calls for the *perceiver* of the object.

When we are aware of an object we are not only aware of the
object but the consciousness has a reflective power: *it is aware of
being aware.* As objects come and go in our awareness *our reflexive awareness continues the same.* This reflexive awareness
(the awareness of being aware!) is a more direct reality than the
objects we are aware of. This awareness differs from awareness of
objects in this fundamental point: an object is thrust upon us
but when we turn away or the object disappears the object is
gone, but *awareness itself* is always there. It has the characteristic
of *being-lived-through.* Here Tennant turns to the German language to pick up the word, *erleben* which means "to live through,

to experience, witness," and the noun, *das Erlebnis,* "experience, occurrence, adventure." These German words reflect better than any English words the quality and the intensity of this "awareness of awareness." Therefore, we have the right to postulate at this point the uniqueness of consciousness with its *erleben*-quality, the subject of this consciousness, and states and activities of this subject (I, 32).

If these theses are denied, confusion results. *All efforts to destroy the notion of the soul involve a soul with such mental powers and activities which can carry out such a logical warfare!* Hume is famous for his attempt to destroy the notion of a soul. Hume said he *searched* for a soul and could not find it. Tennant would ask, "who conducted the search?" Hume "tells us that he never caught himself without a perception; but he might as truly have said that he never caught a perception without himself" (I, 80).

We, therefore, have the right to postulate a soul. Only by attributing to man a soul can we account for man's sense of *continuity* through time; for the manner in which man *unifies* and *orders* his experiences; and for the strong sense of *individuality* which each human person possesses. The soul *acts,* it is, therefore, *actual*; the soul *exists* for there can be no experience without the *Experiencer*; the human being *thinks* but this thinking is but the reflection of the *essence* of the soul. For the very same reason we say that a tree exists to account for the unity of experiences with reference to the tree we also say the soul exists to account for the unity of our personal life. "No one has ever really dispensed with the subject of consciousness whatever terms he may have used to hush up its existence. No one will ever dispense with it, because to do so involves intrinsic impossibility" (I, 18).

Thereby Tennant feels that he has accomplished the first great step in a Christian apologetic. He has shown that upon empirical grounds *man has a soul.* As having a soul he is capable of moral, ethical and religious experiences. The groundwork for a theism has been laid.

However, any attempt to trace the origin of the soul is wrought with difficulties. At best we can claim that man has a soul. Psychology certainly can say no more than this. The origin of the soul and the destiny of the soul is outside empirical knowledge. His only lever for immortality is the biological continuity of life. If animals possessed with souls (as his monadology teaches) lived *before* man, there is no scientific objection to man's soul living *after* his death—a very cryptic argument at best.

2. *The existence of God.* Pledged to that which only an empirical methodology will permit Tennant must now set forth a

proof for the existence of God. The first clue to the existence of God is the order in nature, but the major thesis must be built around *cosmic teleology*. The teleological proof for the existence of God has been one of the most popular from Socrates until the present. Paley gave it a most famous defense in his work, *Natural Theology*. His illustration of finding a watch on some forest path has become one of the most trite pieces of popular apologetics. It was the one proof for the existence of God that Kant was most impressed with even though he did find it necessary to bring it under criticism in his *Critique of Pure Reason*. However in his *Critique of Judgment* it almost becomes a compelling proof.

Paley's formulation was considered the most persuasive given in post-medieval times. However, it was a general conviction of most scholars, especially philosophers and biologists, that Darwin's *Origin of Species* (1859) crushed its cogency. But even though Paley's formulation received the most wide-spread hearing there was another formulation of it perhaps of more enduring importance. From 1833 to 1836 a series of twelve volumes appeared known as *The Bridgewater Treatises*. These volumes were written by some of England's greatest scientists and their one aim was to prove the existence of God from considerations of nature. One of the arguments used in this treatise was the *adaption of nature for life*. This kind of teleology was left untouched by Darwin's theses.

In 1913 L. J. Henderson published *The Fitness of the Environment*. This was an extension and modernization of the thesis first broached in the *Bridgewater Treatises*. This work presents line upon line and page upon page of detailed information of the adaptations of *inorganic* nature which made life possible. It is impossible to convey the weight of what Henderson says without a rather full reproduction of his facts. But after reviewing all the things necessary for life to exist, and while admitting that in no sense could chance explain the happy combination of so many and such divergent factors, Henderson remains agnostic as to how it all happened.

However men like Boodin, Northrop, Barnes, Heard and Tennant feel that they see the very clear implication of the welter of data Henderson has amassed. It amounts to a powerful case for *inorganic* or *cosmic teleology*. It is on this cosmic teleology that Tennant rests the case for his second great section of apologetics, the proof for the existence of God. He builds his case on the "conspiration of innumerable causes to produce, by their united and reciprocal action, and to maintain, a general order of nature" (II, 79).

One might object to cosmic teleology and say that the argument is not valid for it deals with the phenomena upon the crust of the earth and not the whole universe. Tennant is willing to settle for something less than the universe. If we can prove design on the crust of this earth we have at least proved that this earth had a Designer. However the earth is a *representative* fragment of the universe, and this must not be forgotten. Nor must we forget (as Kant argued) that the design-structure of the universe anticipates at the inorganic and organic levels the ethical and moral on the human level.

Tennant rejects Paley's teleology on the ground that it is too narrow, and insists that evolution has nothing to say against cosmic teleology. However something may even be said of design in creatures. Evolution may describe the course of changes but it does not discuss the *origin* of these changes. Evolution may thus be incorporated into the *wider* teleology. This wider teleology was argued first by Aquinas, says Tennant, but it needed the work of Henderson for its modern restatement.

A scientist may object to all of this and say that this matter of coincident of factors necessary for life is real and not apparent for under different conditions a different form of life would appear. Tennant's rejoinder is that the complexity of life is so great that *any* appearance of life calls for more than blind forces or chance. If the scientist retorts by saying that evolution can explain *everything*, then Tennant thinks the scientist is guilty of two things. First, he is assuming that Darwin has said a final and conclusive word about the matter but this is not in keeping with the probability-status of all scientific theories. Second, the scientist is really using the word "evolution" as some cosmic explanatory principle and not in the narrow scientific sense as used in biology. "Presumably," he concludes," the world is comparable with a single throw of dice, and common sense is not foolish in suspecting the dice to have been loaded" (II, 87).

A logician may say that there are such things as lucky throws of the dice. What about this? And in that we have only one universe to go by, how can we speak meaningful of the difference between chance and design? Tennant's reply is that we must not confuse probability in mathematics with probability in the world of fact. The cosmic teleological argument is not concerned with purely mathematical probability but with the "alogical probability which is the guide of life, and which was found to be ultimate basis of all scientific induction" (II, 87). At this point science and theology walk hand in hand and it is unfair to reprimand the theologian and not the scientist. This type of supposition as is found in the cosmic teleological argument is the type upon which all scientific knowledge rests and relies upon and therefore it is not true "that science rests on reason, while, in a corresponding sense, teleology rests on unreason" (II, 89) .

This teleological argument is not like a chain but like chain-armor. It is not constructed so that each link is dependent upon the previous one but it is a webbed argument in which the total pattern of facts form a texture of great strength. In conclusion he writes: "All causal science is, in the last resort, but reasonable and postulatory; teleology is therefore a development from science along its own lines, or a continuation, by extrapolation, of the plotted curve which comprehensively describes its knowledge. And this is the *apologia* of theism such as professes to be reasonable belief for the guidance of life, when arranged by science and logic—or by more pretentious theology" (II, 120).

In the *Philosophy of the Sciences* he makes a statement that is a fitting summary of an apologetic based upon empirical theism. He says that the effort to separate metaphysics from science is suicidal for from science alone "comes the only indisputable facts" (p. 186) from which metaphysical generalizations can be made, for metaphysics "is but a continuation, by extrapolation, or through points representing further observations, or the curve of 'knowledge' which natural science has constructed. In short, science and theism spring from a common root" (p. 185) .

BIBLIOGRAPHY

Bertocci, P., *The Empirical Argument for God in Late British Theology*
Buswell, J. O., *The Philosophies of F. R. Tennant and John Dewey*
Fulton, "Teleology," *Hastings Encyclopedia of Religion and Ethics*, XII, 215-32
Tennant, F. R., *Miracle and its Philosophical Presuppositions*
_____, *Philosophical Theology* (2 vols.)
_____, *The Philosophy of the Sciences*
Scudder, D. *Tennant's Philosophical Theology*

Part III

Systems Stressing Revelation

I. AUGUSTINE AND ILLUMINATIONISM

II. CALVIN AND THE HOLY SPIRIT

III. KUYPER AND SPECIAL REVELATION

Chapter VIII

AUGUSTINE (354-430)

I. INTRODUCTION

Outside of the apostolic circle it is difficult to find a man with a greater stature than that of Augustine, bishop of Hippo. He was a mystic, saint, preacher, administrator, scholar, theologian, controversialist, philosopher, historian, letter writer, commentator, teacher, and author. This great genius created the philosophy of history with his *City of God* and introspective religious literature with his *Confessions*. The roots of our modern university curriculum stem from his work, *On Christian Doctrine*. He is the chief parent of medieval mysticism, monasticism, and scholasticism. He dominated the theology of the Middle Ages as its greatest authority. The Reformers claimed that they were doing nothing more or less than returning to Augustine. In fact Calvin said he could write his theology out of Augustine!

He is also considered the founder of modern philosophy in that he struggled so creatively with such concepts as the conscious ego, personality, time, history, free will and subjective truth. What a varied genius who is at the same time the greatest authority for scholasticism, for the Reformers, and the root of modern philosophy! Out of Augustine we can defend (apparently!) authoritarian Roman Catholicism and the great doctrine of the grace of God as taught by the Reformers.

However, Augustine has not been without his critics. He has been accused of sponsoring the type of artificial thought which became so characteristic of medieval scholasticism. Because Augustine had such a turbulent problem with sex in his own life he is accused of giving it a morbid interpretation and thus adversely influencing Christian thought. It is claimed that his radical views of original sin and human depravity broke with the historic tradition of the Christian theologians so that his net contribution to theology was for the poorer rather than for the better. In his Platonism which put such a high value on thought and concept and so little on sense and experience he is judged as retarding the growth of the sciences. In his debates with the various heretics he is charged with creating a spirit of ecclesiastical dogmatism within Christendom. And to others his views of ecclesiology were far too Romish and authoritarian.

Although Augustine was a man with a mighty intellect he nevertheless was also a mystic. Confessions, prayers, and adorations were his daily spiritual fare. When he was dying he had the penitential Psalms written on his walls with large letters so that he could read them while he was in bed. There he rested in tears, in prayers, in confessions, in reading the Psalms as he awaited his exodus from this life.

Augustine allowed no gossip around the table at meal times. He had written over the table the words: "Whoever loves to speak ill of an absent life with his words acknowledges this table to be unworthy of himself." If some one forgot the motto Augustine would arise and say, "Either that inscription must be erased or I must leave the room."

The various influences upon Augustine are too complex to trace out in any detail here. Generally his education was more Latin than Greek. He was influenced little by Aristotle and much by Plato. He remarks that Plato apparently worshipped the true God and says it "is evident that none [of the philosophers] come nearer to us than the Platonists" (City of God, VIII, 5). He also asserts that the Platonists are to be ranked before all others and that they are "the noblest of the philosophers" (City of God, X, 1). Furthermore the Christian has every right to the use of the correct conclusions of the Platonists because they "have unlawful possession" of the truth (On Christian Doctrine, II, 40). Such appreciation of Plato does not mean that Augustine does not see his shortcomings from the perspective of the Christian revelation.

His Christian influence stems, of course, from his very devout Christian mother, and very directly from Ambrose of Milan. His love for philosophy he traces to Cicero's Hortensius which inflamed him with a love for the subject.

There is a complex problem in deciphering Augustine's philosophy, theology, and apologetics from his voluminous writings. He wrote as the problems arose, and also over the entire period of his active life as a bishop. The materials are many, the topics diverse, and this is complicated by changes and developments in his thought. But one major theme keeps shining through his works: the quest for certainty.

The Confessions—the combination of personal testimony autobiography, report of his spiritual pilgrimage—reveal the powerful hungerings of Augustine for certainty as well as his fruitless search in contemporary philosophies. Two factors are suggested as disturbing Augustine in a profound manner and thereby exciting this quest for certainty. First, the doctrine of sin cast a deep shadow over man's intellectual powers. If sin weakened the will and excited the passions would it not also cloud the mind? How can a *fallen* intellect have any assurance of the truth? *Secondly*, Augustine had evidently given much time to the study of the skepticism of the *New Academy*. According to this school man could not trust *sense* or *mind*. If both are untrustworthy where does one find bedrock? Augustine's apologetics is really tracing out the answer to the skepticism suggested by both sin and philosophy!

II. FROM DOUBT TO GOD

1. *From doubt to the self.* The *New Academy* advocated universal doubt. Let us let them have their say and agree that we must doubt all things. But let us not stop here. Let us analyze what the process of doubt involves. According to the skeptic we come to the conclusion that we know nothing. The only guide of life consists of sensible guesses—probability statements!

Augustine, however, does not come out with this conclusion. If I doubt, he argues, I must *remember*, I must *understand*, I must *will*, I must *think*, I must *know*, and I must *judge*. Doubting necessarily implies all of these acts of the self. But all of these actions imply the *Actor*, the *Doubter*. Universal doubt cannot lead to universal skepticism. Doubting involves the existence of the self that doubts, and the *valid mental processes* which set up the structure of the process of doubting. In a word doubting leads to the exact opposite conclusion that the *New Academy* thought it did. Here is the argument in Augustine's own words:

> But, without any delusive representation of images or phantasms, I am most certain that I am, and that I know and delight in this. In respect of these truths, I am not at all afraid of the arguments of the [skeptical] Adademicians, who say, What if you are deceived? For if I am deceived, I am. For he who is not, cannot be deceived: and if I am deceived, how am I deceived in believing that I am? Since, therefore, I, the person deceived, should be, even if I were deceived, certainly I am not deceived in this knowledge that I am. And, consequently, neither am deceived in knowing that I know. For as I know that I am, so I also know this also, that I know (*City of God*, XI, 26).

And,

> Yet who ever doubts that he himself lives, and remembers, and understands, and wills, and thinks, and knows, and judges? Seeing that even if he doubts he lives; if he doubts he remembers why he doubts; if he doubts he understands that he doubts; if he doubts, he thinks; if he doubts, he knows that he does not know; if he doubts he judges that he ought not assert rashly. Whosoever therefore doubts anything else, ought not to doubt all of these things; which if they were not, he would not be able to doubt of anything (*On the Trinity*, X, 10).

The conclusion, certain and unavoidable, is that *I exist*—an

"I" that can think, remember, and judge! *In doubting the mind thus knows itself.* It knows that it exists, it knows that it lives, it knows that it understands, and it knows all of this certainly.

However, Augustine agrees with the skeptics at one point. Being a good Platonist he believes that we have full right to be skeptical about our senses. If there is any truth at all it will not be found in them. We must move on to another territory if we wish to find truth and that *is the realm of the inner world.* "Do not go outside, come back into your very own self, truth dwells in the inner man," he wrote (*The True Religion*, XXXIX, 72). Speaking to sinners Augustine asks them to seek God. But how shall they seek him? "He is within the very heart. . . . Return to your heart, O ye transgressors!" (*Confessions* IV, 12). This call to retreat within is based on Augustine's conviction that truth is located within the self and not within the senses. For this reason Augustine's philosophy has been called by the great historian of philosophy, Windelband, *the metaphysics of subjectivity.*

It would not be quite proper to say the location of the truth was in the mind and the mind alone. Rather it is in the self which includes the mind. For Augustine thinks of the total self as having the truth and grasping the truth. By making truth the function of the total man Augustine advances over Plato and the neo-Platonists.

In summary it may be thus said that truth is *inward* (in contrast to the senses) and *personal* (in contrast to a Platonic intellectualism).

2. *From doubt to truth.* If doubt implies the reality of the doubter, it also implies the reliability of the faculties involved in doubting, and thereby implies further the *truthfulness* of the propositions these faculties work with. Doubting, the doubter, the faculties involved in doubting, and truths imbedded in the doubting process belong together. The end-product of doubting, namely *the doubt,* involves the use of *truth-along-the-way.* Or to put it another way, proposition X can be doubted only if we presume the veracity of propositions Y and Z. *The doubter does possess knowledge.*

If he possesses knowledge, he possesses truth. Or as Augustine framed it, "Everyone who knows that he is in doubt about something knows the truth, and in regard to this he is certain" (*The True Religion*, XXIX, 73).

Acidic doubt may successfully eat away the evidence of the senses; it can show a thousand ways in which our eyes, ears, sense of smell or touch or direction, deceive us daily. But exposing the flux of the senses we use a non-sensuous faculty, the soul or the mind. That which judges is superior to that which is judged; therefore, the mind which judges the senses is superior to the senses. If doubt implies truth, doubt also implies that truth is not of the senses. The standards for truth are not in the senses. Nor do they come to us by the senses. They are laid up in the mind, at hand, ready for use. Doubt may corrode the deliveries of senses but these internal standards are not derivable from the senses and therefore they are not affected by the senses.

True, we learn things from the senses. The body through its senses puts the soul in touch with the world around us. The mind operating with its inborn categories does examine the world about and thus creates *scientia*. It is necessary for the routine of earthly existence. But it is *practical* knowledge. The really important knowledge is not *scientia* but *sapientia* (wisdom). This is the realm of eternal and spiritual truth and is far superior to the practical truth of *scientia*. There is only one possible good in *scientia* and that is it might be the source of some proof for the existence of God. But apart from that *scientia* does not contribute to our salvation and it must be judged as barren. It is at this juncture that criticism has been leveled against Augustine. By devaluating the senses and sensory knowledge he inhibited that kind of research and learning necessary for the development of science.

In philosophical language Augustine is a *rationalist*, i.e., one who believes that the criteria for truthfulness are to be found in the mind and not in the senses. Truth is that which holds together, that which is consistent, that which makes peace with the law of non-contradiction. And being a Christian theist he adds one more characteristic to truth: *it is divine.*

Along with his *rationalism* he also carried a *realism*. In this connection *realism* means the real existence of the principles of thought. Thus the law of contradiction is not a convenience of language or thought but part of the real order of things. This is part of Augustine's Platonic and neo-Platonic heritage. These principles of thought, these standards of right and wrong, these innate ideas have a very important function for Augustine. *They are part of the soul's environment.* Just as the body lives within the universe of objects so the soul lives within the universe of thoughts, concepts or ideas. Through reason the soul perceives these realities. But these realities do not float around in nothing but they are sustained and impressed upon man by God.

Furthermore, if we collect these ideas and classify them we get the following divisions: logic, predication, numbers, morals, and beauty. The classical division is that of Plato's: the true, the beautiful, and the good.

These ideas are not then conventions or sociologically conditioned *mores*. They are engraved on the heart and they are part of the nature of things. Number, for example is not invented by man but is *discovered* by man. Logical order is not devised by man "for it exists eternally in the reason of things, and has its origin with God" (*On Christian Doctrine*, II, 32) .

This retreat of Augustine within man is not the same as subjectivism. The objects which exist *before* the mind have an unquestionable objective status for they cannot be manipulated, distorted, or shoved around by the will of man. On the contrary, all proposed objectivity is dependent upon the objectivity of the universe of ideas! Unless we all shared in the objective universe of our ideas we would be shut up to our own ideas and we would never know if we had the same meaning or thought that another person did.

It has been pointed out a number of times in the exposition of Augustine that his "I doubt, therefore I am," anticipates Descartes' "I think, therefore I am." (However the argument had already been used by Campenella, 1568-1639.) The report is that Descartes was irritated when this was pointed out to him. It may be argued that Augustine was more profound than Descartes in this matter. Descartes moved from thought to existence whereas Augustine moves from doubt to truth, as well as to personal existence. Furthermore, Descartes must bring God in artificially but Augustine brings Him in naturally as the Author and Ground of truth. One of the most fundamental axioms of Augustine is: "Behold, there is He wherever truth is known" (*Confessions* IV, 12) .

3. *From truth to God*. It has been affirmed that Augustine accepted the traditional proofs for the existence of God, but it is the inner proof he defends with fervor and with consistency with the total system of his thought. The revelation of God *through nature* is a condescension to our weakness; the clarity of the knowledge of God comes from the presence of God to the inner eye when it is sound and clear.

If doubt exists, then knowledge exists, then truth exists, and *therefore God exists*. This is based on the premises that God is the True, the Beautiful, and the Good and therefore, where the truth is, God is. Furthermore, God exists in each human person as the supporting Being. He prays: "Why, then, do I ask Thee to come into me, since I indeed exist, and could not exist, could not exist at all, O my God, unless thou wert in me" (*Confessions* I, 2). God also supports within the mind, the *eternal concepts*, and is thereby the Light of the mind. He writes: "And being thence warned to return to myself, I entered into my inward self, Thou leading me on; and I was able to do it, for Thou wert my helper. And I entered, and with the eye of my soul . . . saw above the same eye of my soul, above my mind, the Unchangeable Light" (*Confessions*, X, 10).

The knowledge of God is accordingly not inferential but innate within the soul. God is both Guide and Goal of the search for Him. There is no interval in Augustine's thought between the soul, the existence of truth, and the existence of God.

Augustine's proof is, fundamentally, a proof for the existence of God from considerations of the possibility of knowledge. It is a proof from the character and function of the *eternal concepts*. It is the belief that God, the truth, and certitude of the truth implicate each other.

There are also some traces of Platonism in his proof for the existence of God. For example Augustine sees God as the Form or Forms, i.e., the Form over all the forms (or concepts, or ideas) and this is Platonic. The implicit Platonic and ontological argument is in the words "For never yet was, nor will be, a soul able to conceive of anything better than Thou, who art the highest and best good" (*Confessions*, VII, 4). Thus there is "an eternal, immutable Form which is neither extended nor varied in time, and through which all mutable things can receive a form and according to their kind fulfill and accomplish their ordered rythms in space and time" (*Confessions* IV, 12).

In summary it may be said that truths imply both a system of truths (the eternal concepts) and the Unchanging Truth, namely, God. Thus the movement of doubt which would boast in the denial of the reality of God unexpectedly ends up by proving His very Being!

4. *God as World Ground.* Augustine's philosophy is a robust theism. To him God is Creator and Lord of all. When God created He had certain patterns, certain forms, certain ideas in mind, and after these the creation was formed. God is thereby the Support of both the *truth* and the *being* of the universe. He is also the source and the support of all good.

In fact, so strong is the theism of Augustine that he has to prevent it from slipping into pantheism. One manner in which he prevents this is to develop a doctrine of the Trinity. Although Plotinus did have a Trinity of Mind, Soul, and World it cannot match the Christian Trinity of Father, Son, and Holy Spirit. Augustine's Trinity is a Trinity of redemption and revelation. Augustine also secures himself against pantheism with a strong doctrine of creation. He avoids dualism which would assert that there was both a good and evil principle within the universe, and he avoids pantheism by making it clear that God and his creation are absolutely two different entities.

Augustine's doctrine of revelation has similarities to the neo-Platonic doctrine of illumination but once again Augustine's doctrine is enriched by the data out of Scripture. Augustine saw a revelation in the human soul, in creation, in Scripture, in Christ, and in the soul in regeneration.

However, it is generally granted that Augustine was also weakened in his thought by neo-Platonic elements. His doctrine of sin as negation or lack or privation is neo-Platonic and not Scriptural. His doctrine of the ineffability of God is neo-Platonic. Plotinus said that God is so much The Other that our knowledge of Him is better gained through negation than affirmation, the so-called "negative theology." Augustine affirmed that none of the categories of Aristotle applied to God, nor can we apply the category of substance to God.

He is generally Platonic in his doctrine of *existence*. God is the origin of all Being and all Truth. In eloquent words Augustine informs us that God's supreme character is existence: "For to Him it is not one thing to be, and another to live, as though He could be, not living; nor is it to Him as one thing to live, and another thing to understand, as though He could live, not understanding; nor is it to Him one thing to understand, another thing to be blessed, as though He could understand and not be blessed. But to Him to live, to understand, to be blessed are to be" (*City of God*, VIII, 6).

God is thus the source and foundation of existence. He is the only really true being and to think "God" and to think "non-existence" is to think the infinitely opposite. In the light of God's being all else is in change. Every man has his own existence in this Fountain of being, even the sinner (*Confessions* IV, 12). God is the foundation for all physical causation: "Whatever bodily or seminal causes, then, may be used for the production of things, either by the co-operation of angels, men, or the lower animals, or by sexual generation; and whatever power of the desires and mental emotions of the mother have to produce in the tender foetus, corresponding lineaments and colours; yet the natures themselves, which are thus variously affected, are the production of none but the most high God. It is His occult power which pervades all things, and is present in all without being contaminated, which gives being to all what is, and modifies and limits its existence; so that without Him it would not be thus nor thus, nor would have any being at all" (*City of God*, XII, 25).

God is the foundation of all morality and all spirituality. God is the author, supporter, and impressor of the eternal concepts. Therefore, He is the source of all truth and all human rationality. We have here, then, a full-orbed theism and a singularly great Christian philosophy.

III. ILLUMINATION AND REVELATION

1. *All truth is illumination.* The eternal concepts are either grasped directly by intuition as the mind finds them ready at hand or Augustine says we may account for them by the presupposition that God constantly impresses them upon our minds. Although Augustine teaches both his emphasis is upon the latter. All truth is an illumination of the mind by God, whether the truth is secular or sacred or whether the mind is that of the sinner or saint. The neo-Platonic illustration of the shining sun illuminating all in our world is frequently in the back of Augustine's mind as he thinks on this topic.

The basis of Augustine's doctrine of illumination is that God is Truth, God is Light, and God is Eternity. These three terms penetrate each other. Truth is Light, and Light is Eternal. Augustine adds yet another word, Love. Augustine's praise to God is "Love knoweth [truth]. O Eternal Truth and true Love, and loved Eternity! Thou art my God; to Thee do I sigh night and day" (*Confessions* X, 10). God is the sun of the soul and the soul only sees because the sun enlightens it. Corollary to this is the Augustinian interpretation of John 1:9 which teaches that Christ is the Logos which enlightens the mind of every man born into the world. The deduction is that a soul cannot see by its own light but "needs to receive illumination from another, the true Light" (*City of God*, X, 2).

The human mind is therefore constantly dependent upon the Light. The human mind is a light but it is wise only as it partakes the Supreme Light. To understand the truth the soul must be enlightened by another light for the depravity of the soul has taken truth out of the nature of the soul. But whether it be secular truth or spiritual truth, whether it be the saint or the sinner, *the preception of truth is always by illumination.* At this point there is universal agreement among Augustine's interpreters. Human knowledge may be called *discovery* as we see it, but in that God is truth and the Author of all truth every bit of truth we happen to possess is ours in virtue of divine illumination. Therefore, there is no "brute fact" or "neutral truth" to Augustine.

Augustine's work, *The Teacher*, is a very interesting one. For one thing it contains a very astute theory of signs and language which anticipates the modern discussions in analytic philosophy. The other thing is that it defends the thesis that Christ is the interior Teacher of man.

2. *Divine revelation.* Although all men have the Light of the Logos in their soul, and their power to judge is proportional to the degree to which they let truth radiate their minds, there is yet another territory requiring a special divine illumination. This is the illumination of the truths of revelation. There are a number of reasons for this. The human cannot cope with the infinity of facts within the universe; even if we knew all the facts our immaturity prevents us from making the proper interpretation of them; and most damaging of all our sinfulness darkens our minds and alienates us from the Truth.

This suggests that a natural theology or a philosophy of Christianity separated from revelation is impossible. Man's rational powers desperately need the revelation of God! This revelation is the torch guiding the reason of man. This revelation for our purposes is the Scriptures, for the Scriptures have been "communicated by the supreme and true God through Holy men" (*City of God*, XX, 1). God's truth has been insinuated into these holy souls making them "the friends of God and His prophets" and through whom He "noiselessly informs them of His works" (*City of God*, XI, 4). However this revelation is in need of revelation! Illumination is the interior revelation of the heart enabling the sinner to see the exterior revelation in the Scriptures. This illumination is part of the blessedness of the human salvation. It is imperative for grace to include a revelation of God for unless we know God we cannot choose him.

IV. FAITH AND REASON

1. *Faith defined.* Augustine does give us a short definition of faith; *it is to think with assent.* But if we stop here we do not do justice to the richness of his thought. Faith, according to Augustine, has many facets to it. *Faith is faith in a teacher.* Unless one trusts the teacher he cannot learn. *Faith is faith in a friend.* There

can be no friendship unless their is mutual trust. *Faith is accepting authority.* Upon the investigation of the credentials of an authority we give an authority our faithful obedience. *Faith is the compulsion of truth.* When the mind is presented with clear truth it can do nothing else but believe. *Faith is the provisional acceptance of something* which yet awaits more thorough investigation. *Faith is insight* in which something heretofore unknown is grasped with clarity. *Faith is a surrender* to the will to God.

2. *Faith as acceptance of credible authority.* As previously indicated faith is acceptance of credible authority. The authority in question is the authority of revelation. In Augustine's writings authority means testimony. Hence faith and reason differ chiefly at this point. Faith is accepting the truthfulness of testimony whereas reason is accepting something through provable propositions (or sight). The two great testimonies for Augustine are the Church and the Bible.

We hear about Christianity's claim to be the revelation of God. We examine these claims and come to a satisfactory decision about them. We have established Christianity as *authoritative.* From thence the truths of revelation stand certified and are to be accepted by faith for they are validated by authority. This authority is the combined voice of the Bible and the Church.

Augustine accepts the Christian Scriptures as the veritable word of God. The reason God has graced humanity with a Bible is that "we were too weak by unaided reason to find out the truth, and for this cause needed the authority of the Holy Writings" (*Confessions* VI, 5). Writing to Jerome he says that "I confess to our Charity that I have learned to yield this respect and honour only to the canonical books of Scripture: of these alone do I most firmly believe that the authors were completely free from error. . . . Better far that I should read with certainty and persuasion of its truth the Holy Scripture, placed on the highest (even heavenly) pinnacle of authority, and should, without questioning the trustworthiness of its statements [accept]" (*Letters,* LXXXII, 3 and 5).

The exact place that the Church plays in Augustine's doctrine of authority is a matter of sharp difference of opinion. Augustine claimed that he would not have believed the gospel unless the Church had spoken it. He also frequently is quoted as having said, "Rome has spoken; the case is ended." These statements of Augustine may be taken as favoring the view that eventually developed in Roman Catholicism. Others do not see any particular significance in Augustine's remarks in settling the claims of the Roman papacy. However, both interpretations agree that in the

Church Augustine found the true, unbroken testimony of the apostles and of Jesus Christ. Hence the reliable tradition from God's Son through the apostles and then through the Church had an authority to Augustine very close to that of Holy Scripture.

Faith at this level is faith in *credible authority*. It is the faith of any person who would seek to learn. Without a positive disposition, a favorable inclination, a tentative acceptance of a new hypothesis, *nothing* can be taught, learned, or verified.

3. *The relationship of reason to faith.* It is a firm and often repeated conviction of Augustine that faith precedes reason. There is only one conceivable sense in which it could be said that reason precedes faith. Revelation can come only to a rational person. Revelation must say something which a human being can grasp at the level of the bare words. Reason is the point of contact in revelation in the sense that the message of revelation cannot be meaningless hash. There is then a preliminary critical sifting of what is heard, and this decides the direction faith is to take.

Otherwise, faith precedes reason. The key to Augustine's apologetics is the motto: *faith leads the intellect.* For example he wrote: "If you are not able to know, believe that you may know. Faith precedes; the intellect follows" (*Sermons*, CXVIII, 1). Augustine reasons at this point that it is impossible to see the truth in any system if the mind is in a state of unbelief. The person dominated by an acidic skepticism can learn nothing. A friendly disposition is the prerequisite for all learning. Furthermore, no hypothesis is ever verified without a provisional acceptance of its truthfulness else we would never have the motivation to test it. In the spiritual realm the necessity is greatly increased. The intellect needs the aid, insight, and illumination of faith: "Faith gives the understanding access to these [Christian] things, unbelief closes the door" (*Letters*, CXXXVII, 15). "We believed that we might know; for if we wished first to know and then to believe, we should not be able either to know or believe" (*St. John's Gospel*, XXVII, 9). Similarly with reference to the existence of God: "Nor does anyone become fit to discover God unless he shall have first believed what he is later to come to know," (*The Freedom of the Will*, II, ii, 6), and, "Understanding is the reward of faith. Therefore, seek not to understand that thou mayest believe, but believe that thou mayest understand" (*On Christian Doctrine*, I, 10).

The reason faith must precede reason in the area of Christian truth is that the unregenerate mind cannot be trusted with the truth. The mind must be purified and it is purified through faith. Speaking of the unchangeable truth, and the Triune God who counsels us with this truth Augustine declared that "the soul must be purified that it may have power to perceive that light, and to rest in it when it is perceived" *(On Christian Doctrine, I, 10)*. Commenting on the mind, he says though it is naturally capable of reason it has been crippled by sin and vice. In order to be healed and see the eternal Light, the mind must "in the first place . . . be impregnated with faith, and so be purified" *(City of God, XI, 2)*.

Tertullian is purported of having said that he believed because the gospel was absurd. What he most likely had in mind was nothing more or less than the scandal of the gospel. To the mind in rebellion against God the truth of God can appear only as absurd. However Augustine sounded one Tertullian-like note when he compared a Roman fish story with that of Jonah. He remarks that "that story of ours about the prophet Jonah is far more incredible [than the Roman fish story]—more incredible because more marvelous, and more marvelous because a greater exhibition of power" *(City of God, I, 14)*. However, Augustine's more consistent opinion is *that faith represents no stulification of the intellect.* Faith does not end nor terminate thought but is the presupposition for thought. Reason comes to the service of faith. Therefore, faith cannot be a generous surmise, a fond wish, or a leap into the dark. As Augustine wrote: "The mysteries and secrets of the kingdom of God first seek for believing men, that they may make them understand. For faith is understanding's step and understanding is faith's attainment" *(Sermons [N.T.], CXXVI, 1:1)*. Therefore, faith commits itself only to that which is worthy of belief: "No one believes anything unless he has before thought it worthy of belief" *(Of the Predestination of the Saints, ii, 5)*.

The ground underlying the assertion that faith does not stultify reason is because Augustine sees philosophy and theology in such a close harmony. To Thomas philosophy and theology were independent disciplines which supplement each other. To Occam they are independent disciplines which hardly supplement each other. *But to Augustine philosophy is the handmaiden of theology!* Perhaps it is over-statement but it might be said that the true theology is the true philosophy. If such a harmony exists between the two disciplines then faith and reason, revelation and philosophy cannot be thought of as fundamentally antithetical to each other.

"Far be it," cries Augustine, "that we would have faith without accepting or demanding reasons for our faith" *(Letters, I, 3)*. Constructive thought is possible only on the presupposition of belief. Reason functions only when interested and faith gives reason its interest. But reason may have good reason to reject that which faith proposes. Augustine positively affirms that "far from us the thought that God detests that whereby he has made us superior to other animals; far from us an assent of pure faith which dispenses us from accepting or demanding reasons" (*Letters,* CXX).

Faith without the scrutiny of reason is credulity. Genuine faith demands reasons and reason demands adequate grounds for faith. Faith is grounded, tested, verified testimony and achieves the status of being free from doubt. Faith in authority is faith in *reliable* authority. Faith is faith in an authority which would be *unreasonable* not to trust.

However reason is never reason isolated from morality. Just as sin and vice blind and cripple the reason, faith and hope enlighten it. Furthermore one cannot talk of reason or faith without talking of the *will*. Augustine has a very pronounced doctrine of the will. In fact the will is the most powerful of the human faculties. Faith is itself a species of the will for the will dictates to faith prior to knowledge. Otherwise will would bow to reason and lose its autonomy. But grace touches the will and teaches it to forsake its pride and thus comes to know the truth. Although it may appear that Augustine has made the human person arbitrary this is not quite the point. By making the will central in his anthropology he has made it moral. Coming into the truth is not mere intellectual vision but demands the act of the will in an act of moral obedience.

If the will is wrong the motions of the soul will be wrong; but if the will is right the motions of the soul will not only be "blameless, but even praiseworthy. For the will is in them; yea, none of them is anything less than will" (*City of God,* XIV, 6).

V. MIRACLE AND PROPHECY

Setting a pattern for centuries of apologetic writing Augustine brings prophecy and miracle into his system of Christian apologetics. The only demur is that in the total structure of his apologetics he puts much more stress on philosophical apologetics than upon Christian evidences.

1. *Miracles.* Augustine defines a miracle in a very modern fashion when he wrote: "But when such things happen in a continuous kind of river of everflowing succession, passing from the hidden to the invisible, and from the invisible to the visible to the hidden, by a regular and beaten track, then they are called natural; when, for the admonition of men, they are thrust in by an unusual

changeableness, then they are called miracles" *(On the Trinity, III, 6)*.

Augustine will not accept the report of any miracle. He mentions miracles of his own time but tells his readers that they are not to be gullible and accept these reports. He believes only those that "come under my own observation, or which any one can readily verify" *(City of God, XXI, 7)*. Biblical miracles presumably pass such tests. Further miracles cannot be rationally explained or else they would lose their miraculous character. The Christian knows that God does nothing without reason so there is a reason in miracles even though our frail minds cannot discover it. But one cannot boggle at this point because there are many things which reason cannot account for but which are true. Skeptics ask that miracles be "explained and because we cannot do so, inasmuch as [miracles] are above human comprehension, they suppose we are speaking falsely" *(City of God, XXI, 5)*.

However the universe is the greatest miracle of all! The world is filled with countless miracles "in sky, earth, air and waters, while itself is a miracle unquestionably greater and more admirable than all the marvels it is filled with" *(City of God, XXI, 7)*. Why then should men balk at miracles at all? The wonder of creation as a whole and in its parts constitutes a sufficient proof of the Biblical wonders. Miracles, therefore, are God's means *of attesting promises.*

2. *Prophecy.* It has been claimed that Augustine stated as clearly as it has ever been stated the argument from prophecy. Two such representative statements are: "But they are much deceived who think that we believe in Christ without any proofs concerning Christ. For what are clearer proofs than those things, which we now see to have been foretold and fulfilled" *(Concerning the Faith of Things not Seen, 5)* ; and, "What man might not be moved to faith in the doctrine of Christ by such a miraculous chain of events from the beginning, and by the manner in which the epochs of the world are linked together, so that our faith in regard to present things is assisted by what happened in the past, and the record of earlier and ancient things is attested by later and more recent events" *(Letters, CXXXVII, 15)*.

The two greatest works of Augustine are his *Confessions* and the *City of God.* The permanent enduring worth of the *Confessions* is the report of this man of this ancient classical period who could find no peace of heart or mind in the religions and philosophies of classical antiquity, but who in turn finds all he sought for in Jesus Christ and Christian truth. The great value of the *City of*

God is certainly first of all in the comprehensive Christian interpretation of history it gives, a contribution which is still being felt today. The work is also important for the massive attack it contains on the polytheism, immorality, and logical inconsistencies of Roman religion as it is contrasted with the grace, light, and truth in Christianity. The momentum of this man is yet with us for the spirit of Augustine was much alive in the Reformation, and also in the theology and apologetics of the contemporary Christian scene.

BIBLIOGRAPHY

The works of Augustine in translation may be found in such series as *Library of Christian Classics, Ancient Christian Writers, The Fathers of the Church, The Works of Aurelius Augustine, The Nicene and Post-Nicene Fathers.*
Adam, K., *St. Augustine*
Allin, A., *The Augustinian Revolution in Theology*
Battenhouse, R. W., editor, *A Companion to the Study of St. Augustine*
Bourke, V. J., *Augustine's Quest of Wisdom*
Burnaby, J., *Amor Dei. A Study of the Religion of St. Augustine*
Cochrane, C., *Christianity and Classical Culture*
Hessen, J., *Augustins Metaphysik der Erkenntnis*
Maritain, J., et al., *Monument to St. Augustine*
Richardson, A., *Christian Apologetics*
Pope, H., *St. Augustine of Hippo*
Warfield, B. B., *Studies in Tertullian and Augustine*
West, R., *St. Augustine*

Chapter IX

JOHN CALVIN (1509-1564)

INTRODUCTION

The Protestant Reformation is summed up in the names of Luther and Calvin. Luther stands at the head of the great Lutheran bodies of the world, and Calvin at the head of the more diverse Reformed movement. Although each Reformer was a genius in his own right—sketched out by Henry Strohl in his *La Pensée de la Réforme*—and each made a very unique contribution to the Reformation, yet it was Calvin who was the thorough systematizer and logician. The great foundations of Reformation apologetics was set forth by Calvin in the first few chapters of his *Institutes of the Christian Religion*. Unfortunately Protestant bodies have not been true to this apologetic system of Calvin's and even among the Calvinists and Reformed it has either been neglected or altered.

The main outlines of Calvin's life are well-known. The definitive life of Calvin is E. Doumergue, *Jean Calvin, Les hommes et les choses de son temps* (seven volumes). A brief and very sympathetic account of his life is provided for us in Emanuel Stickelberger's *Calvin, A Life*. His theology in its entirety and in its parts has been the subject of continous scholarly research. With the revival of Reformation research inspired by the emergence of neo-orthodox theology there has been a renaissance of Calvin study. The details will be found in Wilhelm Niesel's recent work, *The Theology of Calvin*.

Calvin's literary output was enormous. His *Institutes* run to over a thousand pages of crammed Latin text. His *Commentaries* are not only classics in exegetical skill but set a magnificent pattern for subsequent Protestant exegesis. Here is laid the scientific foundations of Protestant hermeneutics and biblical interpretation. We also have the *Letters* of Calvin and His *Tracts and Treatises*. And his literary output was matched by his preaching, teaching, and administrative activities. How he got so much done is unbelievable! And this in spite of his wretched health. Stickelberger describes it as follows:

> Subjected to maladies of the trachea, he had with pains in his side to spit blood when he had used his voice too much in the pulpit. Several attacks of pleurisy prepared the way for consumption whose helpless victim he became at the age of fifty-one. Constantly he suffered from the hermorrhoidal vein, the pains of which were unbearably

increased by an internal abscess that would not heal. Several times intermittent fever laid him low, sapping his strength and constantly reducing it. He was plagued by gallstones and kidney stones in addition to stomach cramps and wicked intestinal influenza. To all of this there was finally added arthritis. It was no exaggeration when he parenthetically wrote in a letter, "If only my condition were not a constant death struggle . . ." (*Op. cit.*, p. 86).

There were certain remarkable features about Calvin which help explain his great ability and influence. (i) Calvin was an expert *logician*. When in law school he excelled as a student. When Calvin writes he drives us all to the wall. If our facts are shoddy, or our reasons feeble, or our inductions faulty, Calvin will spot them. And if we wish to disagree with him we find we must think harder and reason better than we ever have before in our lives—if we wish to make a credible opposition or a decent case to the contrary! (ii) Calvin was an *exegete* of first class ability. Scholars feel that his greatest genius is in his *Commentaries* and not in his *Institutes*. In Biblical exegesis only Bengel and Calvin receive serious attention today of men who wrote before the rise of critical Biblical exegesis. (iii) Calvin was a *humanist* in his learning. The liberal arts supplied the requisite learning and tools for the service of theology. In contrast to the scholarship represented by the Roman Catholic scholastics Calvin (and Melanchthon, too) made a synthesis of the new learning of humanism with profound Reformation theology. (iv) Calvin was a *patristic scholar*. He attended the famous Lausanne conference in which Farel was debating the Roman Catholics. Calvin held his peace for four days and then when he spoke he revealed a masterful knowledge of the Church Fathers. A moments consultation of the index of his *Institutes* will verify that. (v) Finally, Calvin was a *versatile genius*. Classics? At the age of twenty-three he wrote a commentary on *De Clementia* in which he cited fifty-six Latin classical authors, and twenty-two Greek. He refers to thirty-three works of Cicero, all the works of Horace, Virgil and Ovid. He refers to Terence, Homer, Aristotle, Plato and Plutarch. Languages? His *Commentaries* reveal his skill in Hebrew, Greek and Latin. Law? When the legal experts of Geneva failed to write a new code of the city Calvin produced one in two weeks. Memory? He did all his first-rate work *before* the days of concordances and all the research tools available in our libraries! Practical? Calvin designed the sewer system of Geneva and started small industries to improve the economic situation of the city, some of which are still functioning today. Education? He laid the foundations of the famous Geneva Academy (curriculum, faculty members) which attracted students by the hundreds from all over Europe.

Luther and Calvin share two important theses together in their attitude towards Christian apologetics: (i) They both agreed that the synthesis of theology and philosophy achieved by the great scholastics of the Roman Catholic Church was more mischievious than helpful. It obscured both the authority and the clarity of the Word of God. Furthermore, Roman Catholic theologians had not fully explored the significance of the doctrine of original sin in its relationship to human reason. As Roger Mehl has pointed out in famous work, *La Condition de Philosophe Chrétien,* it was the Reformers who first attempted to explore systematically the serious consequences of sin upon the human reason. (ii) They both agreed that the Christian faith was autonomous. It did not need the support of a philosophy nor a battery of human arguments to make it credible. The Christian faith was sealed with the name of God! What more can be demanded than this? This too represented a radical break with the methodology of Roman Catholic theologians.

There are different schools of the interpretation of Calvin's apologetics. We note that even Warfield and Kuyper differed in their interpretation of the *Institutes* at this point. In recent times Barth and Brunner differ over Calvin's doctrine of "natural theology." And the recent scholarship is generally opposed to the older and more traditional Calvin scholarship. We shall give the interpretation of the apologetics of Calvin which we feel is closest to the opening chapters of the *Institutes* with proper understanding that there are alternate interpretations. We shall profit from the use of the latest translation of the *Institutes* and its scholarly apparatus (in the *Library of Christian Classics*, John T. McNeil, editor; F. L. Battles, translator).

I. THERE IS A VALID GENERAL REVELATION TO WHICH ALL MEN ARE ACCOUNTABLE

Calvin did not use these words but they are the contemporary counterparts to Calvin's thought. A *general* revelation is a revelation made to *all* men. It is a revelation man possesses because he is man, i.e., God's creature. If this revelation is properly apprehended it issues in two things: a valid knowledge of God, and a proper piety and worship of God. Calvin taught rather forcefully that such a general revelation did exist. But where did it exist? What is its locus?

1. *There is in man's nature a general revelation of God.* Calvin finds a number of elements in man's nature which are revelation-bearing. Man has a knowledge of God by natural endowment. Be-

cause he is man he has *a sense of deity*. This is not exactly the philosopher's doctrine of the innate idea of God. It is more the witness of God within the creature. It is more a continuous reflection of the divine majesty upon the consciousness of man than an idea deposited within man and abiding like a man's will or memory. There is a dynamic element here which typical philosophical doctrines of the innate idea of God miss. There is an "ever renewing [of] its memory" (I, iii, 1) .

This sense of deity creates in man the *seed of religion*. The divine witness produces the religious attitude, so to speak. If the sense of deity comes through unhindered, and if the seed of religion flourishes without interference, then there issues *true religion* (both in knowledge and worship) . To put it tersely: the sense of deity creates within man the seed of religion and the seed of religion creates religion as belief, practice and worship. This sense of deity is not learned nor acquired but it is present at birth. It is continuously impressed upon man during his total life-time, and it is impossible to efface it (I, iii, 3) .

Man's *talents or gifts* are revelation-bearing in that they point us to the Gracious Giver (I, v, 5). Man's skill in the arts, music, and sciences reveals to him *that he is gifted! But a gift is given!* The gift suggests the Giver, God himself. What a genius is born with is not his accomplishment and therefore must be reckoned as a gift from a higher source.

Man's *intelligence* is revelation-bearing. The nimbleness of the soul manifest in man's scientific research and other attributes of the soul in gaining knowledge are "unfailing signs of divinity in man" (I, v, 5) .

Man's *moral sense* is revelational for our moral experience is meaningless unless there is a Judge in heaven: "Shall we, indeed, distinguish between right and wrong by the judgment which has been imparted to us, yet will there be no judge in heaven?" (I, v, 5) .

Man's very *existence* is a witness for the existence of God. No man can look within himself—and here is a strand similar to Augustine's inward retreat—and contemplate his own existence without turning his heart towards God in whom he "lives and moves" (I, i, 1) .

Finally, man's sense of *depravity* is revelational. As again we look within and find out what we are we are caused to "recognize that true light of wisdom, sound virtue, full abundance of every good, and purity of righteousness rest in the Lord alone" (I, i, 1) .

2. *There is in creation a general revelation of God*. Although

we do not know God in himself because his essence is transcendent we do know God in his creation: "But upon his individual works he has engraved unmistakable marks of his glory, so clear and so prominent that even unlettered and stupid folk cannot plead the excuse of ignorance" (I, v, 1) . . . "this skillful ordering of the universe is for us a sort of mirror in which we can contemplate God, who is otherwise invisible" (I, v, 1). There are "innumerable evidences" (I, v, 2) in heaven and on earth which bear witness of God to the total human race. It is true that some features of God's great creation are known only to men of learning who can perform the proper research. There is much that such a person can learn of the divine wisdom and glory. But the universe as the work of God is so obvious that the dull and unlettered cannot miss its message. Pagans, sunk in terrible idolatry, are surrounded by the work of God speaking the lie to them of their idolatry. Neither dullness of wit nor primitive jungle existence are sufficient to cloud the obvious revelation of God in creation.

The conclusion is that a general revelation in creation does objectively exist. It exists so obviously no normal person can escape it. But here there is a compounding of the witness. The man who gazes upon nature is the man with the sense of deity and seed of religion within him. This inner witness of God concurs with the witness of God in creation to form a most certain witness to the being of God. Therefore, no man can plead ignorance from a knowledge of the being of God.

3. *There is a general revelation of God in God's providential care of man.* To the doctrine of creation must be added the doctrine of providence. God's providential actions are revelational for they reveal the goodness of his heart and the wisdom of his rule. There, accordingly, is an intense *activism* is Calvin's doctrine of God. God is *continuously* at work in his creation. He is no absentee landlord, nor indifferent Aristotelian God. His work is seen in the *seasons* whose alteration is the foundation of man's agricultural life and, therefore, reveal the kindness of a heavenly Father. His work is seen in the *animals* for they are given to man some to eat and some to bear his burdens. God's providence is seen in the *food* we eat for it is his gift for our sustenance. The *natural order* of the world around us with lakes and mountains, trees and minerals is still a further token and revelation of the providential care of God.

God's providence also extends to *history.* According to Calvin nothing happens willy-nilly. It all happens under the providential eye of God. Calvin emphasizes in particular the moral providence of God. The sinner *generally* ends up unhappy and wretched; the *believers* generally are rewarded for their righteousness and this reward is a revelation of the "unfailing rule of his righteousness" (I, v. 7). Calvin knows that there is the occasional Job who suffers though righteous, and that there is the wicked king who nevertheless prospers. Yet even this is part of the providence of God and does not obscure his righteousness. But when God so wills it and does grant his children a remarkable deliverance this is a revelation of a fatherly kindness (I, v, 8). The conclusion Calvin then reaches about the providence of God is that "Indeed, his wisdom manifests his excellence when he dispenses everything at the best opportunity; when he confounds all wisdom of the world; when 'he catches the crafty in their own craftiness.' In short, there is nothing that he does not temper the best way" (I, v, 8).

II. THE GENERAL REVELATION OF GOD IS RENDERED HELPLESS BY MAN'S DEPRAVITY SO THAT IT DOES NOT PRODUCE A TRUE KNOWLEDGE OF GOD OR A TRUE WORSHIP OF GOD

The *Institutes* commence with a discussion of the relationship of the knowledge of God to the knowledge of the self. Is God understood first, and then the self? Or is the self understood as the means of understanding God? He answers his own question by saying that "Yet, however the knowledge of God and of ourselves may be mutually connected, the order of right teaching requires that we discuss the former first, then proceed afterward to treat the latter" (I, i, 3). We cannot undestand the creature until we first understand the Creator. The knowledge of the lesser depends upon the knowledge of the Greater.

To know ourselves we must first know God. But what does it mean to know God? The expression, "God exists," is too barren for this weighty consideration. Calvin says much of the knowledge of God (which obviously includes God's existence) and little of the existence of God (which may not lead on to the crucial issue of the knowledge of God). We must not thus rest with the question of the existence of God but must press on to ask ourselves *what does it mean to know God?* Calvin's thesis is basically that if we know God who is a spiritual being then our knowing God must possess a spiritual character. We simply cannot say, "I believe God exists" in the same manner in which we say, "I believe atoms exist."

Calvin believes that *knowing* God demands a certain subjective state of piety and outward form of worship. This piety is a reverence and love for God (I, ii, 1). Where God is known he is loved, worshipped and trusted. Calvin emphatically asserts that *where there is no piety, God is not known!* (I, ii, 1). Therefore, *if general revelation is reaching man as it should, mankind would be properly knowing God and manifesting the piety and worship which necessarily attends the knowledge of God.*

But any survey of the religious life of man reveals everything to the contrary. There is a great diversity of opinions; there is an endless confusion of theologies; and there are numerous corrupt practices under the name of religion and God. Calvin draws the inevitable conclusion that general revelation is not getting through. Something is clogging up the channels and jamming the message! That something is human depravity.

The human race has degenerated from the law of its creation (I, iii, 3). The degeneration from this law means the corruption of the knowledge of God. Book I, Chapter IV is devoted to showing that man's depravity so corrupts man that the general revelation of God does not create the proper knowledge of God. On the contrary, the religious potential in man expresses itself in false religions. True religion conforms to the will of God (I, iv, 3) and no religion is genuine unless it is joined with truth (I, iv, 3). *Therefore, the corrupted religions of men cannot be based upon the knowledge of God.*

Human depravity spoils it all! Man himself is a sure work of divine wisdom. He is a "clear mirror of God's works," (I, v, 3); his bodily parts are witnesses of the exquisite workmanship of God (I, v, 4). Yet man cannot read this clearly. Creation is a clear manifestation of God's might (I, v, 6); it is filled with testimonies of God's power (I, v, 6); it is a revelation of the goodness of God (I, v, 6); and it is a record for all the world to see. Yet because man is depraved these "manifold testimonies . . . flow away without profiting us" (I, v, 11). Depravity expresses itself in many ways: in our hypocrisy, our whims, our pride, or our superstitions. In this depravity our minds create a "boundless filthy mire of error" (I, v, 12) and when they are not guided by divine truth they wander about in a labyrinth of error and confusion.

The conclusion is that the general revelation in the human being, in creation, and in providence fail to create a true knowledge of God in the human breast. Therefore, "it appears that if men were taught only by [general revelation] they would hold nothing certain or solid or clear-cut, but would be so tied to confused principles [in virtue of their depravity] as to worship an unknown God" (I, v, 12).

From the objective character of general revelation and the depravity of the human mind three things follow in Calvin's thought:

1. Even though man is depraved he is without excuse. The sense of deity is fixed deeply within us, "as it were in the very marrow" (I, iii, 3). No effort of man—no matter how strong—can efface it or avoid it. If man violently denies it or vigorously represses it, yet at critical experiences it reasserts itself. Thus the soldier who thinks he has once for all suppressed this inner witness of God suddenly finds it popping to the surface when the terrors of war rip off his own self-composure. Hence there are no atheists in fox-holes. Only when outward peace is restored can the soldier return to a somewhat successful suppression of this witness. But when calamity, dire sickness, or death's approach again crush the shell of self-composure he is again faced with the inward sense of deity.

Creation is filled with God's burning lamps showing forth the radiance and glory of the Creator. Sin has not changed these witnesses! The conclusion is that "although we lack the natural ability to mount up unto the pure and clear knowledge of God, *all excuse is cut off* because the fault of dullness is within us. And, indeed, we are not allowed thus to pretend ignorance without our conscience itself always convicting us of both baseness and ingratitude" (I, v, 15, italics are ours).

2. Intense *philosophical thought* cannot remedy the darkness occasioned by our depravity. That the rude and superstitious views of the uneducated should be condemned goes without saying (I, v, 12), but what about the views of learned and enlightened men? Here depravity reigns, too, unbroken! *The knowledge of God has been corrupted by all the philosophers* (I, x, 3).

This does not mean that Calvin has no relationships at all with the philosophers. *First*, we can trace philosophical elements of the scholastic, classical and contemporary periods in Calvin's writings. For some of his definitions he is as dependent upon philosophers as he is upon Scripture. *Secondly*, in that philosophers, too, are under the pressure of the sense of deity, they can possibly say some things which approximate the truth of God.

However, the important thing here is that critical, powerful, and enlightened human reason, as exhibited among the philosophers, is no match for human depravity. The philosophers who attempt to penetrate the secrets of heaven present us with a shameful diversity (I, v, 12), a diversity which a true knowledge of God cannot tolerate. If their offerings are carefully examined they will be found to be fleeting unrealities, another sign of the depravity of the philosopher. Stoics, Egyptians, Epicureans all wander in the labyrinth!

Even when the philosopher under the sense of deity approximates the truth of God he cannot prevent it from suffering corruption. "In this regard how volubly has the whole tribe of philosophers shown their stupidity and silliness" (I, v, 11). Even such a great mind as Plato is not exempt! If even the great ones like Plato stumble and fall in their "inclination towards vanity and error" (i, v, 11) what can be expected of ordinary people? In fact the human race is so confused that it can make no more sense out of the providence of God than it can if "all things were turned topsy-turvy by the heedless will of fortune" (I, v, 11). *The labyrinth prevails! Philosophers cannot decipher it!*

3. There will always be *corrupted religion*. Because man has an inerradicable sense of deity, because this creates an enduring seed of religion, *man is incurably religious*. He will worship something, and believe in something. But the depravity of his heart prevents him from coming to a true knowledge of God. In pagan religions there is a great *uniformity*. There is the uniformity of corrupt religion. There is also a great *diversity*. Depraved man creates endless numbers of religions and gods. Therefore, the knowledge of the true God given in Scripture "excludes and rejects all the gods of the heathen, for religion was commonly adulterated throughout almost all ages" (I, x, 3).

Calvin could never take a sympathetic view of comparative religions. All roads do not lead to God! If the belief in God includes *true piety and true knowledge of God* how can any one say that all religions are on the way to God if instead of true piety there is superstition and corruption and instead of a knowledge of God there is idolatry? One could only speak sympathetically here if one were to radically redefine what it means to believe in God and to know God and to worship God.

The most general conclusion is then (in modern terms) Calvin accepts a valid objective general revelation but due to man's depravity there can be no natural theology.

III. IT IS SPECIAL REVELATION WHICH ALONE CAN OVERCOME THE DEPRAVITY OF MAN AND RESTORE A TRUE KNOWLEDGE OF GOD

It is first of all to be noted that Calvin does not speak of apologetics as such. The apologetical issue to Calvin was whether there is a true knowledge of God or not. And the task of apologetics is to show that this is the case in Christian faith. Secondly, he does not use the expression "special revelation" but in our terms this is what he means. And thirdly, we note a lack of philosophical approach. Calvin was not ignorant of the philosophers, nor as we previously indicated is he completely free from their influence. But his method is certainly non-scholastic. He gives us no philosopher as his guide as Thomas pledges himself to Aristotle. Nor does he offer us any theory of knowledge or theory of reality as the pre-condition for writing theology.

Calvin's point is that when general revelation failed (the knowledge of God the Creator) God then came to man's rescue with "the light of his Word by which to become known unto salvation" (I, vi, 1, the knowledge of God the Redeemer). This is *special* revelation for its meets man's special condition, namely, his depravity. It is thus *soteric* or *redemptive* revelation. The theme of Book II, by the way of illustration, is the knowledge of God the Redeemer in Christ.

The patriarchs did receive the Word of God by many different modes (I, vi, 2). The Word which they received made their faith clear and unambiguous. It was handed down from generation to generation so that each generation could have it for its heritage. Whatever rays of light were left over from general revelation were not sufficient to save. These are reënforced by special revelation and added to the redemptive knowledge of special revelation form the total corpus of special revelation. It is that "inner knowledge" of special revelation alone which mediates the knowledge of God as Mediator and Redeemer and thus saves the soul (I, vi, 1).

Two things must be noted here: (a) The emphasis on revelation as redemptive is very important and very strong. Revelation is not dishing out truth as such, but truth as it heals and corrects our depravity. (b) Although Calvin does not give any extensive treatment he discusses *soteric revelation in principle* before he discusses Sacred Scripture. There is special, soteric revelation *before* there is Scripture.

Calvin is aware that the depravity of man can corrode an oral tradition. It was therefore necessary that the special redemptive revelation be put into written form: "In order that truth might abide forever in the world with a continuing succession of teaching and survive through all ages, the same oracles he had given to the patriarchs it was his pleasure to have recorded, as it were on public tables" (I, vi, 2).

Certainly some Israelites heard the word of God directly from the prophets. Others heard the word second hand or third hand from those who heard the prophets. But most of the Israelites came to know the word of God in the writings of the prophets for their writings "were passed down to posterity in but one way:

from hand to hand" (I, viii, 9). In virtue of having been written down the heavenly doctrine of special revelation will not perish through forgetfulness nor will it be corrupted through error nor will it be altered by the audacity of men (I, vi, 3). *For all concrete purposes, for all practical purposes the written Word is exactly the Word of special revelation to Calvin.*

The objectivity of a word of special revelation is no less than the general revelation engraved upon the immense frame of the visible universe. It is a revelation called into being by reason of man's depravity. It was forged and fashioned to remedy that corruption. Of course it presumes both the reality and the priority of redemption. But Calvin is not here dealing with justification or regeneration but with salvation as it pertains to the knowledge of God. If the cross overcomes our guilt, and if the resurrection overcomes our spiritual death, then special revelation overcomes our sinful ignorance. This special revelation is then for us sinners "the rule of eternal truth" (I, vi, 3). It is the thread of Ariadne which lead us out of the "inexplicable labyrinth of the mind" (I, vi, 3). It is the spectacles which enables a man to read the record of general revelation correctly (I, vi, 1).

Calvin does not split up his apologetics. He does not prove that God is, then that the Christian God is the true God. He does not prove the formal inspiration of Scripture, and then the Saviorhood of Christ. It is one piece to Calvin. The knowledge of God is the knowledge of God as Redeemer; the revelation of God is revelation of redemption; the redemption of God is the redemption in Jesus Christ.

IV. SPECIAL REVELATION AS OBJECTIVE REVELATION PRESERVED IN THE FORM OF SCRIPTURE NEEDS THE WITNESS OF THE SPIRIT TO ESTABLISH IT IN THE HEART AS THE TRUTH OF GOD

Calvin would not tolerate the implicit suggestion of some recent writing in theology that the witness of the Spirit somehow *makes* the Bible the Word of God. This would run counter to his arguments against the Romanists in which he insisted that the Word of God is the Word of God in itself. Scripture is Scripture because it is Scripture! The Church cannot make it something that it really is not; and if it is really Scripture the Church cannot add anything to its certainty as Scripture. Calvin's favorite word here is *majesty*. The Scripture has an inherent *majesty* which so effectively impresses the mind that no ecclesiastical imprimatur is at all necessary.

The clear word of God in Scripture needs an inward assist due to the depravity of man. The true word of God must be seen as the Word of God. Revelation must be grasped as revelation. Revelation must be grasped with a divine certainty. *We cannot rest divine truth upon human opinion.* Thus in Calvin's great doctrine of the witness of the Spirit we have the cure. *The Holy Spirit enables us to see revelation as revelation; and the revelation is received with a divine certainty.* This witness of the Spirit is thus an *illumination* and a *persuasion.*

Of course Calvin is not speaking of a mere formal certification of the Scriptures as the Word of God. Special revelation is *soteric* revelation, and its theme is *the knowledge of God as Redeemer through Christ!* It is a recognition of Scripture as the *redemptive* Word of God.

Calvin is constructing here the Protestant doctrine of certainty (and biblical!) in contrast to the Roman Catholic doctrine. The break-through of course came with Luther and one can find it in his great commentary on Galatians and in his theological masterpiece, *The Bondage of the Will.* But Calvin gives it theological precision and exposition. According to the Roman Catholic teaching the Scriptures do not give a certain witness of their divine origin. The magisterial word of the Church is necesary to remove doubt about the Scripture's supernatural origin. Christian certainty is then ultimately the certainty arising from a divine and infallible society, the Roman Catholic Church. Calvin counters this by asserting that the Word of God possesses its own inherent *majesty.* This *majesty* is greater than any word of the Church. Rather than the Scripture's needing reënforcement for its *majesty* by the word of the Church, the Church needs the Scriptural word to know that it is the Church. But human depravity does blind the heart of man to the *majesty* of Scripture. Here is the difficulty and not in the so-called ambiguous character of Scripture—as the Romanists assert. The cure proper to the malady is the inner witness of the Spirit where the depravity of man is directly overcome and releasing him to see the *majesty* of the Scripture!

The witness of the Spirit is truly a divine persuasion. The Church is composed of sinful men and can only give a corroborating witness—which Calvin admits it can give (I, viii, 12). But the Spirit alone can give the divine witness and so end all doubt. There will be doubt until a man hears the word of Scripture as if God himself were reciting it. This doubt cannot be removed by human reasons nor reasoning. It is only the witness of the Spirit which makes us feel as if God were reciting the Scriptures to us.

In this all doubt is overcome and the Christian possesses a certainty which is truly divine.

Calvin in effect thereby places the Church and human reason *beneath* the Scriptures and as inferior to the witness of the Spirit. The Church is *beneath* the Word of God for it is the Word of God which creates the Church! Reason is beneath the Word of God for it can never escape its own human limitations nor overcome its own weakened depravity and so give the human mind a divine certainty about divine things.

However, Calvin might be cornered from another direction. It might be agreed that the Church is composed of sinners and therefore needs the assurance of the divine Word that it is the Church rather than giving the divine Word its imprimatur; and it might be agreed that sinful man, even in the role of learned and astute philosopher, cannot decode the secrets of heaven; yet a fusion of human reason and divine truth in the form of Christian evidences could lead the human mind to full certainty. To this problem Calvin devotes Book I, Chapter VIII.

Calvin believes that there are substantial reasons or evidences which in themselves manifest the divine origin of the Scriptures and the Christian faith. Christian evidences do provide "wonderful confirmation" and show that the Scriptures do "breathe something divine" (I, viii, 1). The Scripture does have a *majesty* and *dignity* of its very own which is not obscured by its "mean and lowly words" nor by its "rude and unrefined style" (I, viii, 1, 2). The Christian may appeal to the well-ordered divine providence, to the heavenly character of the Scriptural doctrines, to the agreements of the parts of Scriptures with each other, to the antiquity of Scripture, to the remarkable preservation of the Scripture, to miracles, to prophecy, to the unbroken witness of the Church to the Scripture ("it has obtained its authority by the holy concord of divers people," I, viii, 12), and to the attestation of the blood of martyrs.

All of these show the "heavenly inspiration" of the Scriptures; that the Scriptures are the oracles of the Holy Spirit; that the Scriptures are oracles of God; that the Scriptures bear a heavenly majesty; that the Scriptures are supported by solid props; and that the Scriptures are "brilliantly vindicated against the wiles of its disparagers" (I, viii, 13).

But these evidences are no match for human depravity. If we use them as battering rams against unbelief they simply bounce back! The wall remains firm. Therefore Calvin does not appeal to them as the means whereby human unbelief is crashed through. Arguments, the common agreement of the Church, or other helps are not strong enough for this task (I, viii, 1). After passing the evidences in review Calvin says that "of themselves they are not strong enough to provide a firm faith," and that it is foolish to try to use them to prove to unbelievers that the Scriptures are the Word of God (I, viii, 13).

It is the witness of the Spirit which is the match for human depravity. It is the Spirit who can give the believer a certainty "higher and stronger than any human judgment" and which removes the issue from all doubt (I, viii, 1). It is the witness of the Spirit which not only evicts from the heart all doubt but lets the truth shine in its own light, and lets it stand without external props (I, viii, 1). By the witness of the Spirit the Heavenly Father reveals his majesty in Scripture and raises the authority of Scripture beyond all controversy. The conclusion is then that the "Scripture will ultimately suffice for a saving knowledge of God only when its certainty is founded upon the inward persuasion of the Holy Spirit" (I, viii, 13). This is the chief and highest testimony to the Scriptures!

However, Calvin does not thereby totally discount evidences. Both at the beginning and at the end of Chapter VIII he expresses their function. Christian evidences play a confirming role *after* the Spirit has sealed his witness in our hearts. In fact they point in a different direction. Whereas the Spirit gives the soul a profound inward assurance of truthfulness in the gospel, the evidences direct our eyes towards more external, more objective verifications. Therefore, to neglect them in theology would be to invite the serious charge of subjectivism. But in themselves they are not strong enough to fix the certainty of Scripture in our minds, but after the Spirit has done this they are "useful aids" and "wonderful confirmation[s]," I, viii, 1). Or, as he says at the conclusion of the chapter, Christian evidences function as *secondary aids* to our feebleness [*imbecillitas*, weakness, helplessness, feebleness] in confirming the Scripture as God's truth.

Here the Augustinian character of his thought again shines through. The opening words of the *Institute* are Augustinian. The quest for happiness in terms of *wisdom* is Augustinian as is the correlation of the knowledge of God with the knowledge of man. In agreement with Augustine Calvin says that our methodology in this matter must conform to Augustine. To attempt to prove Christ to unbelievers is to presume that the unbeliever can see, know, and understand *prior to faith*. To attempt this is certainly foolish (*enepte*, impropriety, absurdly)!

According to Augustine *first* must come godliness and peace of mind (i.e., faith), and *then* comes understanding!

But there is yet another way to err in this matter. The Church cannot give us certainty because it is founded on the Word of God and it is confusion to think the building is the foundation of the foundation! Reason cannot give us certainty because it is caged in by human depravity. Christian evidences is rejected as the first line of defense because it presupposes that man can know prior to the illumination of the Holy Spirit. But can we not go one step more and say that the work of the Spirit is so *direct* and so *powerful* that it does not even need the Scriptures? To this claim Calvin devotes Book I, Chapter IX.

The thesis of the fanatic is that they think that it is unworthy of the Holy Spirit to limit themself to Sacred Scripture (I, ix, 2). The Spirit works directly and impressively upon the human heart and out of this great religious experience arises our Christian certainty. This Calvin calls a forsaking of the Scripture and a guidance by frenzy (I, ix, 1).

Calvin attacks them with the principle of consistency. The Holy Spirit is consistent with himself. The Spirit of Christ, the Spirit of Sacred Scripture, and the Spirit of Christian experience is one. To claim that the Spirit of Christ in religious experience is different from the Spirit of God set forth in Scripture is to chop up the Spirit. Calvin appeals to Isaiah 59:21 to show that God guides his people by his Spirit *and* his Word. To separate the Spirit from the Word is "heinous sacriledge" (I, ix, 1). The ministry of the Spirit is not to teach new doctrines nor to give radically new revelations. The ministry of the Spirit is to seal "our minds with that very doctrine which is commended by the gospel" (I, ix, 1), i.e., by the written Word of God.

But, Calvin asks, how do we identify the Spirit? There are many spirits but which is the Spirit of God? There are many religious experiences but which one is inspired by God's Spirit? Calvin's answer is that the image of the Spirit is traced for us in the Sacred Scriptures. If the Spirit we relate ourselves to has the same contours as the image of the Spirit in Sacred Scripture *then* we have to do with God's Spirit. If we can trace our religious experiences to the Spirit of Christ and the Spirit of Sacred Scripture *then we are never deceived in our experiences.*

Thus Calvin writes: "For by a kind of mutual bond the Lord has joined together the certainty of his Word and of his Spirit so that the perfect religion of the Word may abide in our minds when the Spirit, who causes us to contemplate God's face, shines; and that we in turn may embrace the Spirit with no fear of being deceived when we recognize him in his own image, namely in the Word" (I, ix, 3).

The Spirit does work with God's people. But when he works with them the Word of God is his instrument (I, ix, 3). And therefore the only Spirit Christians may recognize in truth and in good conscience is the Spirit whose image conforms to the image of the Spirit in the Word of God.

Therefore the certification of the Christian faith is not to be found in the utterances of a proposed infallible Church; nor in rationalistic Christian evidences; nor in the appeals of philosophers to reason; nor is ecstatic experiences of the Holy Spirit. It is to be found in the knowledge of God as Creator and Redeemer; it is to be found in the union of Word and Spirit; it is to be found in special revelation centering on the person of Christ and affirmed by the inner witness of the Holy Spirit.

The *sum of all our wisdom* (I, i, 1) is then the knowledge of God in special revelation; the knowledge of our selves through Christ our Lord; and the knowledge of God, man and Christ in the pages of Scripture illuminated by the Holy Spirit.

BIBLIOGRAPHY

Calvin, John, *Institutes of the Christian Religion*. Library of Christian Classics, Vol. XX

Hoitenga, D. J., "Calvin and the Philosophers," *The Reformed Journal*, pp. 11-13, February, 1958

Hunter, A. M., "The Erudition of John Calvin," *The Evangelical Quarterly* 18:199-208, July 1946

Kantzer, K. S., "John Calvin and the Holy Scriptures," *Inspiration and Interpretation* (J. Walvoord, editor)

Krusche, W., *Das Wirken des Heiligen Geist nach Calvin*

Niesel, W., *The Theology of Calvin*

Parker, T. H. L., *The Doctrine of the Knowledge of God*. A Study in the Theology of John Calvin

Stickelberger, E., *Calvin, a Life*

Strohl, H., *La Pensée de la Réforme*

Torrance, T. R., *Calvin's Doctrine of Man*

Wallace, R. S., *Calvin's Doctrine of Word and Sacrament*

Warfield, B. B., *Calvin and Augustine*

Chapter X

ABRAHAM KUYPER (1837-1920)

A couple in Holland had a young child whose head seemed too large for such a youngster so they took him to a German specialist to see if the cause might be water on the brain. The verdict of the doctor after due examination of the child's head was "Bewahre, das ist alles Gehirn"—"By no means! It is all brains." And truly it was all brains for the youngster was Abraham Kuyper and all of Holland came to know the products and the powers of these brains.

Without question one of the greatest men that Holland has ever produced was Kuyper. If there was ever a match for Calvin, point for point, it would be "Bram" Kuyper. His preaching was the finest in the land and a full church attended his pulpit ministry. His political addresses were masterpieces of logic and oratory. The amount of material he wrote is staggering—thousands upon thousands upon thousands of pages. Year after year he wrote for the *Heraut* and the *Standaard* besides writing lectures, political speeches, sermons, and books. As an educator he not only founded the Free University of Amsterdam, taught such a diversity of subjects as Hebrew, Homiletics, Aesthetics, and Theology, but later as prime minister saw a bill through the legislature which reconstructed the educational system of Holland. As politician he was active most of his life. Besides writing politically in his journalistic work, he served in the legislature as a member, then as a prime minister, but always as the head of his party either in name or in spirit.

Besides being a preacher and minister he became a strong leader in the Reformed Church in Holland. He was really three men in one—politician, professor, and pastor! As pastor he gave his church distinguished service until he was called to a more general service. As church leader he attempted to guide his church through difficult theological waters. As theologian he not only founded a university on Christian principles but he also became its first professor of dogmatics and its greatest author. His life's masterpiece was his great *Theological Encyclopedia*, the central part of which is translated into English as *Principles of Sacred Theology* (or, in the first printing, *Encyclopedia of Sacred Theology*). His other great work is *The Work of the Holy Spirit*. Besides being an expert in theology (and also very capable in comparative philology) he was a great Christian devotionalist. After reading one of Kuyper's devotional works one finds most other volumes rather trite. The deepest water is in Kuyper.

Kuyper was raised in a typical Dutch orthodox home. However in university days he became fascinated with the modernist theology of the day and swung over to it. Vanden Berg cites Kuyper as writing: "I entered the university a young man of orthodox faith, but I had not been in the school more than a year and a half before my thought processes had been transformed into the starkest intellectual rationalism" (*Abraham Kuyper*, p. 19). However, in his first pastorate he contacted a very devout and very orthodox group in his Church and through their witness and his many discussions with them he found his way back to the faith of his youth and home. Having understood orthodoxy from the inside both in youth and adult life, and having entertained modernism and "dreamed the dream" of modernism and thereby knowing it too from the inside, he was prepared to be a giant in the defense of historic Calvinism. After his conversion back to his earlier orthodox faith he set himself to master Calvin and this he did. But there is a sweetness to Kuyper's Calvinism. Calvinism can show a hard cold edge in its attempt to separate truth from error, in its attempt to defend the glory of God in terms of absolute decrees and unconditional covenants, in its attempt to show the depravity and finitude of man. But this edge cannot be found in this man for he sets his thought well within a devout Christological frame of reference.

I. CALVINISM, A LIFE-SYSTEM

One of the trite testimonies one hears is "Jesus saves, keeps and satisfies." Kuyper would have no problem in agreeing to this but as a sum of Christian experience he would most likely declare it wretchedly short-sighted. In giving his Stone Lectures at Princeton Theological Seminary he commenced with a lecture entitled, "Calvinism A Life-System" (*Calvinism*, p. 9). Calvinism was not exhausted in our doctrine of salvation. It called forth the entire man and the entire man in his cultural commitments—politics, science, art, education. His entire educational philosophy which he built into the curriculum of the Free University was that Christianity calls us to a total life-perspective, a total way of living, to a *Weltanschauung*.

Certainly Kuyper was a Christian and he knew, well that Christian faith dwelt in all kinds of hearts which entertained a great diversity of theological beliefs. He by no means identified saving faith and Christian conviction with a certain creed or confession. But he felt that the purest form of Christian theology was Reformed Theology (*Principles*, p. 50). Of course, Reformed Theology and Calvinism were one and the same to him. So he could write in his work, *Calvinism*: "In Calvinism my heart has found rest. From Calvinism have I drawn the inspiration firmly and resolutely to take my stand in the thick of this great conflict of principles" (p. 12). His apologetic at this point is rather clear and straightforward: only the Reformed Faith, only a full-orbed Calvinism, can offer the most satisfactory interpretation of man, his nature, his culture, his civilization, and his religion. Nor must we stop here! Calvinism is not merely a victor in consistency of thought. Calvinism is the best guide of life, the most satisfactory rule of living, and the best plan of action for individual, church or state. It alone offers unity of thought and action, and of culture and social change. Kuyper thus argues that the harmonies of life individually or corporately, scientifically or ecclesiastically, politically or artistically are to be found in Calvinism. Any other world-view seriously defaults at many critical points.

II. THE UNIVERSALIZING OF THE CONCEPT OF FAITH

There are two prevalent notions about faith which Kuyper challenges: (a) that the human race may be neatly divided into two groups—those who have faith and those who do not; and (b) that all clear logic and scientific research is free from the leaven of faith.

1. Kuyper—taking a cue from Augustine—asserts that faith is a structural part of universal human nature. Faith is not that which divides the religious from the irreligious. Certainly the human race is properly divided on the issue of *saving* faith but not on faith in itself. Saving faith is but a special function of general faith. To be a human being is to have a faith-structure in one's nature for this faith-structure is part of universal human nature (*Principles*, pp. 125-126).

If this is true any discussion of faith cannot commence with the presupposition that religious people have faith and unbelievers do not. It must begin with the conception of faith as a "formal function," as a "universal character" (*Principles*, p. 125). Because faith is a structural part of universal human nature it is elusive. That which is a common denominator is taken for granted and not usually the subject of a critical analysis. It is because faith is such a common denominator that it is not really properly recognized for what it is.

The faith-structure functions in all human knowing. Philosophers have pointed out that our convictions about things are always in advance of the evidence. For example in our *sensory experience* we believe that we are seeing things and not little pictures in our minds (even though a few philosophers may defend the latter). But whenever we carefully attempt to track down the evidence for this conviction we stumble. Yet we really do believe that we see trees or cats or rivers. Or consider our treatment of *the laws of science*. We hold that the generalizations of the scientists are true for all places and all times—yet their evidence is based upon so few experiments in such few places. Wherein comes our boldness to convert such meagre evidence into such comprehensive assertions?

Kuyper's answer to the problem of the certainty of our sensory experience, and the universalizing of our laws of science is *the faith-structure*. Faith is "that function of the soul by which it obtains certainty directly and immediately, without the aid of discursive demonstration" (*Principles*, p. 129). Kuyper would thus agree that Hume and Russell were correct in spotting the discrepancy between our convictions and our sense data, but failed in their answer when they retreated to a barren, negating skepticism. Further, Kuyper would agree with Kant that the glue which puts our universe together is a structure within the mind but Kuyper located it in the faith-structure and not in Kant's battery of categories.

Accordingly, when I look at a tree and believe that I see a tree, and that I am not deceived in seeing a tree, it is faith assuring me of the report of my senses.

2. Faith is, furthermore, the root of science. Kuyper argues this on three grounds.

(a) Observation is grounded in faith. In that science deals with empirical reality—the space, time, material universe—it is helpless without observation. But only as the ego assures us *in faith* that our senses are telling us the truth can we proceed with our observations. Kuyper's argument here is quite forceful. Observation is itself not scientific. Nor is the sheer use of instruments in observation scientific for that is but the extension of observation. It is the ego which must assure us in virtue of the faith-structure that we really see things which enables science to get off the ground. Without faith giving us certitude in our observations science would not exist and could not exist.

(b) The forming of axioms is grounded in faith. Axioms cannot be demonstrated. For example to prove any of the basic rules of

logic *involves those rules in the proof.* One cannot prove the law
of identity, that A = A, without assuming it throughout the
proof. But we possess an absolutely fundamental conviction of
certitude with reference to axioms. Where does this certitude come
from? It is a product of the faith-structure in man! Just as the ego
binds us to the faithful delivery of our senses, it also binds us to
the trustworthiness of our axioms, and it does both of these in
virtue of the faith-structure.

(c) Only in faith is there a motive for science. Science seeks
the general law. But science can only work with a small handful
of incidents. Science is always violating the strict rule of logic and
making universal statements out of a very limited number of
instances. For example if a new drug works on five hundred cases
then we presume it will work on all possible cases. There is no
logical justification in moving from five hundred to all. Yet
science must do this very thing. If we deny the right of science to
go against the stream of logic in proceeding from a few instances
to a universal law then there simply can be no science. The
resolution of the difficulty is the introduction of the faith-structure.
It is the ego's faith which provides the justification. Kuyper does
not absurdly argue that the ego makes up evidence for the process
of generalizing in science, rather "the idea itself that there are
such laws, and that when certain phenomena exhibit themselves,
you are certain of the existence of such laws, does not result from
your demonstration, but your demonstration rests, and in the end
it appears the means by which your certainty is obtained. Without
faith in the existence of the general in the special, in laws which
govern this special, and in your right to build a general conclusion
on a given number of observations, you would never come to
acknowledge such a law" (*Principles*, p. 139).

For apologetical theory the concept of faith is very important.
It sets forth faith as the root of our rationality and not as a jello-
like subjectivity. If there is faith in religion it is there in integrity
for it is part of the universal character of human nature. The
antithesis is not between faith and reason, but between faith and
demonstration. Faith is the presupposition of all demonstration.

III. THE TRAGEDY OF SIN AND THE RESTORATION IN REGENERATION

As a disciple of Augustine and Calvin, Kuyper finds it necessary
to calculate the extent of the destruction in human nature wrought
by sin. In his estimation one cannot write about apologetics without taking the measure of sin's ruin. Its "fatal effects" (*Principles*,

p. 107) must be counted up. Kuyper finds *fatal effects* in three areas.

1. Sin works a destructive effect *in our minds*. Kuyper spells out a seven-fold corrosion of the mind by sin. It makes us assert falsehoods; it makes us subject to unintentional mistakes; it leaves us exposed to self-delusion and self-deception; it distorts our powers of imagination; it makes us ready victims to the evil communications of other minds; it exposes the soul to spiritual maladies which arise from corresponding physical maladies; its works destructively in our relationships with other peoples; and it fractures the inner harmony of the self.

2. Sin works a destructive effect *in our moral motives*. Whenever man interprets, whatever the subject matter happens to be, he interprets from his own perspective. In that it is *his* perspective he interprets it from his personal interest. Interpreting from personal perspective and personal interest is not an evil of itself, nevertheless it is a very soft spot in our defenses against sin. Sinful men are prone to make selfish interpretations. Thus our moral motivation is *ambiguous at the root*. This does not mean that we are conscious of sinful motivation. It means that sin exerts its continuous pressure upon us and, therefore, our motivation and decisions are sinful.

3. The most drastic effect of sin upon us is with reference to the darkening of our natures *in their understanding*. The trouble here is deeper than any possible effect of sin upon our ability to think logically. For knowledge to exist in its fulness there must be a rapport between the knower and the object. This rapport is fundamentally a species of love. Sin is estrangement (not rapport) and man in estrangement loses his power of love, Therefore, man is estranged from the objects he would wish to know. He is estranged from *creation* for he does not know creation as he should. He is estranged from *himself* and the life-harmony of the ego and of his being is fractured. There is a discord within the innermost being of man. He is estranged from *God*. Sinful man cannot know the soul, the world, nor God as he should.

This frightful condition is the state of *unregeneracy*. The entire race is plunged into this condition by human sin. All scientists, all philosophers, all theologians, all scholars are (apart from the grace of God) unregenerate. The humanity of creation—Adam and the race to be produced by him as a race-family—is fractured by sin into a aggregate of individuals.

The cure of unregeneracy is regeneration! *Palingenesis*—the transliteration of the Greek word for regeneration. The Holy Spirit works the work of regeneration making sinners new men in Christ and thus they differ at root from men in sin. Although this difference is fundamental, decisive, and indelible there is no absolute difference between the unregenerate and the regenerate: (a) In that Christian principles have been deeply imbedded in western culture both regenerate and unregenerate have conducted social and personal affairs in terms of these principles. True, since the advent of modern philosophy and science this common area of Christian principles is appreciably shrinking. (b) In that Christians and non-Christians can agree on the elementary deliveries of the senses and the simple judgments of weights, times, and measurements the difference is not absolute. And (c) the Christian himself is not radically remade but in most ways remains continuous with his old self.

However, even though this difference is not absolute it is *decisive*. As soon as there is any discussion between regenerate and unregenerate about something which involves principle the difference between the two consciousnesses or mentalities immediately appears. Any apologetics which does not reckon with this decisive difference will be routed. Concessions to please the unregenerate mind can be no part of real Christian strategy.

This may seem to argue for two truths—truths for the unregenerate and truths for the regenerate. But truth is one and not two. The duality is not in the truth but in the radically different set of presuppositions between the Christian and the non-Christian. To deny that such a radical difference obtains is to miscalculate the corruptive and depraving influence of sin.

IV. SPECIAL REVELATION, THE CENTER OF GRAVITY IN CHRISTIAN APOLOGETICS

If Kuyper's over-all perspective is Calvinism or Reformed Theology, his concrete working principle is the principle of special revelation. Although this is working out the basic theses of Calvin it cannot be denied that Kuyper gave them the touch of his own genius.

1. *The objective genealogy of revelation.* As a good Calvinist, Kuyper locates the origin of all God's actions, including those of revelation, in the glory of God. Unless God did things for his own glory he would not be God. If God is the supreme Being,

then it is axiomatic that his supreme motive for acting is his own glory.

When a man speaks he speaks out of his fund of knowledge. He has *something* to say because he *knows* something. What does God speak out of when he speaks? According to Kuyper he speaks out of the perfect knowledge that he has of himself. Using the terminology of older theologians Kuyper identifies this perfect self-knowledge of God as the archetypal knowledge of God. This is the ultimate and common root of all revelation and, therefore, of all knowledge of God. If we cannot trace back our theological beliefs to this ultimate source they are nothing but human opinions. If we can trace them back to this root then we know that we know God!

However, God does not give us a complete volume of all the divine knowledge! Only a small part of the self-knowledge of God is conveyed to man. Furthermore, it cannot be given in any divine or heavenly form, but only in a form suitable to man—in a cosmic or anthropomorphic form, or, in an adjusted or accommodated form. This segment of the archetypal knowledge of God cast in the form of human language and accommodated for the proper assimilation of human beings is the *ectypal* knowledge of God. The archetype is the original, and the ectype is the copy. The knowledge of God is drawn from the archetypal knowledge of God, conveyed through the processes of revelation, and comes to man as ectypal knowledge.

Kuyper is no narrow biblicist. He knows that revelation may exist as tradition and says that at the formal question of the existence of tradition as a form of revelation we have no debate with the Roman Catholics (*Principles*, p. 399). Abraham, Isaac, Jacob and Joseph lived out their years without a Sacred Scripture, but certainly in virtue of ectypal knowledge of God. Special revelation is wider than Sacred Scripture, and takes its first embodiment as *tradition*.

Taking his cue from Calvin, Kuyper follows through that the difficulties in preserving a revelation as tradition call for a revelation as Scripture. Kuyper has a wide and a narrow definition of inspiration. In the wider sense inspiration is the various actions of God upon man which are necessary to produce a revelation. In the narrow sense it is *graphic*, i.e., it has to do with the production of an inspired Scripture. Mankind's weakness through sin, and mankind's rebellion against the truth of God would eventually corrupt an oral tradition. The inspired Scripture renders the revelation as objective, durable, catholic, and pure.

2. *The subjective genealogy of revelation.* According to Kuyper revelation is soteriological. He follows Calvin in dividing our knowledge of God into our knowledge of God as Creator and our knowledge of God as Redeemer. This is but another way of spelling out the distinction between general and special revelation. Special revelation is *soteric.* It is *remedial* of the consequences of sin. This has great importance for the manner in which we regard Scripture.

First of all it means that the Scripture is essentially a book of redemption. Whatever else may be in Scripture it is first of all a record of the gospel. Secondly, the first intention of special revelation is to save the sinner. The sinner does not participate in revelation as a school boy participates in the class lesson, but he participates in it *with his being.* Through revelation he becomes saved!

This means that when the sinner participates in revelation he becomes regenerate. Special revelation comes with the purpose of regeneration. It is the instrument of the Holy Spirit whereby he effects our regeneration. It creates the subjective anchor of theology for only the regenerate can truly engage in Christian theology. It creates the great subjective division of the human race into regenerate and unregenerate. It is the beginning of the new impulse of life which shall not cease until it comes to its final realization in the cosmic regeneration of all things.

A very important element of special revelation must be spelled out and at this point Kuyper makes a noticeable improvement over Calvin (although the seed idea is in Calvin). In passing he also corrects by anticipation some of the things said today incorrectly of the historic view of revelation.

First, revelation must come to the sinner in such a way that he can get his teeth into it. If humans could listen to the chatter of angels they would find it incomprehensible. God's revelation, to the contrary, "corresponds entirely to the character of our human nature and our human consciousness" (*Principles,* p. 217). As Calvin put it, God bends down and lisps his revelation to us as a nurse lisps to the young child in teaching it how to speak. Revelation is no rock thrown over the wall. Revelation is no arrow shot from heaven's ramparts to earth's crust. Revelation is no telegram cabled from heaven to earth. It is something bent down to our level, cast into our language, structured in terms of our culture, diced up small enough for our minds! Therefore, it comes as no foreign substance which our mental tissue perforce would eject.

Secondly, the sinner can get his teeth into special revelation in the sense that believing it, it becomes a principle of the knowledge of God within him. It does create in man, redemptively of course, a restored knowledge of God. The sinner is recreated in being and renewed in ,mind. Thus the revelation is spiritually assimilated by the sinner.

Thirdly, this assimilation is assisted by the help of the Holy Spirit. At this point Kuyper brings to bear with great energy and theological penetration the doctrine of the internal witness of the Holy Spirit. In his works—*Calvinism, Principles of Sacred Theology, The Work of the Holy Spirit*—he reproduces for recent theology Calvin's great doctrine of Book I, Chapter VII of the *Institutes.* If Calvin was the first great theologian of the Holy Spirit of the Christian Church, Kuyper is certainly the second.

V. THE PRODUCT OF SPECIAL REVELATION AS THE KNOWLEDGE OF GOD IS THEOLOGY, THE SCIENCE OF GOD

Kuyper lived in a time of great theological turmoil. He himself went from orthodoxy to modernism and back to orthodoxy. He saw the trend of modernism to define theology as "the science of religion" and not as the science of God. To this redefinition of theology Kuyper reacted with all the powers of his mind and all the artillery of his learning. The entire life-system of modernism came to its logical expression in defining theology as the science of religion. Kuyper did not deny the right of an objective study of religion as a psychological and sociological phenomenon. But it was a terrible betrayal of everything Christian to call the descriptive study of religion by the name of theology. To call the study of religion theology would be like calling the activities of the physicists physics!

By its very etymology theology means the science of God. How can it be the science of religious men? religious cults? religious states? religious activities? This is not just a matter of formal definition with Kuyper. It is not a case of more precisely (or more conventionally) defining theology. It is a matter of substance; it is a matter of the very existence of Christianity. To define theology as the science of religion involves a "metamorphosis of the object" (*Principles,* p. 215). Instead of theology being the science of God it becomes the study of religious man; instead of being governed by special revelation it is governed by human research into religious matters. If this switch is made it ought not be called theology at all. One can catch here anticipations of the great criticisms which Karl Barth brought against modernism's understanding of theology in his *Church Dogmatics.*

On the contrary Kuyper vigorously insisted that theology is the science of God. It is a science because it has a definite object, God in his revelation. It is a science because it has a principle of control, the knowledge of God in special revelation. It is a science because it has a fundamental principle, the recovery of the knowledge of God in the sinner by means of a redemptive revelation. It is a science because it has a pedigree we can trace—from the archetypal knowledge of God, to special revelation, to the ectypal knowledge of God, to Sacred Scripture.

Kuyper was no religious intellectualist. Although he had a weighty doctrine of the knowledge of God and saw theology as a science (and therefore deserving a place in a university in the form of a faculty of theology!), he never cut the nerve of religion as subjective piety and worship. He insisted as vigorously as any of our contemporary existentially-minded theologians that revelation was as much a meeting with God as a knowing of God, that revelation was no doctrinaire communication but part of the redemptive work of God, and that faith was not assent to a Koranish-like truth but living communion with God. However, he saw better than the existentialist for he realized that if one washed out the conceptual element in revelation (i.e., revelation as knowledge) then one washed out all the so-called "existential" elements too.

The Scriptures are not constructed like a text. They do not have the ordered outline like Calvin's *Institutes* nor do they set forth a deductive system like Spinoza's *Ethics*. Nor is there any Psalm that gives us an eagle's eye view of the attributes of God like Hegel's Table of Categories. The Bible is a book of history and literature and therefore the theology buried within the history and literature must be mined out like gold is extracted from a vein. The knowledge of God is in Scripture like gold is in the earth. The careful, thorough theological exegesis of Scripture whose product is the knowledge of God is the parallel to the mining, smelting and refining processes in the recovery of fine gold.

There are two presuppositions to this mining process. *First* the theologian himself must participate in *palingenesis*. Just as blind men cannot lecture on color-matching nor deaf men on music so unregenerate men cannot treat theology (*Principles*, p. 48). If revelation is the knowledge of God for sinners, then the theologian—as a sinner—stands in need of regeneration as the subjective prerequisite for his task. It must be parenthetically added that this does not mean that the Christian theologian is restricted to the use of works of other regenerate men. Kuyper is too good of a Calvinist to say anything like this. God in his overruling sovereignty can use the works of any man for his glory. Did he not use a Pharaoh, a Judas and a Cyrus? If God can so work in the area of sinful men that these men contribute to his purposes and glory why then exclude the books of unregenerate men from the same overruling providence?

Secondly, theology calls for the *logical action* of the regenerate man as he writes theology. *Palingenesis* is the necessary spiritual presupposition for writing Christian theology; the *logical action* is the necessary scholarly activity. By logical action Kuyper means the total application of the Christian mind, with all the scholar's apparatus, to the Christian revelation so as to produce the Christian theology.

Theology is a science because it has a prescribed datum (revelation), a qualified researcher (the theologian), a scientific methodology (logical action), and it produces a body of knowledge (Christian theology). That there is a subjective element in theology not characteristic of other sciences Kuyper was first to assert (cf. *Principles*, p. 48).

Kuyper argues for the dignity of the theology on the basis of the organization of a typical Dutch university. These universities are divided up into faculties and each faculty is no arbitrary demarcation but reflects a fundamental relationship of man either to other men or to the universe. The theological faculty justly deserves a place in the university because it too treats of one of man's fundamental relationships, the relationship of man to God. Therefore, any university that does not have a faculty of theology comes short of the total truth. However one must not have a faculty of religion (the psychological, sociological, and historical study of the world's religious phenomena) but a faculty of theology (i.e., that which is based on the study of God in his special revelation—which may well include the study of religion as an ancillary subject).

The object of theology is God. If there were no proper object to a study it would lose its status as a science or as a worthy human discipline (e.g., as is the case in astrology). If we deny that theology has God as its object, but rather man's religious experiences, we ought to cease talking about God and theology. Only as we maintain that God is the object of our theology do we uphold the dignity, worthiness, and scientific status of Christian theology.

VI. PARTICULAR ISSUES IN CHRISTIAN APOLOGETICS

Having sketched out the broad outlines of Kuyper's thought

we now turn to his opinions on some central and crucial topics to see how he applies his apologetic theory in concrete.

1. *Logic and testing.* Kuyper did not discuss the relationship of logic and faith extensively so no clear picture emerges as to how he correlates the two. He does insist that sin did not effect man's power to reason correctly (cf. *Principles*, pp. 110 and 159). The movement of the mind from axioms to theorems is trustworthy. If a scholar does make a slip another scholar may correct him. Apart from the general destructive work of sin in our natures making us subject to errors of memory, etc., original sin does not effect our logical powers. What we do in mathematics, logic, or geometry is free from the influence of original sin. Logic within its own domain of pure formal thought is therefore not suspect (cf. *Principles*, p. 110).

But if the logical faculty of man is carried over to "divine things" (*Principles*, p. 288) the situation changes. In "divine things" illumination (or *palingenesis*) is indispensable, and therefore, we cannot trust the logical faculty without it. Logic in the area of "divine things" is disturbed by sin. Furthermore, the truth of God stands as truth in virtue of its being the truth of God. If it needed any sort of support, reassurance, validation, it would cease to be the magisterial truth of God. In virtue of the derangement of the logical faculty with reference to divine things, and in virtue of the status of the magisterial word of God, there can be no *testing* or *verification* of Christian revelation, nor do we as sinners possess such *criteria* for validating revelation (cf. *Principles*, pp. 251-252).

Kuyper speaks very emphatically at this point (cf. *Principles*, pp. 380-389). Man as a sinner simply cannot *test* a divine revelation. The function of divine revelation is to heal the sick, to cure our depravity, and to give us a knowledge of God. To permit the sick and depraved to *test* their own cure is nonsense! If they could really test their cure they would not be sick or depraved. Furthermore, the knowledge of God in special revelation in connection with divine redemption through Jesus Christ is the principle of Christian theology. A principle is that which stands *first* in a system of thought. It has the same status as an *axiom* in geometry. It is therefore an *ultimate* and because it is an ultimate we can not get behind it. If this is the very structure of an axiom or a principle then one cannot prove or test them; one chooses them or adopts them. *If our Christian principle were capable of testing or proof it would not be ultimate for it would rest on yet a higher principle.*

By arguing in this manner Kuyper is arguing as a logician. And there are a number of contemporary philosophers who would say formally speaking Kuyper cannot be refuted. Ultimate positions are chosen; they are not capable of proof in any precise sense of the word. But Kuyper also argues this point theologically. Our rescue from ignorance, our rescue from sin, and our rescue from unbelief is the combined product of revelation and redemption, and this is also that which makes us Christians. If one attempts to get behind revelation and redemption one destroys Christianity. A testing of revelation and redemption is an attempt to get behind revelation and redemption to some more ultimate point. This means that God's revelation and redemption are not the final word, and if these are not the final word the Christian creed is not worth the paper it is printed upon.

One cannot deduce from this that Christians cease to think because they are overpowered by revelation and redemption. Along with Augustine, Anselm and Calvin, Kuyper believes that faith is *the beginning of understanding,* not the end of it. The Christian "cannot . . . abandon his reason" (*Principles,* p. 383) but is summoned to the sacred task of understanding the revelation and all its elements to the highest possible degree.

2. *Christian evidences.* Kuyper's stance on Christian evidences is exactly that of Calvin. Human depravity simply prevents the evidences from "getting through." The evidences rest upon Christian principles and, therefore, sinners who reject Christian principles also reject Christian evidences.

The Scripture is the Scripture because it is the word of God. It has its own majesty within it just as a sapphire gleams with its own glory (*Principles,* p. 387). The Scripture, as such, does not need proof to make it the word of God. But when our depravity is healed by the witness of the Spirit the Scriptures shine in our hearts with a higher light than that which radiates from the jewel. God comes to us in Scripture, not with theistic proofs, but with his own overwhelming power and majesty, (*Principles,* p. 243).

Speaking of evidences and their role Kuyper writes the following:

> He only, who in palingenesis had experienced *a miracle* in his own person, ceased to react against miracles, but rather invoked them himself. He who had observed the fulfilment of several prophecies in his own spiritual life, understood the relation between prophecy and its fulfilment. He who heard the music of the Divine melody of redemption in his own soul was rapt in wonder . . . in listening to the Oratorio of Salvation proceeding from the heavenly majesty of doctrine in Holy Scripture (*Principles,* p. 558).

As far as those who are outside of the faith are concerned all appeals to evidences is futile because the appeal presupposes that man's depravity does not really turn man from God but he does have an ear with which he can hear the appeal of Christian evidences. However, this is not the case. An argument may develop at some small point which seems neutral and innocent enough but shortly it moves to fundamental principle where the Christian-non-Christian chasm appears.

If supernaturalism breaks up the position of the unbeliever so that to admit *one* supernatural event would collapse his system, then one break in the chain of the Christian faith would be equally as damaging (*Principles*, p. 386). If one "cardinal point" of the Christian systems is uprooted by skeptical biblical criticism, then the Christian principle is fractured. But Kuyper is no obscurantist at this point. He knows that critics have proposed certain "logical incongruities" (*Principles*, p. 386) within the Scriptures itself (contradictions) or in the relationship of Scripture to external sciences (errors). Christians cannot fold their hands and say the Bible is the Bible! Christians must give answer to these accusations or else their confession loses "its reasonable character" (*Principles*, p. 386). This or that logical incongruity may push us hard. We may have to give some ground. We may have to frankly confess that we do not know the resolution of the problem. We may even have to revise our doctrine of inspiration. But we cannot yield one inch at the point of the Christian principle or else we surrender Christianity. Kuyper expressed himself as follows:

> If a man wants to criticize, let him criticize. Such criticism even holds the promise that it will deepen our own insight into the structure of the scriptural edifice. Only no Calvinist ever allows the critic to dash out of his hand, for a moment, the *prism itself* which breaks up the divine ray of light into its brilliant tints and colors. (Calvinism, p. 58, Italics are his).

3. *Miracles.* According to Kuyper the soul, the body, and the cosmos form a nexus. That which affects the soul must affect the body and that which affects the body must affect the cosmos. Man in original righteousness possessed a disease-free body in a paradise. When man sins the sentence of death is passed upon his body and a curse upon his environment.

Redemption follows the same nexus. The regeneration of the soul calls for the redemption of the body and that calls for the restoration of the cosmos. However the redemption of the body and the restoration of the cosmos come at the end of time. In that the Church is the new humanity of God whose members have lived in all the Christian centuries they await their perfection and glorification together.

But we need a sign in this life that redemption does follow this same nexus. The sign that redemption follows through into the realm of the human body and into the domain of nature is the miracle. It is a *power* which shows that God's redemption pursues sin in all its manifestations. The misery of sin is not only depravity and guilt but disease and death. The word of divine forgiveness also calls for the word of healing. Thus Christ's miracles are tokens of that power which shall someday remove from us all the miseries of sin. Without the sign and token of the miracle we might regard the gospel promises as mere words empty of any power of redemption. As tokens and signs miracles then promise us the regeneration of all things. The work of sin in the body and in the cosmos will be undone. Thus miracles are not extras in the divine economy which we may easily neglect, nor are they logical knots in the understanding of Scripture but they are organic to the entire notion of redemption and providence.

4. *Common ground and common grace.* Palingenesis creates a new humanity but this new humanity lives within the civilization of sinful humanity. What sort of relationship obtains between the two? *First,* they subsist together *in common grace.* When man sinned he cut the nerve of all morality and rectitude. If this depravity would have gone without any divine check man would have become totally degenerate. But God prevents this total degeneracy (often and wrongly confused with total depravity) by an act of grace and prevents this from occurring. In that it is an action undeserved it is called *grace,* and in that it is for all men it is called *common.* Kuyper defines common grace as "that act of God by which *negatively* He curbs the operations of Satan, death, and sin, and by which *positively* He creates an intermediate state for this cosmos as well as for our human race, which is and continues to be radically sinful, but in which sin cannot work out its end" *(Principles,* p. 279, italics are his).

Common grace is thus a restraining and a preserving action. As sinners we were preserved in spite of our sinfulness that we might be alive and hear the gospel and believe it. It means that human culture is possible and that a civilization can reflect a measure of justice and that sinners without God's special grace may be good artists, responsible judges, and worthy parents.

Secondly, on certain matters *they have common agreements.* Kuyper spells out three of them: (a) they have in common all matters of observable facts which is the beginning data of the sciences; (b) they have in common the "somatic side" of spiritual sciences, such as the conjugation of some verb in Latin or Greek; and (c) they have in common the rectitude of form in formal logic (*Principles*, p. 160). Thus Kuyper can speak of a "common realm" or of "common fields."

Thirdly, at the point of principle *there is divergence and contradiction*. In matters of fundamental stance the sinner and the saint operate with different axioms. Neither in polemics nor apologetics can a common thesis be found. To postulate such a common thesis is to deny that man is really depraved, and that revelation and regeneration and redemption truly constitute unique Christian principles. If we think that we have found a "neutral matter" which we can debate, we will shortly discover that we lock horns over fundamental principles and all neutrality vanishes! (*Principles*, p. 386).

BIBLIOGRAPHY

Coenen, L., "Abraham Kuyper," *Evangelisches Kirchenlexikon*, II, 1012-1014

Kolfhaus, W., *Dr. Abraham Kuyper, 1837-1920, Ein Lebensbericht*

Kuyper, A., *Calvinism*

_____, *Principles of Sacred Theology*

_____, *The Work of the Holy Spirit*

Masselink, W., *General Revelation and Common Grace*

Vanden Berg, Frank, *Abraham Kuyper*

Vander Linde, S., "Abraham Kuyper," *Religion in Geschichte und Gegenwart* (3rd edition), IV, 191-192

TOPICAL INDEX

Abraham, 62
adequacy, 139
analogy,
    Butler, 118 ff.
    of being, 99-100
anthropology, 70
apologetics,
    major problems, 17-27
    New Testament, 1-2
    origin, 1
    strategy, 13
    systems, 15-17
a priori, religious,
    Tennant, 128 ff.
Arminianism,
    Butler, 114
assent, 59
astronomy, the new, 34
Augustinianism, 176 f.
authority, 157
    Pascal, 44
autonomy, 165

being, 94
Biblical criticism, 75
    Butler, 124

Calvinism and Kuyper, 180
Cartesianism, 152
Catholicism, Roman, 68
certainty, 23, 103, 174
Christian, definition, 63 ff.
Christian evidences,
    Augustine, 160 ff.
    Butler, 123 ff.
    Calvin, 175 f.
    Pascal, 46
    status of, 26-27
    Kuyper, 192 f.
Christological apologetics, 63
    Pascal, 45
Church, 157, 175, 177
common grace, 194 f.
common ground, 194 f.
    problem of, 24
comparative religions, 171
    Brunner, 84 f.
consciousness, 140 f.
contemporary of Christ, 64

cosmic redemption, 193 f.
creation, 170
    and revelation, 166
cross, offense of, 77

Danish Christianity, 51
deism, 108 ff.
depravity and Calvin, 168 ff.
Deus absconditus, 32, 37, 52
doctrine, 63
    Brunner, 74
doubt, Augustine, 149 f.

empirical metaphysics, 137 ff.
empirical rationalism, 135 f.
empiricism, 126
    Locke, 111 f.
    Tennant, 133 ff.
encounter, 71 f.
enthusiasm, 107
epigenesis, 134 f.
eternity, 65
evolution, 143
experience, 133 f.
    Butler, 112
    unique, 15 ff.
existentialism, 53 f., 55 ff., 61, 84
existential shock, 33

faith
    Augustine, 156 ff.
    Brunner, 76 ff.
    Calvin, 177 f.
    character of, 25
    Kierkegaard, 61 ff.
    Kuyper, 181 ff.
    Pascal, 42, 43-45
    Thomas, 100 ff., 103 ff.
fundamentalism, 68-70

general revelation, 165 ff., 169 f.
God, 81, 168
    Brunner, 72
    existence, 141
    Kierkegaard, 51-53
    Pascal, 42, 52
    philosophers, 68
    as Subject, 53, 72
    Thomas, 96 f.